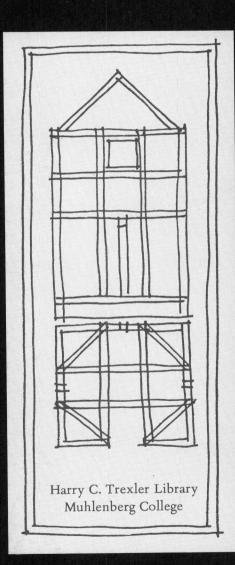

Single Market Europe

Spyros G. Makridakis and Associates

Single Market Europe

*Opportunities and Challenges
for Business*

Jossey-Bass Publishers

San Francisco • Oxford • 1991

SINGLE MARKET EUROPE
Opportunities and Challenges for Business
by Spyros G. Makridakis and Associates

Copyright © 1991 by: Jossey-Bass Inc., Publishers
350 Sansome Street
San Francisco, California 94104
&
Jossey-Bass Limited
Headington Hill Hall
Oxford OX3 0BW

Library of Congress Cataloging-in-Publication Data

Makridakis, Spyros G.
    Single market Europe: opportunities and challenges for business /
Spyros G. Makridakis and associates.
        p.   cm. — (The Jossey-Bass management series)
    Includes bibliographical references and index.
    ISBN 1-55542-343-4
    1. Europe Economic Community.   2. Europe—Economic integration.
3. Europe 1992.   4. European Economic Community countries—
Commerce. 5. Finance—European Economic Community countries.
I. Title.   II. Series.
HC241.2.M2376   1991
337.1'42—dc20   90-24419
                                                     CIP

Manufactured in the United States of America

The paper in this book meets the guidelines
for permanence and durability of the Committee on
Production Guidelines for Book Longevity of the
Council on Library Resources.

JACKET DESIGN BY WILLI BAUM

FIRST EDITION

Code 9146

Published in collaboration with
INSEAD, Fontainebleau, France

The Jossey-Bass
Management Series

Contents

Part Two: Strategic Challenges
of the Single Market

Part Three: Critical Cultural
and Managerial Issues

Part Four: Finance, Banking,
and the Monetary System

Part Five: 1992 and Beyond:
Perceptions and Realities

Preface

Yet another book about 1992? This was our initial reaction when we were asked to write on the subject. The market appeared to be inundated with books claiming to be about the changes ushered in by the creation of the European Community (EC). When we actually tried to find a volume on the topic for use in our seminars at INSEAD, however, we realized that there was in fact a dire need for a book that covered the subject in a straight-forward way, was aimed at business executives, and offered practical advice for firms already operating within Europe or aspiring to take advantage of the single market. The existing works, even those with *business* or *management* in their titles, were essentially economic or political textbooks that skirted the issues of concern to businesspeople. Strategy, marketing, manufacturing, human resources, and so on were covered by no more than fleeting references of little help to the executive. In addition, little was written about "beyond" 1992 and the implications for business.

Single Market Europe: Opportunities and Challenges for Business was written to address this need. Given INSEAD's unique position as Europe's leading business school and the expertise of its faculty, our goal for this book was to present the facts, challenges, and dangers of the single market for an audience of business managers. It was our aim to comprehensively cover all aspects of the single market and their implications for companies and, by so doing, to answer questions repeatedly posed by executives.

We have organized our work into five parts. Part One sets the scene, covering background information and presenting an assessment of Europe up until 1992. This part is intended for the uninitiated, as well as for those whose memories can benefit from a precise review or clarification. The first chapter presents a brief historical overview of the European Community, which is composed of Belgium, Denmark, France, Germany, Greece, Ireland, Italy, Luxembourg, The Netherlands, Portugal, Spain, and the United Kingdom. The progress made thus far, as well as the obstacles, to European integration is discussed. Chapter Two covers the competitive environment — the advantages and disadvantages of doing business in the European Community in relation to its two greatest commercial rivals, the United States and Japan. The chapter then looks to the future and the changes that are most likely to occur in the competitive positions of these three major trading blocs following the implementation of the single market. The final chapter in the section (Chapter Three) examines the political and economic objectives of not only EC countries but also those of the Eastern bloc, notably the Soviet Union. We argue that recent moves toward democratic pluralism and mixed economies have modified the political climate of Europe, raising hopes for a coexistence or even a federation of all European countries extending beyond the boundaries of the EC and the European Free Trade Association (EFTA) to include those of Eastern Europe.

Part Two deals with the strategic aspects of integrating Europe into one economic community. Chapter Four discusses the need for pan-European marketing strategies — the combination of product strength and geographical coverage. This chapter suggests that those in the best position to exploit the opportunities of the single market are the Americans, whose products combine both strength and coverage—to the point that they already can be considered pan-European. European companies, however, are reformulating their strategies, which include expansion plans toward Europe-wide marketing. Their major challenge is determining how to market successful pan-European products and formulate the types of strategies required to best achieve this objective. We then move from marketing to the manufacturing process. Chapter Five considers manufacturing strategy and the major challenges facing firms operating in Europe. Uniform technical standards as well as the free movement of products and people throughout Europe will mean huge economies of scale. If these economies are to be harnessed effectively, pan-European rationalization of both manufacturing and after-sales services will be essential. In addition, new manufacturing technologies must be employed in order to allow for customization and as much differentiation of products as possible.

Chapters Six and Seven deal with business strategy and its increasing importance for European firms. Both chapters maintain that the events of 1992 will provide the means for companies to break free from their constricting domestic markets but that they also will make them more vulnerable to competition from other firms (both European and non-European). Although both chapters discuss the changing role of strategy and how it can best be employed within the European context, the first of the two concentrates more specifically on the organizational aspects of strategy and presents the various choices strategists will have to make when moving their companies from domestic to Europe-wide operations. A major objective is how European companies can gain or maintain competitive advantages and how the importance and value of these advantages have changed and will continue to change. Chapter Seven aims at improving executives' understanding of strategy and helps them concentrate on the important issues they are about to face as the result of single market Europe and the globalization and intensification of competition. This chapter explains why old strategies do not work in today's fast-changing business environment and provides guidelines for the formulation of new strategies appropriate for 1992 and beyond.

Part Three examines the cultural aspects of a European single market. Chapter Eight focuses on the cross-cultural issues of pan-European management. We explain the differing perceptions, backgrounds, and expectations that exist among managers of different national origins and examine the serious problems that such cultural differences can cause when managing across national boundaries. In addition to arguing that a greater cultural awareness is a prerequisite for pan-European success, the chapter also provides guidance, based on the results of extensive research, for operating successfully in multicultural environments. Chapter Nine concentrates on identifying the qualities required of pan-European leaders. Criteria for choosing managers for pan-European and international appointments and recommendations are presented. Chapter Ten is concerned with the European consumer: we discuss the major differences in preferences, tastes, and buying habits among various countries, concluding that it is currently difficult to define the single consumer type versus nationally bound buying habits and tastes. The chapter examines the truth behind the popular Euro-consumer myth and concludes that successful marketing strategies must be based as much on the specific product or service as on the actual target market. Only through a better understanding of the target audience, gained by utilizing information obtained from consumer surveys and selling in different countries, can marketing managers make informed decisions as to whether to employ a pan-European marketing strategy or a more focused approach. The final chapter of this section (Chapter Eleven) describes the demographic, economic, and cultural environment of the twelve EC countries and is written for those who need a reference guide to these various aspects. We conclude that Europe is as different in economic and demographic terms as it is rich in culture, the only commonalities being its aging population and slow economic growth rate. If properly handled, however, this diversity can become a considerable advantage rather than a drawback.

The fourth part of the book deals with the implications of monetary policies and the liberalization of the banking and financial service sectors. Chapter Twelve covers the European monetary system—how it works, its successes and failings, the issue of monetary union between the twelve EC members, and the economic implications of a central European banking system similar to that found in the United States. Chapter Thirteen directly focuses on the financial services industry, and in particular on the evolution of the banking and securities markets. We study the forces driving integration, as well as the legislative measures that encourage it, and the effects such integration will have on the users and providers of financial services and products.

The fifth and final part of the book deals with the perceptions and reality of a single market Europe. Chapter Fourteen is written by businesspeople who present the history of the pulp and paper industry over the last few decades. The chapter shows that the major impact of the Treaty of Rome on this industry was the creation of an export boom in which the major objective of companies was to increase production capacity at home in order to sell products abroad. Such an objective was not balanced by economic or profit-making considerations, thereby creating less-than-optimal production/distribution structures. The prospect of the single market has changed the strategic orientation of the pulp and paper companies, which are now in the process of rationalizing their European production and distribution networks. In so doing they are investing heavily throughout Europe, creating a huge capital spending boom that is about to change the industry's competitive position vis-à-vis EFTA and other non-European countries. Chapter Fifteen presents the opinions of government officials and business leaders on three major areas related to the unification of the European Community. The first topic is Japan and the challenges and threats it represents for the Community. We then tackle the question of "Fortress Europe," the most widespread concern outside the EC. The opinions of people inside and outside the EC are presented, and the major arguments and counterpoints on whether the EC will turn into a protectionist fortress are summarized. Finally, this last chapter looks beyond 1992, examining the long-term implications, prospects, and challenges of a single market Europe. We conclude with the opinion of a ten-year-old Spanish girl, who expresses the greatest hope of all for the united and prosperous Europe of tomorrow.

Paris, France   Spyros G. Makridakis
March 1991

The Authors

Michelle Bainbridge studied at the University of London (WLIHE). After leaving England, she worked for HDM (Havas Dentsu Marsteller), a leading international advertising agency in Paris, and then as a research assistant in areas as varied as the French sailboat market, pulp price forecasting, and, most recently, the impact of telecommunications on society and management. She has also been employed as research assistant at INSEAD.

Arnoud De Meyer is associate dean for the M.B.A. program and professor of technology management at INSEAD. He holds a degree (1976) from the School for Management, Belgium, in electrical engineering, and he obtained his Ph.D. degree (1983) from the State University of Ghent, Belgium, in management information flows in industrial R&D departments. He has published widely about the flow of information in R&D departments and the use of information systems in manufacturing and the internationalization of the R&D function. He is actively involved in the European Manufacturing Futures Survey, a survey administered annually at INSEAD to monitor the development of manufacturing concerns in Europe.

Yves Doz is professor of business policy and associate dean for research and development at INSEAD. He obtained his D.B.A. degree (1976) from Harvard University in business policy. His extensive research on the strategy and management of multinational corporations, specifically examining high-technology industries, has led to numerous publications, including three books: *Government Control and Multinational Strategic Management: Power Systems and Telecommunication Equipment* (1979), *Strategic Management in Multinational Companies* (1986), and *Multinational Mission: Balancing Local Demands and Global Vision* (1987, with C. K. Prahalad). His current research work concentrates on the problems of innovation in large, complex firms and on collaboration among companies.

Robert Gogel, senior vice-president in the MAC Group's Paris office, directs client assignments in the areas of strategy formulation and implementation for large multinational corporations. He has twelve years of consulting experience and has published a number of books and articles in the field. Gogel received his A.B. degree (1974) from Harvard College, his M.B.A. degree (1976) from the University of Chicago, and a Licence en Sciences Economiques Appliquées (1976) from the Université de Louvain.

Gabriel Hawawini is director of the Euro-Asia Centre, associate dean, and Yamaichi Professor of Finance at INSEAD. He received his M.B.A. (1974) and Ph.D. (1977) degrees from New York University in finance and economics. He has written and edited eight books and published over fifty articles in finance and economics journals. His research interests include the structure and performance of financial markets, valuation of risky assets, risk estimation in financial models, and organizational decision making under uncertainty. He is currently studying the price behavior of European and Japanese common stocks, mergers, and acquisitions in the banking sector and the transformation of the European financial services industry.

Dominique Héau is associate dean for executive education and professor of business policy at INSEAD. He has a diplôme from Haute Ecole de Commerce in Paris and a degree in public law from Paris. He received his M.B.A. (1969) and D.B.A. (1976) degrees from Harvard University in business policy. His current research activities involve planning practices in multinational diversified firms.

Manfred Kets de Vries is professor of organizational behavior at INSEAD. He obtained his M.B.A. (1969) and D.B.A. (1970) degrees from Harvard University. He is author, coauthor, or editor of seven books: *Power and the Corporate Mind* (1975, with A. Zaleznik); *Organizational Paradoxes: Clinical Approaches to Management* (1980); *The Irrational Executive: Psychoanalytic Explorations in Management* (1984); *The Neurotic Organization: Diagnosing and Changing Counterproductive Styles of Management* (1984, with D. Miller); *Unstable at the Top: Inside the Neurotic Organization* (1987, with D. Miller); *Prisoners of Leadership: Charting a Course Through the Corridors of Power* (1989); and *The Handbook of Character Studies* (1991, with S. Perzow). He also has written nearly fifty articles dealing with clinical approaches to management. He is a practicing psychoanalyst and a member of the Canadian Psychoanalytic Society.

Jean-Claude Larréché is professor of marketing at INSEAD and a specialist in strategic marketing. He obtained his M.B.A. degree (1970) from INSEAD, his Ph.D. degree (1974) from Stanford University in business, and his M.S. degree (1969) from London University in computer science. He is a qualified electronics engineer and author or coauthor of five books, including three marketing simulations: *Markstrat* (1987, with M. Gatignon), *Industrat* (1987, with D. Weinstein), and *Markops* (1988). His articles have appeared in the *Journal of Marketing*, *Journal of Marketing Research*, and *Management Science*, among others. Professor Larréché is a consultant to several international corporations and a member of the boards of Reckitt & Colman, plc London, and the MAC Group London. He is president of Strat*X, a company specializing in strategic marketing training.

André Laurent is professor of organizational behavior at INSEAD. He obtained his Ph.D. degree (1963) from the University of Sorbonne in psychology and his Diploma I.T.P. (International Teachers Program) (1972) from Harvard University in business administration. He has published widely on the methodology of the survey research interview and on managers as subordinates. His present research is primarily concerned with assessing and identifying the impact of national culture on the management of organizations. The focus of his current work is exploring the implications of national differences in managerial ideologies for multicultural organizations.

Bernard Majani is a consultant to the world's leading pulp and paper companies. He received his B.S. degree (1954) in pulp and paper technology and his M.S. degree (1955) in chemical engineering from the University of Maine. He began his career as a pulp engineer, making a significant contribution to the development of blade coating in the United States, and has worked for Aussedat Rey, first as director of marketing and then as vice-president of corporate planning. Majani founded, and has published for the past ten years, *Economie Papetière* and, more recently, *Papercast*, two of the most highly regarded trade newsletters. He is a member of the French Association of Business Economists, the American Institute of Chemical Engineers, and the Technical Association of the Pulp and Paper Industry.

Danielle Majani graduated from EDHEC (1988), a leading French business administration school, where she majored in finance and commercial law. She first became involved with the paper industry in 1985, when she worked in the marketing headquarters of the Weyerhaeuser Paper Company in Pennsylvania. Later, she joined the Corporate Marketing and Economic Research Center of Weyerhaeuser in Tacoma, Washington. She has worked for the MAC Group in London and, most recently, as research analyst for *Papercast*.

Spyros G. Makridakis is research professor at INSEAD. He obtained his M.B.A. (1968) and Ph.D. (1969) degrees from New York University. He has authored or coauthored eighteen books including *Forecasting Methods for Management* (1989), which is now in its fifth edition and has sold more than ninety thousand copies in nine different languages. Makridakis has written over one hundred articles in various journals and was also the founding chief editor of the *Journal of Forecasting* and the *International Journal of Forecasting*. His latest book is *Forecasting Planning and Strategy for the Twenty-First Century* (1990).

Christine Mead is a practicing psychotherapist in London concerned with postdisaster counseling. She received her B.A. degree (1987) from New York University. Mead has worked for the Institute of Cultural Affairs and has been a research assistant at INSEAD.

Eric J. Rajendra is a senior consultant in the financial institutions practice at the Paris Office of SRI International management consultants. He had been on a leave of absence from McKinsey and Company (Europe) to undertake research at INSEAD in the European financial services industry. He received his B.A. degree (1980) from Brandeis University in economics and political science. He also holds an M.A.L.D. degree (1983) from The Fletcher School (Tufts University and Harvard University).

Jonathan Story is professor of international business at INSEAD. He received his M.A. degree (1970) from Trinity College, Dublin, in international politics and his Ph.D. degree (1973) from Johns Hopkins University in international politics. His latest book is *Western Europe in World Affairs: Continuity, Change and Challenge* (1986). He has published widely in the area of European affairs and in journals such as *International Affairs, Politique Etrangère, Western European Politics*, and the *SAIS Review*.

He is a member of the Institut Francais de Relations Interna-
tionales (IFRI), the Royal Institute of International Affairs,
London, and other professional organizations dealing with politics and political analysis.

Pierre Valette-Florence is professor of marketing and
quantitative methods at the Ecole Superieure des Affaires of the
University of Grenoble, France, where he is also head of the
marketing department. He holds an M.A. degree (1977) from
the University of Paris in mathematics, as well as an M.S. degree
(1977) from the Ecole Superieure des Travaux Publics de Paris
in civil engineering and an M.B.A. degree (1978) from York
University. He obtained his Ph.D. degree (1985) from the University of Grenoble in marketing and statistics. Valette-Florence is a
member of the editorial board of *Recherche et applications en
marketing*, the leading French academic marketing publication,
and has published over fifty articles in journals such as the
Journal of Advertising Research and the *Journal of Business Research*.

Charles Wyplosz is professor of economics at INSEAD.
He received his civil engineering degree (1976) from the Ecole
Centrale des Arts et Manufactures, Paris, and his Ph.D. degree
(1978) from Harvard University in economics. He has served as
associate dean for research and development at INSEAD, chairman of the Second Congress of the European Economic Association, and consultant to various French and European agencies. He is a founding managing editor of *Economic Review* and
the *Annales d'économie et de statistique*. Professor Wyplosz is also
director of study at the Ecole des Hautes Etudes en Sciences
Sociales in Paris.

Single Market Europe

PART ONE

Setting the Stage:
European Business Before 1992

CHAPTER 1

Evolution of the Single Market

Spyros G. Makridakis, Michelle Bainbridge

A day will come when you, France; you, Russia; you, Italy;
you, Britain; and you, Germany—all of you, all nations of
the Continent will merge tightly, without losing your
identities and your remarkable originality, into some higher
society and form a European fraternity. . . . A day will come
when markets, open to trade, and minds, open to ideas,
will become the sole battlefields.

> Mikhail Gorbachev, quoting Victor Hugo, in a
> speech delivered to the Council of Europe in
> Strasbourg

At the Yalta Conference in 1945 the world was divided into
political spheres of influence to be shared by the superpowers.
Just as the Yalta discussions were kept secret at the time, so were
those of another meeting held a little more than thirty years
later in Tokyo between Japan's major industrialists and Ministry
of International Trade and Industry (MITI) officials. The Tokyo
conference visualized a division of the world into three major
areas, each specializing in its own field of competence. North
America, with its vast agricultural plains, was to become the

Note: Throughout the book, we use the term *European Community (EC)*
to refer to all three of the political and legal entities—the European Economic Community (EEC), the European Coal and Steel Community (ECSC),
and the European Atomic Energy Community (Euratom)—established by
the signing of three separate treaties.

3

breadbasket of the world, supplying cheap and abundant food. Europe, rich in culture and haute couture, was to become the cultural museum and high-life entertainment playground for the rich and successful. Finally, Japan was envisioned as the manufacturer and supplier of conventional and high-technology products for the entire world. Financial and other services were not included in the division preparing the ground for competition among North American, European, and Japanese firms.

There is little doubt about Japan's increasing dominance in manufacturing, particularly in computer- and information-related industries, its willingness to spend huge sums to become a primary player in the area of biotechnology, and its heavy investment on a worldwide basis in the service sector in an attempt to achieve equal status with American and European giants. Japanese companies have set ambitious, long-term objectives (usually in terms of 20 to 30 percent market share) and then slowly and patiently developed and implemented strategies to achieve these objectives. The Japanese have shown little or no concern for financial outlays or for the short-term losses they might incur in order to achieve their long-term market share objectives. The acquisition of CBS Records and Columbia Pictures by Sony illustrated once again the Japanese attitude toward long-term investment and determination to dominate high value-added sectors no matter what the initial costs were. Moreover, Japanese acquisition of huge chunks of real estate in various Western countries (for example, the Rockefeller Center in New York City and the Forum Des Halles in Paris) and their worldwide expansion policies have raised many critical questions about their long-term goals and willingness to play by accepted rules. What remains to be seen is the possible response of European and North American countries to the Japanese challenge. There is no doubt that the speed-up in the creation of a single market throughout the twelve EC countries and the United States–Canada trade agreement have been direct responses to the Japanese threat.

The Single European Market: Expectations and Reality

What have been the effects of the creation of the European Community (EC)? What about the outcome of further attempts at European integration? As with all such important questions, there is a wide divergence of views. Some argue that a common European market is merely a grand illusion, that nothing much has changed or will change, and that the unification of Europe is a well-orchestrated advertising campaign resembling an empty balloon, having no substantial value beyond its large volume (Minc, 1989). Experts on the European Community claim that though in theory its objectives might seem great, in fact, bureaucracy, national scrambling, and contradictory practices have reduced its effectiveness and produced a different reality from that envisioned by the creating fathers of a unified Europe (Van Meerhaege, 1989).

Those on the opposite end of the spectrum view the EC as creating a "Fortress Europe," using a central legislative and executive body to protect Europe from outside competition. More and more Europeans believe in a united Europe that goes beyond an economic community or single market, looking for a political, not just an economic, union. The desire to be European, rather than a specific nationality, is increasingly voiced within Europe, particularly by young Europeans who do not understand or identify with the nationalistic chauvinism of their parents and grandparents.

Although there may be elements of truth in these opposing views, the reality lies somewhere in between. As is often the case, the goal of the common market is to facilitate the achievement of economic objectives and permit European firms to compete on equal terms at a global level with North American, Japanese, and other national firms. If short-term action is needed to achieve such objectives, there is little doubt that certain measures will be employed, much as the American Congress or the Japanese Diet do not hestitate to pass legislation with which to protect—or even help—their national companies or interests. European leaders and prominent businessmen have been against protectionism (see Chapter Fifteen), being suspicious of reciprocity and wanting to be treated as the negotiating equals of the Americans and Japanese in regard to trade issues and other disputes. Although many idealists believe in a "federal state of Europe," such a dream, if it can indeed become a reality, will take a long time to come to pass.

There is little doubt that European economic integration can be made smoother, possibly more efficient, and definitely less bureaucratic. However, it would be a mistake to dismiss the considerable progress already made. Airbus Industries, the four-nation European consortium, has gained competitive equality with Boeing; the Ariane satellite launching project has become the most successful in the world; and Euratom has become a leader in basic research in physics. Among others, these prominent endeavors have achieved success owing to other large-scale resources made available to them as a result of European cooperation. Whereas single companies or countries could not afford the huge costs and risks involved, several can do so when joining together. Moreover, critics who accuse Europe of unfair competition as a result of governmental subsidies must be reminded of similar practices of the U.S. Department of Defense or Japan's powerful Ministry of International Trade and Industry. Although the Defense Department or MITI might not make direct subsidies, their help has a similar effect. Thus, Europeans feel that their actions are in response to U.S. and Japanese practices and protectionist measures, rather than a type of protectionism they have initiated themselves. Fortress Europe is not one of the principal aims of the European leaders, nor is it being advocated by high-ranking business executives. At the same time, Europeans do not want to be dependent on either the Japanese for microchips or the Americans for computers. It is quite clear to the leaders of the EC that the country that manages to achieve a position of dominance in the high-technology areas will also dominate all industries that depend on them.

At the business level, the trend toward European market integration has produced innumerable concrete results that cannot be denied. Cross-country operations; the free movement of people and the opportunity to work anywhere within the countries of the EC; the complete elimination of customs barriers and the swift progress toward the reduction and eventual removal of other ones; product and component standardization; harmonization of health and safety regulations; increasing numbers of cross-border mergers and acquisitions, alliances, joint ventures, and agreements; the free flow of capital; and similar accomplishments have become a reality producing considerable economic benefits for both business firms and consumers. Thus, any attempt to slow down the momentum toward the creation of a single market will run into strong opposition first and foremost from businessmen, whose firms will be the greatest losers if the road leading to a truly common market is blocked. Moreover, European leaders have been made painfully aware of the fact that, in today's competitive environment, no European country (not even the largest, let alone the smallest) can successfully compete with the Japanese and American giants; they therefore have no illusions about the necessity of joining forces and are themselves pushing for swift European integration.

Background of the Single Market Movement

The European Coal and Steel Community (ECSC), established in 1951 in Paris, was the first attempt at European cooperation. Its goal was to pool and better manage the coal and steel production of the six signing countries. The Treaty of Rome was a natural extension of the ECSC (signed in 1957, effective from January 1, 1958), creating both the European Economic Community, or Common Market, and the European Atomic Energy Community (Euratom). The Treaty of Rome is heralded as the birth of the movement toward a common European market. Its purpose was to achieve not only economic and monetary union but eventually also political union of the European states.

The progress between 1958 and the end of 1985 was slow and uneven. This period was primarily marked by legislative efforts aimed at reducing tariff and customs barriers in order to create a freer flow of goods and people. However, myriads of nontariff obstacles existed to bar foreign rivals and, by so doing, to offer protection to national firms from competitors both inside and outside Europe. Moreover, most services were excluded from the reduction of tariff and customs barriers. In addition, preferential treatment of national suppliers for government procurements in defense and other sensitive or critical areas was common practice: such contracts were not open to competition from firms of other EC countries.

During the "golden sixties," when most European countries experienced smooth and strong growth rates, there was little motivation for European unity. Following the 1973 energy crisis, Europe experienced a slowdown in economic growth, high inflation, and double-digit unemployment. During the early eighties, the economic scene had gone from bad to worse so that debates about "Eurosclerosis" had become commonplace (referring to the fact that Europe's institutions and firms had become unable to adapt to the economic difficulties and rise to the competitive challenges facing them). By the middle of the 1980s, it was clear that no single European country could achieve competitive parity with North America and Japan. Initially, leading European businessmen (both from within the EC and outside it), became convinced of the necessity for a single market if Europe was to survive the global competitive game. Later on, political leaders joined them.

In December 1985, the European leaders adopted the White Paper, which contained 279 proposals aimed at achieving a single market by December 31, 1992. Less than two years later, the Single European Act (SEA) came into force, amending the treaties of Rome and Paris. Among the stipulations included in this act, one of the most important was that a qualified majority voting rule for most (although not all) proposals should supersede the unanimity previously needed by the Council of Ministers to adopt proposals. The majority rule unblocked the decision-making process at the community level, as individual countries or a minority of countries could no longer veto measures that they disagreed with. Consequently, more progress has been achieved in those few years than in the thirty-odd years since the signing of the Treaty of Rome.

The purpose of the European Community extends well

beyond simply creating a free-trade zone. The ultimate objective is to achieve an economic integration among the member states that will eventually lead to some form of political unity. To this end the following goals have been articulated:

1. Complete elimination of customs duties among member states.
2. Unqualified restriction of obstacles to the free flow of import and/or export of goods and services among member states.
3. Common customs duties and unified industrial/commercial policies regarding countries outside the community.
4. Free movement of persons and capital.
5. Common agricultural and transport policies.
6. Common technical standards as well as health and safety regulations.
7. Common measures for consumer protection.
8. Common laws to maintain competition throughout the community and fight monopolies or illegal cartels.
9. Regional funds to encourage the economic development of certain countries/regions.
10. Greater monetary and fiscal coordination among member states and certain common monetary/fiscal policies.

Although fifty-eight of the original 279 proposals outlined in the White Paper have been adopted by the Council of Ministers, major issues remaining are the harmonization of value-added tax (VAT) and excise duties, the adoption of a unified monetary system and common economic policies, and the achievement of political integration of the twelve EC states.

Progress Toward a Single Market Europe

How much progress is made toward a single market Europe depends on many unpredictable and unforeseen factors (for example, the impact of the latest developments in democratization) and the implications for issues affecting the EC. Considerable progress has been made since 1985 and pivots on three major accomplishments that have had a snowball effect on European business: the free movement of goods, changes in financial and banking services, and the practice of government procurement.

The Free Movement of Goods. The Treaty of Rome postulated the progressive reduction of customs duties among EC states. This objective was achieved among the original six members on July 1, 1968, and continued as new members joined the EC. There have been no customs duties on exports between the original ten EC members and Spain since March 1, 1986, and the same will be true for imports into all countries (except Portugal). However, the free movement of goods has been hampered by a plethora of other barriers whose aims were to help local industries by obstructing the import of goods. These obstacles can be included in one of the following three major types: differences in technical standards and regulations, administrative barriers (including frontier formalities), and fragmented local markets.

Although differences in technical standards or in regulations governing product specification could not completely stem the flow of goods, their pupose was to slow down imports by favoring national producers. Thus, the production of cars, electrical appliances, and food and medical products, to mention just a few, was governed in each country by elaborate technical regulations and others that were preferential to national manufacturers (the same national producers very often were instrumental in drawing up the regulations with which to protect themselves). Foreign-made products could be imported with no duties payable but could not be sold in a given country unless they conformed to the technical, health, safety, and other standards and regulations particular to that country. Moreover, they had to be certified by a government agency as conforming to all such standards and regulations. The consequences of having to manufacture products with diverse country-specific requirements and the certification procedures necessary before one could sell the product in a given country dramatically increased costs, introduced delays, and, in some cases, effectively barred actual entry into certain markets.

Great progress has been made toward adopting common technical standards and ratifying community-wide health, safety, and other regulations. As integration continues, there will be few differences left involving standards or regulations, except those impossible to change (for example, the steering wheel being on the right side in English cars). In a single market Europe, the principle of mutual recognition of products will mean that a product certified in any one EC country can be sold in all of the others. There are considerable benefits to be had by adopting uniform standards and regulations across Europe. Production and distribution costs will be reduced as firms rationalize their manufacturing, distribution, and after-sales service networks on a Europe-wide scale.

The aim of administrative barriers was to hamper foreign competition in indirect ways. For example, the Germans categorically refused to admit beers containing additives and sausages containing soya bean meat substitutes, thus successfully barring entry of foreign brews and produce from certain sausage manufacturers into the German market (the largest in Europe). The Italians claimed that accepting pasta made from common wheat rather than 100 percent durum wheat was detrimental to Italian consumers' health, whereas just across the border, a certain type of Italian salami was not permitted on French soil. Most of these administrative barriers have been removed (for instance, a country cannot refuse the import of any food or drink products made within the EC unless there are sound reasons concerning health, safety, or consumer protection). All twelve members of the EC have agreed to the principle of mutual recognition, although some countries are not willing to fully apply the principle to all products. Thus, consumers will decide whether they want to buy meat-substitute sausages, pasta made from common wheat, or Italian salami. Obviously the price, quality, and other characteristics of the products being offered will become the critical factors determining whether a product or service will be bought, rather than the legislation and other protectionist barriers that decided in the past.

A great step forward was made in January 1988, when a single customs document, the single Administrative Document (SAD), was introduced to replace the fifty-seven-odd documents previously in existence. This administrative measure immensely facilitated the import of goods from one EC country to another by reducing not only the work involved in filling out the various forms, but also the actual waiting time at border checkpoints.

Another noncustoms barrier is market segmentation by country. Such a barrier can be inferred by the huge price differences among countries for the same commodity (even standardized ones such as electrical appliances and pharmaceuticals). If free trade among member states were uninhibited by nontariff barriers, then no price differentials could be justified in excess of those imposed because of differing VAT rates. However, manufacturers and distributors alike have reaped higher profits in some countries. Even though the same item might be less than half the price in a neighboring nation, by exploiting language differences and unofficial cartels in distribution channels producers have been able to set artificially high prices that the consumer has no choice but to pay.

As economic unification approaches, parallel trade will increase as entrepreneurial intermediaries buy goods in a country where they are relatively cheaper and resell them in another, bypassing language barriers and avoiding established distribution channels. Thus, discount stores, mail order houses, and cross-border buying deals will flourish until price differentials are reduced to the point at which this parallel trade is no longer profitable.

Financial and Banking Services. The highly fragmented European financial and banking sectors have been undergoing sweeping changes introduced by the White Paper directives. These changes affect the free flow of capital, the unification of the financial markets, and the standardization of the banking sector.

Since July 1990, free capital movement among EC member states has become a reality (with the exception of Ireland, Spain, Portugal, and Greece). Freedom of capital movement puts severe pressure on the monetary policies of individual countries (see Chapter Twelve) and necessitates a much greater degree of coordination among central banks. In addition, it raises a number of important issues related to the taxing of capital income, interest, and dividends in EC countries, issues which will in turn necessitate the harmonization of monetary and fiscal policies among the twelve.

Freedom of capital movements coupled with the removal of obstacles to operation among different European countries have cleared the way for many more Europe-wide financial service corporations. The benefits for the consumer could be huge, since the large price differentials for financial services that currently exist among various countries are no longer feasible. Moreover, since the product of financial services does not involve physical movement of goods or people, it will be relatively easy to sell such services across borders. Thus, an English building society could sell mortgage loans in Naples through the mail, or a French company could sell life insurance to Germans through a branch in Brussels. Similarly, a Luxembourg bank could offer, by mail, higher interest rates for Euro-deposits in European currency units (ECUs) than could a bank in Madrid. These and similar services have become commonplace, leading to increased pressure for greater financial and economic integration among the twelve and, ultimately, to higher interdependence of their economies, paving the way for the eventual adoption of a common European currency.

Free capital movements and the smooth operation of financial firms and institutions would not be possible without some form of standardization of the banking industry. Practical ways of accepting checks from other countries and processing them quickly and efficiently in a European clearinghouse are a necessity. Considerable progress has been made in standardizing credit cards for both automatic retrieval of cash and approving purchases of goods and services across borders, and check clearance and credit card usage have improved international travel and facilitated trade.

Government Procurements. Public procurements by governments are substantial, accounting on average for close to 10 percent of the total gross national product (GNP) (15 percent if the purchases of nationalized corporations are included). Opening up these procurements could change the face of competition in industries such as telecommunications, transportation, arms manufacturing, and water and electricity supply. The savings from more open competition may be substantial. The Cecchini report, one of several funded by the commission, directed by Paolo Ceccini, and conducted by independent consultants seeking to establish the present costs of the European Community's market fragmentation, estimated that such benefits could save as much as 30 billion ECU (or increase overall GNP by 0.6 percent), in particular in areas where huge overcapacities currently exist (such as boilermaking, turbines, and locomotive construction) or where national production hampers global competition (for example, in telecommunications). Because of the importance of these industries, governments have favored national companies, citing reasons of defense and/ or national independence to explain these choices. At the same time, some areas of public procurement have been used for intergovernment cooperation to help European industry compete on a worldwide basis (for example, aeronautics, space satellites, and weapon systems). Thus, it may not be impossible for government procurements to be used for enhancing international cooperation rather than for a means by which European industries protect themselves from one another.

Legislation has been drafted in Brussels that will oblige national governments to advertise public procurements and offer equal chances to tenders received from nonnational companies. A great deal still needs to be done, however, particularly in the primary areas mentioned above. Although there will be delays in some public procurements becoming completely open, since vital national interests will be put before competitive or free-trade objectives, it will nonetheless not be long before procurements are within the reach of all EC firms.

Tough Issues Confronting a Single Market Plan

This section describes the three major problems that remain to be overcome for a single European market, similar to that of the United States, to become operational.

Nationalism. For historical reasons, Europeans often see themselves as adversaries rather than allies. The more critical and pessimistic members of the community are quick to point out that the last person to attempt to unify Europe was Adolf Hitler. Although huge changes in the attitudes held by Europeans have occurred, the wounds left by wars and other national rivalries have not completely healed. As the age composition of the European population changes, however, fewer people will be alive who can actually recall the world wars, and perceived national rivalries will thus become less pronounced. At the same time, there is little doubt that the English see themselves as different from the French or Germans, whereas Northern Europeans distinguish themselves from the Latins, who live around the Mediterranean. Moreover, areas of national concern differ quite widely among the English, the French, the Germans, and the Dutch. Each country is trying to safeguard its national interests while maintaining its freedom to conclude bilateral agreements with countries from outside the EC — a case of wanting to have the proverbial cake and eat it, too. The European economic union might therefore present for each issue or decision taken a minimum standard that each of the states will agree to rather than a concerted effort toward economic or political integration.

European integration has been progressing at two speeds. On the one side is England, whose trust in community decisions has not yet recovered from the shock of the runaway Common Agricultural Policy (CAP) costs. Former prime minister Margaret Thatcher, speaking at the October 14, 1988, Conservative Party Conference, took a cautious approach, exhibiting a particularly unyielding attitude toward relinquishing national sovereignty to the benefit of Brussels: "We haven't worked for all these years to free Britain from the paralysis of socialism only to see it creep in through the back door of central control and bureaucracy from Brussels." On the other side are the French, Italians, Spaniards, Belgians, and Dutch, who have been trying to "spur on the Brussels horse," in some cases professing a desire to move beyond the proposals included in the White Paper (although there has been little overlapping of the areas in which these countries feel that progress is most pressing). Some countries (Belgium, for example—which is hardly surprising when one considers where the commission has its offices) have openly advocated political union of Europe's twelve to complement economic integration.

The strong economic position of Germany has provided it with a powerful European-level voice. However, the Germans have vacillated. On the one hand, they have believed that their export-oriented economy would benefit from a single market Europe consisting of 325 million, but on the other hand, they have been concerned about the economic problems of their EC fellow nations (notably inflation) and the low level of economic development of some of them. In addition, Germans have been worried about their Eastern neighbors, particularly the U.S.S.R., and have not been willing to jeopardize the recent unification with East Germany by promoting ever closer political ties with Western European nations. This contributes to a "wait and see" attitude and explains why the French (particularly President François Mitterrand) have pushed for a deeper commitment from the Germans, demanding that they state their position vis-à-vis the Eastern bloc and the European Community without ambiguity.

The extent and speed of European integration very much depend on English convictions and German attitudes. With the change in the English political scene and the emergence of the new prime minister, John Major, it would seem likely that the English stance toward European integration will become more positive than it was under Thatcher. As important questions dealing with tax matters (value-added tax [VAT] and excise tax) and monetary issues must be decided by unanimous votes, there must either be a convergence of views among European leaders or a "two-speed" Europe will emerge with some countries left behind. Whether such a dual approach would work is another question. Nationalism and perceived national interests have been responsible for prevailing attitudes and are, as such, major obstacles to achieving a single European market.

Tax Harmonization. Tax harmonization has presented one of the biggest hurdles to achieving a single market. Governments have been accustomed to receive all revenue from direct or indirect taxation; thus, any threat of reducing such revenue has involved extremely sensitive political issues. There have existed major differences in the taxation systems of the twelve EC members, as well as in the proportion of direct versus indirect taxes in each country's total revenue. At the same time, economic experts — and the commission itself — are well aware that without some form of tax harmonization the chances of achieving economic integration are wafer thin. The issues are complex and extend beyond Europe's boundaries. Although it is clear that direct taxes (income and corporate taxes, social security, and unemployment contributions) must be covered in the not-so-distant future, the commission has concentrated its effort until now on indirect taxation (VAT and excise taxes). However, the commission aims at standardizing the rates of such taxes, as well as those of capital income taxes, by using compromise rates based on the average of the existing rates applied by the twelve governments. This is an approach that may well offend each of the national governments and please none.

The commission has proposed two VAT rates: a reduced one and a standard one. The reduced rate, which will apply to food and water, heating and lighting, pharmaceuticals, passenger transport, and books, newspapers, and magazines, will be between 4 and 9 percent. (The British, who have imposed no VAT taxes at all on children's clothing and shoes and basic food items, may prove less than willing to accept such a compromise.) All remaining items (except those covered by excise duties) will be taxed between 14 and 20 percent of their price. Another proposal for harmonizing VAT rates was put forward by the commission in 1989. However, no consensus has been reached.

Excise duties vary much more widely than do VAT or direct taxes. The commission has put forward a three-stage proposal to harmonize excise duties. During the third stage, the excise tax on alcohol should be 12.71 ECU per liter, the total VAT and duty on cigarettes should be 53 percent of the retail value, and that on unleaded gasoline should be 0.31 ECU per liter. Moreover, no excise taxes on items other than alcohol for consumption, cigarettes, and gasoline or oil should be imposed.

The proposed changes in VAT and excise taxes could have significant effects for certain countries. Denmark, for instance, stands to lose significant revenue from its excise tax on alcoholic drinks (which is the highest in the community), while Greece, which has the lowest rate (more than eighty times lower than that of Denmark), will probably see demand dry up if huge price increases are introduced. Similar but even more pronounced effects will be observed if the proposed VAT rates are to be uniformly applied among the twelve member states. Some VAT revenues will be substantially reduced, thus necessitating alternative sources of revenue, whereas the transitory effects of substantially higher product or service prices might adversely affect demand. Thus, what might seem a rational approach could have disastrous consequences for those countries at either extreme. Unless some form of convergence of rates of VAT and excise duties is achieved, it will be difficult to abolish border controls for goods transported from one country to another, thus thwarting the ultimate objective of a truly free market. However, it seems unlikely that all twelve EC nations will agree to harmonize their VAT and excise taxes.

Inability to reach a consensus leaves four alternatives. First, the commission might modify the proposed rates of 4 to 9 percent (reduced) and 14 to 20 percent (standard) by either increasing their ranges or allowing individual nations to use them as minimum rates. Second, the commission might decide to delay the harmonization issue until the economies of the member states are more integrated. Third, the commission might propose transition periods for certain countries whose governmental receipts cannot afford the steep reductions resulting from the proposed rate changes. Fourth, a de facto, two-tier

EC could emerge. One tier would include Italy, France, Germany, Belgium, Luxembourg, Holland, and probably Spain. Since these countries are geographical neighbors, they must harmonize their VAT and excise taxes in order to open their borders to each other. The remaining countries—Ireland, the United Kingdom, Denmark, Portugal, and Greece—might have to content themselves with border controls for imported goods and less-than-total membership unless their VAT and excise duties fall within the range of those of the other members.

European Monetary Union. Another prerequisite for true economic union of the twelve European nations is a single currency or at least a common monetary policy. Although the European monetary system (EMS) (see Chapter Twelve) has enjoyed a certain degree of success since its establishment in 1979, England has never joined, and Greece, Spain, and Portugal, although members of the EMS, do not participate in the exchange rate mechanism (a de facto two-tier solution). Some countries have had some difficulties since July 1, 1990, the date capital controls were lifted by all member states with the exception of Greece, Ireland, Spain, and Portugal. The problems involved in the implementation of common monetary policies for the twelve might actually be fewer, and the willingness of member states to achieve a unified monetary uninon stronger, than is the case with VAT and excise tax harmonization.

Free capital movements may put the governments of the EC in a position where they are forced either to devalue or to appreciate their currencies when faced with changes in currency demand. One way of reducing pressures for devaluing and appreciating a country's currency (at least in the short term) is through increasing or decreasing interest rates in the country concerned. Unfortunately, this has not often proved a successful solution, as external pressures can force other countries to follow suit and thus nullify the effects of increases or decreases in the country whose currency is under pressure. On a longer-term basis, the only way to avoid pressures on national currencies is by achieving and maintaining inflation rates compatible among community members. Any differential will sooner or later force those currencies with higher rates of inflation to devalue vis-à-vis the countries with more modest rates.

Historically, the German mark and the Dutch guilder have enjoyed lower and more stable rates of inflation than, say, the French franc, the Italian lira, or the Spanish peseta; the latter currencies have thus been devalued in comparison with the former. In order to avoid further devaluation pressures, the French, Italian, and Spanish governments have been following the German lead in determining monetary growth targets and setting up interest rates. As a result, inflation has decreased to levels close to those of the German mark. However, low monetary growth and high interest rates have slowed down economic growth and kept unemployment high. Community governments are therefore concerned about the preeminent role of the German central bank in determining European monetary policies and its ability to dictate European economic growth rates indirectly. Hence, there is considerable readiness on the part of non-German Europeans to move toward a monetary union as soon as possible. If such a union is achieved, the German preoccupation with low inflation can be expected to be balanced by the higher economic growth objective shared by most other EC countries.

England's former prime minister Margaret Thatcher was the major force blocking a European monetary union. She feared loss of sovereignty as well as inflationary pressures on the pound. In addition, she demanded the complete removal of controls on movement of capital existing in countries such as France and Italy, as well as the harmonization of capital income taxes, before a monetary union is implemented. July 1, 1990, marked the liberalization of capital movements, and because the policies for the convergence of taxation rates for capital income are still on the drawing board, it may yet be possible to see a change in the English position. This could result in a European monetary union that would bring economic integration a step further. If the English position does not change, it is very possible that a two-tier monetary union could come into being, with England staying outside the union, along with Greece, Portugal, and Ireland, while the remaining members proceed with the White Paper directives.

Interestingly enough, Nigel Lawson, England's chancellor of the exchequer (the position corresponding to the secretary of the treasury in the United States or economic minister in the vast majority of European countries), resigned in late October 1989 because Thatcher did not follow his advice to join the EMS and support an independent central European bank. Lawson felt that England stood to gain a great deal in terms of reducing inflation and influencing the initial stages of monetary policy-making by doing so. However, Thatcher appeared to be relaxing her position and seemed willing to accept not only a monetary union but even the possibility that the ECU would become legal tender and the single European currency. (An English proposal has been advanced to have banknotes with ECUs on one side and the national EC currency on the other.) With the change in prime ministers, England's position on this and other issues remains to be seen.

The Benefits and Costs of a Single Market

Much of the progress toward economic integration and the creation of a single European market will depend on the perceived benefits that such a market will bring to each of the twelve EC members and the costs that it will involve. The predominant feeling is that the creation of a single economic market will lead to higher growth and lower prices. Although precise figures cannot be presented, several estimates of the effect of the single market exist. Prominent among such estimates are those included in the Cecchini reports, sixteen hefty volumes of sector-by-sector analysis of the costs of not having a single market. Sponsored by the commission, these reports are considered to be optimistic and should therefore be taken to denote the upper limit of the expected benefits.

The Cecchini reports estimate that overall growth in GNP will be accelerated by about 6.5 percent because of the single market. Of this, 2.4 percent will be due to the adoption of

common technical, safety/health, and other standards; 2.1 percent will come from the exploitation of economies of scale; and
the remaining 2 percent will come from other sources such as
elimination of border formalities and decreases in current inefficiencies that hamper competition. In addition, Ceccini envi-
sions a 6 percent price reduction as a result of freer competition,
a 5 percent increase in demand, and correspondingly higher
profits for businesses. Even though the selling price of goods
and services will be reduced, effectively shrinking their revenues, businesses will still be able to achieve higher profits because of lower costs of capital, greater demand, increased efficiency, and a host of other factors. The reports see no obvious
costs and conclude that the opportunity costs of non-Europe
are too large (more than 250 billion ECUs) to let the opening of
a single market pass unexploited.

Critics of the Cecchini reports have pointed out that they
were not objective since they were financed by the commission
itself. Even the staunchest critics have agreed, however, that the
single market will provide significant benefits to both businesses
and consumers, the level of which benefits they foresee as about
half of that predicted in the Cecchini reports. From the two
estimates one could conclude that the benefits from the single
market would be around 4 percent of GNP — although here it is
important to stress that this middle-of-the-road figure is being
challenged by new studies.

An area that the Cecchini reports did not touch on is the
long-term effects of a single market. As prices drop and consumers are provided with a wider choice, demand will undoubtedly increase, as will investments. Moreover, if European firms
become more competitive worldwide there is little doubt that
their riches will be ploughed back into Europe, increasing the
standard of living and further stimulating demand. Uniform
product and safety standards as well as greater economic and
political stability will decrease the potential risks as they are
perceived by firms and contribute to higher levels of investment
in all EC countries. Finally, the substantial help offered to the
less developed countries (such as Portugal, Greece, and Ireland)
and the impoverished regions of the community (such as South-

ern Italy and Northern Ireland), in the form of regional or structural funds, will stimulate higher growth rates in these countries or areas, further adding to overall demand. For these reasons it might be possible to envision long-term growth rates and other benefits well above those announced in the Cecchini reports. In a recent study, for instance, an American researcher concluded that long-term benefits might be as high as one-third of the total GNP of all twelve countries, revealing huge opportunities for Europe and perhaps even a cure for the Euro-sclerosis responsible for the fact that per capita GNP of the twelve ($11,600) represents only 60 percent of the per capita GNP of the United States ($19,800) (Baldwin, 1989, p. 9).

In addition to those mentioned above, the single market will bring another critical benefit that is essentially intangible and bound to the long term and thus much more difficult to quantify. A single market of 325 million consumers fostering very close links with the 33 million EFTA consumers is approximately the size of the U.S. and Japanese markets combined. In addition, if the four Eastern European countries likely to develop strong trading links with the EC (Czechoslovakia, Hungary, Poland, and Yugoslavia) are added to the total European market, this figure rises to close to half a billion consumers. Europe could therefore become *the* economic superpower of the 1990s. More important, however, such a huge market and economic strength will put the Europeans in a very strong bargaining position on political—and especially commercial or economic—issues. Whereas individual European countries have been ignored or pushed around, as part of a real European union they will necessarily be taken seriously. Europeans will be in a position to demand parity with, and impose reciprocity on, the United States and Japan. If they are ignored they can threaten to retaliate, and their market is too large for anyone to take their retaliation lightly. In addition, although European technical standards were ignored prior to 1984, they are now considered world standards, thus providing European firms with a definite competitive advantage. It will be interesting to see which standards are adopted with regard to high definition television (HDTV), although at present Europe would seem to have an edge.

Another long-term benefit will be derived from the ability of European companies to compete in research-and-development (R&D) output. If Europe provides a single market with unified standards and communitywide regulations, companies will be able to concentrate their R&D efforts on turning out commercially successful products rather than on overcoming the bureaucratic peculiarities of each national market. Moreover, a market ranging from 325 to 500 million people will provide a huge testing ground before they are launched on the global market. R&D will become an indispensable factor for industrial success, particularly in the high-tech areas. No single European country will be able to cultivate (or sustain) companies that are competitive vis-à-vis U.S. or Japanese companies, as the R&D costs and potential risks involved will be too large for any individual country to assume on its own. The twelve EC countries and the six EFTA countries, however, can pool their resources and become, we believe, world leaders in critical high-tech areas (see Chapter Two).

The costs of the single market are frequently borne by those countries that pay more to the EC budget than they get from it. Since 1979 the United Kingdom and West Germany have tended to be the only net contributors to the community budget (mainly because of the large proportion of the EC budget accounted for by agriculture), while all the other countries have generally received more from the budget than they pay to it. Apart from actual financial outlays, however, there are other costs that may well concern some of the less economically developed countries more than their industrial neighbors (for example, Greece, Portugal, and Ireland). We feel that the less economically developed countries may see their industries dominated by powerful competition from firms from the large EC nations. As the companies that are less able to compete (for example, those currently protected by favorable national legislation and regulations or who hold monopolistic positions in their home country) are frequently to be found in the less economically developed countries, further internal costs are expected. There is little doubt that the majority of weaker and less efficient firms will have to find specialized niches, become more competitive, sell out to larger firms, or go bankrupt. But this is seen as a price worth paying in order to achieve higher competitiveness at the overall EC level.

For the less developed EC members, there are possible long-term benefits as well as the costs mentioned above. The regional and structural funds available, if combined with specialization (to help them carve out market niches), should help the less developed countries accelerate economic growth by concentrating their efforts. At the same time, leaving the door open to outside competition could wipe out local industries or reduce them to a position where they are no longer able to fend off foreign predators. In the long run, the most likely scenario is that the benefits will compensate for the costs involved; but there are no guarantees that some of the national economies will not suffer, at least in the short term. The same is true for less developed regions of richer countries or the smaller and medium-sized firms that pepper the European corporate map. If they are unable to adapt quickly enough to the new realities of the integrated business environment, they will be gobbled up by other EC-based corporations hungry for efficiency.

There is no doubt that there will be a great deal of very significant change during the period of transition leading up to and following the creation of a single market Europe. However, it must be accepted that the forces leading to a single market are now irreversible (as was unanimously agreed by the European leaders in Hanover in 1988). What remain to be seen are the speed of economic integration and the extent of the benefits and costs that it will bring to the various EC economies. The alacrity with which the single market is achieved will prepare the ground for the eventual political unification of Europe.

Conclusions

Since 1985 the progress toward a single European market of 325 million people has accelerated. The economic realities of the 1980s and the globalization of competition have convinced business and political leaders of the urgency of unifying Europe and have resulted in concrete legislative steps to accomplish that goal. Such legislation aims at eliminating all tariff and nontariff barriers to the free flow of goods, services, capital, and people, and the standardization of technical, safety and health, and other standards. In addition, attempts are being made to create a monetary union and to harmonize VAT, excise, and capital income taxes. Although monetary and fiscal problems might not be resolved at the time of official unification, progress toward a single market will undoubtedly continue.

There are different estimates of the benefits (and costs) of a single market. The short-term upper boundary of such estimates indicates an additional 6 percent growth in GNP and a 6 percent reduction in the prices consumers pay for goods and services. The lower boundary of these short-term estimates is a 3 percent growth and a 3 percent price reduction, whereas more realistic values point to a 4 percent growth in GNP and a 4 percent reduction in prices. In addition, there will be some substantial long-term benefits resulting from increased investment, efficiency in production, and economies of scale, as well as heightened proficiency in R&D expenditure and other benefits related to Europe's bargaining power vis-à-vis the Americans and Japanese. Although these long-term benefits cannot easily be quantified or accurately estimated, they might be much vaster than Cecchini and his team of researchers even dreamed about. Thus, Europe may well be about to witness another Renaissance — economic and political as well as cultural this time.

References

Baldwin, R. "The Growth Effects of 1992." *Economic Policy*, Oct. 1989, pp. 247–281.

Minc, A. *The Grand Illusion*. Paris: Grasset, 1989.

Van Meerhaeghe, M. "The Awkward Difference Between Philosophy and Reality." *European Affairs*, 1989, *3* (1), 18–23.

CHAPTER 2

Competition and Competitors

How the European Community Compares with the United States and Japan

Spyros G. Makridakis

Eternal Europe, now that you take shape, now that muscles come to you, you have still ahead of you so many dreams to realize, such grandeur to reveal on earth, that tomorrow you may well open a new era of humanity.

Paul Ramadier

A toothbrush that costs about thirty French francs (more than $4.50) in Paris can be bought for less than $1.00 in New York. A Toshiba 5100 computer costs some 55,000 Fr in Paris (about $9,000) but can be purchased for less than half that price in New York. At the same time, New York department stores are full of Paris-designed clothes, the prices of which are considerably higher on the U.S. side of the Atlantic than they are on the European side.

Huge price differences have also existed among various countries of the European Community, even close neighbors such as England and France or Belgium and Germany. For instance, pharmaceutical products can be more than twice as expensive in Germany as they are in neighboring France, domestic electrical appliances can be 30 percent more expensive in France than in Belgium, and life insurance can be almost three times as expensive in Italy as in the United Kingdom. Even the price of Italian-made cars can be more than a third higher inside Italy than it is in Belgium. This price differential becomes

close to 50 percent when Italian cars are sold in the United
Kingdom. But even pretax car prices, which theoretically should
be identical, can vary widely between EC countries. For instance,
the pretax price of the average car can be more than 60 percent
higher in Great Britain than in Denmark (the cheapest place in
the EC to buy a tax-free car for export), about 50 percent higher
in Italy and Spain, and between 20 and 40 percent higher in all
other EC countries with the exception of Greece, where pretax
prices are only 7 percent higher than in Denmark.

Once economic integration is achieved, these price differentials cannot continue to exist nor can they be accounted for
on economic grounds. Furthermore, even price differences between the United States and the EC countries, in excess of those
due to transportation costs and import duties, will no longer be
justified.

A major challenge is to identify substantial price differences among various EC countries and increase profits by finding effective ways of lowering them. An important contest for
domestic producers and providers of services will be to fend off
outsiders who aim at reducing prices through a panoply of
nontrade barriers (for example, by gentlemen's agreements between wholesalers and distributors favoring local firms). The
challenge to others (both outside and inside the community)
will in turn be to nullify the effects of these barriers to as great an
extent as possible. Until all, or nearly all, price differentials have
ceased to exist, true economic integration of the twelve EC
members cannot be considered effective, and a prolonged battle among national firms, certain countries, European entrepre-
neurs, and the commission in Brussels is to be expected. The
European Court is to be the final arbitrator in the case of
disagreement.

The prime beneficiaries of the reduced price differentials
should be the European consumers, who will be able to choose
from a wider variety of goods and services at potentially much
lower prices. The biggest losers will be local (national) companies that are currently protected by the de facto fragmentation of EC markets, or by the tariff or nontariff barriers accorded to them by national governments, either directly (in the

form of subsidies, grants, and tax concessions) or indirectly (through public procurement policies). The European Commission has been actively breaking down all kinds of barriers by enforcing articles 85 and 86 of the Treaty of Rome, which outlaw monopolies, cartels, and other restrictive practices the purposes of which are to maintain artificially high prices or unfairly restrain competition.

The European companies that survive the intense post-unification competition within the community will have to be highly efficient and, in most cases, strong enough to do business beyond their national boundaries. They will have access to a huge market of 325 million people (the largest among industrialized nations), plus more than 30 million consumers from the EFTA countries. In addition, they will cease to be at a disadvantage when operating outside Europe, as the Brussels commission is now in a position to demand for European firms trade reciprocity and free access to foreign markets. Thus, they will have a much greater chance of competing on an equal footing with their North American and Japanese counterparts. At the same time, there is little doubt among European executives that as their markets open up internally to companies from other EC countries, the likelihood of a free-for-all situation in which extra-European firms find it easier to attack internal community markets will be greatly increased (see Chapter Fifteen).

This chapter provides an assessment of Europe's competitive advantages in comparison to those of the United States and Japan. This is done by taking an overview of practices common to the EC countries in terms of labor, education, and industrial and welfare policies, and comparing them with those found in the United States and Japan. In addition, expected changes such as technological innovation and the emergence of larger trading blocs between now and the beginning of the twenty-first century are discussed; their influence on the economic, trade, and competitive environments is described in terms of their impact on the global competitive position of the European Community.

Single Market Europe

Figure 2-1. Number of Days (per Employee) Lost Each Year on Strikes.

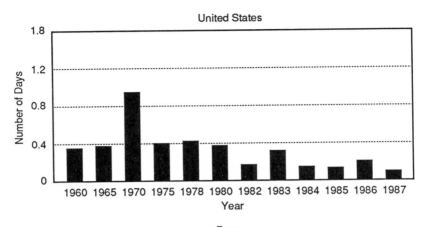

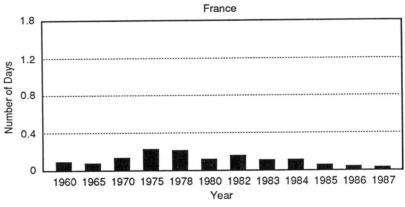

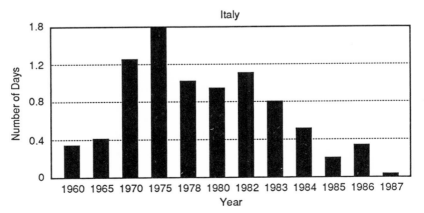

Figure 2-1. Number of Days (per Employee) Lost Each Year on Strikes, Cont'd.

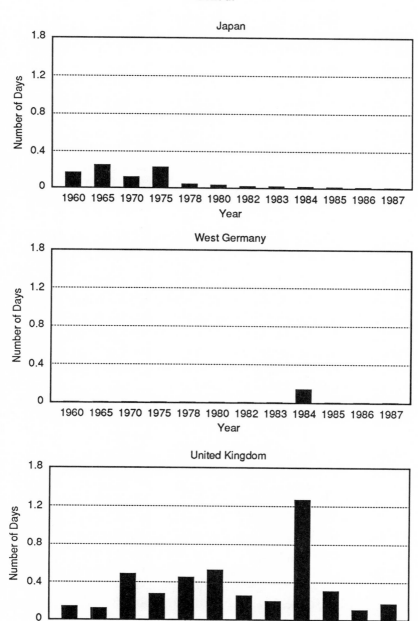

Source: Adapted from statistics from Liesner, 1989.

EC Countries Versus the United States and Japan

Although the twelve EC countries differ greatly both culturally and economically, they share a number of characteristics
that set them apart from the United States and Japan, Europe's
main commercial rivals.

Labor Conditions. The average European works the least
hours per week (between thirty-five and forty), takes the longest
paid vacations (between four and six weeks annually), and en-
joys more fringe benefits than the average worker in any other
place in the world including Japan and the United States. Although wages and other benefits vary greatly from one European country to another (for example, the gross monthly salary
of a Portuguese manufacturing worker in 1988 was 506 ECU
[one ECU equals $1.10], while his German counterpart receives
more than four times that amount, 2,216 ECU a month), they
are, on average, higher than the corresponding costs in either
the United States or Japan. It is standard practice in most EC
countries to adjust automatically wages and salaries to match
increases in the consumer price index. Although the popularity
of such a practice has declined over the last few years, it has
meant that actual wage and salary increases related to merit
have to be added to cost-of-living increases, which is not the case
in either the United States or Japan.

High labor costs have not necessarily resulted in greater
labor productivity or improved labor relations in many European countries. In France and Italy, for instance, labor unions
are dominated by left-wing sympathizers, or, often, actual members of the Communist party itself, who are as interested in
perpetuating the struggle between labor and capital as attaining
benefits for their members.

With the exception of Germany, the number of days lost
in strikes has been extremely large in the EC countries, in
comparison to Japan (see Figure 2-1). Italy, with a working
population almost one-third of the size of Japan's, lost seven
times more days in strikes than did Japan; similarly, the number
of days lost in strikes in the United Kingdom was four and a half

times higher than that of Japan. Furthermore, if the number of days lost in strikes is expressed per employee, Japan's ability to avoid labor strife is exemplary. Figure 2-1 shows the number of days lost in strikes for the four major EC countries as well as the United States and Japan. Japan's improvement over the last couple of decades is inspiring. Even though in 1960, 1965, and the first half of the 1970s Japan's strike performance was not far from the European average, it dropped to close to zero in the 1980s. Even Germany, a country that has exhibited excellent labor relations (labor has seats on boards of supervisors of large companies), could no longer match the Japanese success. The United States, on the other hand, did not fare as well: its incidence of strike action did not decrease as much as that of Japan or the majority of EC countries.

Although good labor relations are not the only factor explaining high economic performance, they still tell us something significant about how employees feel and their willingness to identify with their firms. For instance, the Japanese system of wearing black arm bands to show that employees are "on strike," while working just as hard as ever, seems a remote possibility for most European countries, where striking workers still occupy factories to prevent other workers from entering the work area, thus disrupting the operation of their employers as much as possible. Similarly, although the standard of living of U.S. workers is one of the highest in the world, the high level of strikes seems to indicate that something is amiss with the system.

Labor laws in all EC countries have made it extremely difficult to fire workers once they have been employed in a company for more than a given period of time (usually around a year). In addition, any firing is expensive, as those fired must be compensated. Thus, firms cannot close plants at will nor can they adjust their labor force to meet new requirements during recessions or other periods of economic difficulty. European governments have been faced with high levels of unemployment and have, therefore, restricted the freedom of individual firms to fire workers except in extreme cases and after appropriate government agencies have been consulted and have agreed that the firings are absolutely necessary.

Existing labor laws frequently have led to the equivalent of "life employment," as workers wishing to stay in the company until retirement can generally do so; however, life employment in the community countries does not seem to have produced the same results as life employment in Japan. As a matter of fact, absenteeism is often high and productivity low, since workers know that they cannot easily be fired. Indeed, even if they are, the social security system is such that the economic benefits (in terms of unemployment compensation and so on) may even work as a disincentive to finding alternative employment.

As opposed to companies operating within the EC countries, U.S. companies have had much greater freedom and flexibility in firing their workers at short notice. They can therefore more easily adjust to economic downturns or other unforeseen decreases in demand. Japanese companies are not obliged by law to provide life employment, but it has been their standard practice to do so. Japanese workers are grateful to their companies for such a practice and seem willing to work harder and increase their productivity in return. They strongly identify with their companies, whose long-term survival and profitability are closely linked to employees' own long-term interests and success.

A major challenge for EC firms (and governments) will be to check growth in wages and salaries as well as in fringe benefits, as they are at a disadvantage vis-à-vis U.S. and Japanese companies with considerably lower social security contributions and fringe benefit payments. Unless this is achieved, companies will remain at a competitive disadvantage with higher labor costs and productivity well below that of the United States or Japan, which stand practically equal in terms of both average wages and average productivity.

Table 2-1 shows the 1985 labor productivity for the United States, Japan, and the three largest EC economies—the United Kingdom, France, and West Germany. Japan's lead in the strong demand sectors (particularly electrical and electronic goods) has been close to six times greater than that of the United Kingdom, France, or even West Germany. At the same time, the highest ranking of the EC countries, France and Germany, attain only 65 percent of the labor productivity realized in the United

Table 2-1. Labor Productivity of Various Industries (1985).

	U.K.	France	W.G.	U.S.	Japan
Strong demand sectors					
Electrical and electronic goods	28	47	43	100	236
Office and data-processing machines	37	43	45	100	94
Chemical and pharmaceutical					
products	54	79	75	100	119
Moderate demand sectors					
Transport equipment	23	54	60	100	95
Food, beverages, tobacco	56	73	47	100	37
Paper and printing products	43	67	76	100	89
Industrial and agricultural					
machinery	20	49	46	100	103
Weak demand sectors					
Metal products	38	60	54	100	143
Ferrous and nonferrous ores					
and metals	66	72	92	100	149
Textiles, leather, clothing	59	62	71	100	53
Nonmetallic minerals	40	64	71	100	43
Average	42	65	65	100	100

Source: Services of the Commission of the European Communities, 1989.

States or Japan. (In other words, Japan and the United States presently have a 35 percent advantage over the best of the EC countries in terms of average labor productivity.) This situation gets even worse in the strong demand sector (see upper part of Table 2-1), where the American and Japanese leads are even more pronounced. Obviously, European countries must improve the productivity of their labor, which will necessitate, among other things, improvements in labor relations as well as increasing levels of investment and more relevant education and training. Thus, Japan not only loses fewer days in strikes but also reveals a productivity level considerably higher than that of the countries of the EC.

From a competitive point of view, huge gains could be made if improvements in productivity (which in our view are indispensible) are realized in the future. On the other hand, with increasing automation the percentage of labor cost to total cost is decreasing, making the European disadvantage less pronounced.

Business Practices. In most European countries, there are still a large number of government-owned companies whose main objective is (or has been) to maintain employment rather than to be efficient or maximize profits. Many industries (for example, airlines, transportation, telephones, banks, and so on) are highly regulated, fending off any form of competition including internal competition from other national producers. In addition, most industries have been characterized by oligopolistic competition and/or gentlemen's agreements in price fixing or restricting operations to certain geographical locations. These facts are to a great extent responsible for the huge price differences mentioned above, which still exist despite efforts toward economic integration at the European level.

Historically, government policies have been geared less toward increasing competition and more toward increasing or maintaining employment. Similarly, governmental policies have been aimed at providing acceptable minimum standards of living for as great a proportion of their voters as possible. Over time, the effect of reduced competition has made business executives feel secure. This has further reduced the ability of their companies to compete with outsiders, making them even more vulnerable and dependent upon additional legislation or other measures to protect them from imports. Firms continue to exist in Europe that are as bureaucratic and unable to adapt to the changing environment as are the governments that protect them from outside competition.

Competition is much stronger in the United States, where government interference is minimal — even to the extreme, when issues such as environmental protection are involved. Furthermore, foreign competitors find it easier to enter and compete freely on the U.S. market. In Japan, competition is of a different type: There is strong competition among various trading houses but little competition within them. Cartels are stronger in Japan than in Europe or the United States, and gentlemen's agreements and unwritten rules regulate competition among Japanese firms at home. The Japanese also have their share of protectionist policies, hidden agreements, and widespread practices for controlling distribution and restricted bidding procedures (for example, Toshiba, bidding one yen for a municipal contract worth more than $250), which keep outside firms from actually entering and competing freely in Japanese markets. Finally, it remains yet to be verified to what extent Japanese companies are charging higher prices at home (where competition in certain industries is somewhat restricted) than abroad in order to gain, or maintain, large market shares in foreign countries, one source of Japan's sizable trade surpluses. This can be inferred when Japanese tourists are spotted purchasing a Sony Walkman or Casio digital watch in New York.

The vast majority of firms in almost all EC countries are small or medium-sized and operate within a single country only. This is a distinct disadvantage for Europe as a whole, as economies of scale and R&D expenses can be better absorbed by larger firms. In comparison, the average firm is bigger in both the United States and Japan. In the United States, the reason for this is that the market is considerably larger than the individual markets of single countries making up the EC; whereas in Japan, it is because of the essentially global outlook that firms adopt, often visualizing the entire world as a single market.

Nationalism. There is little doubt that the French, Italians, and Germans, for example, put their own national interests above those of other nationalities or those of the community as a whole. Thus, there is little question as to what they will do in the case of conflict: attempt to maximize their own benefits or minimize their own losses. Recently, the European Community took Denmark to the European Court of Justice because of a clause in a bridge construction contract. In the clause the Danish government stated that Danish labor and materials had to be used "to the greatest possible extent" — which was in direct violation of the 1957 treaty, which demands nondiscrimination among community members. These government procurements are perhaps the greatest test of national governments' commitment to create a single market, and the example stated above is by no means an exception. In Germany, telecommunica-. tion contracts tend to go to companies like Siemens, and big military contracts in Italy are invariably won by Fiat. Moreover, there is no doubt that, for example, the English are often suspicious of the French or the Italians. Such cultural or historically bound conceptions hinder European cooperation and considerably diminish the effectiveness of decision making at a pan-European level.

The commission in Brussels has issued a large number of directives in order to reduce friction and allow for as free a flow of goods and services across borders as possible. The commission and the council have very little actual executive power. Between them, they issue the directives (such as those aimed at completing the single market) that are supposed to achieve specific results within a given time frame (for example, the 1992 time frame of the White Paper). Thus, the directives included in the White Paper are not legally binding until they have been ratified by the national parliament of each member country. Because the ways and means of implementation are left up to the national governments, if national governments choose to slight a directive, they can do so at no apparent cost at least for a period of time (although there are proposals to link the payment of community funds and grants to compliance with the directives). The commission, in its role as guardian of the treaties, can take the case involved to the European Court of Justice, but the process is long and compliance is not guaranteed, even if the court rules against a given country.

Self-compliance therefore becomes an indispensible aspect of the smooth operation of the community. Unfortunately, the perception of various governments is that, if one country does not comply, then they should follow suit so as to reap the advantages of noncompliance. This creates a vicious circle, as the more infractions occur, the more there is an incentive not to comply. Furthermore, it forces the commission to take the role of having to resolve conflict by taking a middle-of-the-road position in order to offend the least number of countries, much as it has decided to do with VAT, excise tax, and customs duties.

Alternatively, the commission sidesteps controversial issues by pushing them further into the future or by providing less rigid guidelines, which in turn leads to yet more infractions. This last solution seems to be a favored measure, as it enhances the chances of reaching a majority position (or unanimity, if required): specific interpretations are then spelled out by the Court of Justice, as in the Cassis de Dijon case, where the court ruled that Germany could not stop Cassis (a French liquor) from being sold on the German market because its alcohol content was lower than that required in order to classify as a liquor in Germany.

As single countries, the United States and Japan are in a better position to maximize national interests. The objective of government decisions and legislation is to balance business, consumer, and environmental concerns without undue worry about sharing the benefits or costs equally among regions. In this respect the United States and Japan have an important competitive advantage over the countries of the EC, whose inability to reach a consensus is hindering their pursuit of common goals, no matter how important they may be. A major question that remains to be answered is whether the EC will be able to put perceived sovereignty and narrow national objectives aside in order to achieve common community goals. Unless the national governments are able to do so, there is little chance that Europe will become a real economic or political entity.

The Role of Governments: Industrial Policy. The U.S. and Japanese governments have used an array of measures to advance industrial policy and help their companies to gain or maintain global competitive advantages. The major vehicle of EC countries has been intracountry cooperation on important commercial projects. Table 2-2 presents a list of major cooperative programs sponsored by more than one country. (These programs are also open to non-EC countries.) The long-term benefits of such projects are enormous, as the examples of Airbus Industries and the Ariane project have shown.

The EC currently is supporting a host of major research projects ranging from research into climatology and natural

**Table 2-2. Major Collaborative Programs Sponsored
by More than One Country.**

Areas Covered	*Cooperative Programs*
Aerospace	
European Space Agency	
Commercialization of the launcher Ariane	Arianespace
Meteorological satellites	Eumetsat
Satellite telecommunications	Eutelsat
Basic nuclear research	Cern
Nuclear energy	
Construction and commercialization of a fast reactor using advanced techniques for extracting energy from a conventional reactor	Superphenix-Nersa
European aeronautical industry	Airbus Industrie
High technology and innovation	
Information and communication technology, robotics, biotechnology, lasers, marine technology, energy, environmental protection, and transportation	Eureka

Source: Office of the European Communities, 1989.

Note: All programs are open to non-EC countries.

hazards (Epoch program) to bio-based agro-industrial concerns (Eclair program) and the application of information technologies and telecommunications of advanced learning systems (Delta). The principles behind these programs are essentially collaboration and the pooling of resources, hence the general requirement that the organizations work with partners from at least two other member states. Qualification can mean funding of up to 50 percent of the research costs involved if the applicants are companies and up to 100 percent if the applicants are academics. As Table 2-3 shows, the total funding of the R&D projects collected under the Framework Program amounts to 5.4 billion ECU for the period 1987–1991, a considerable increase from the 3.7 billion ECU for the 1984–1987 period.

**Table 2-3. Community Funding of Research and Technological
Development Under the Framework Program 1987–1991.**

Priority Areas	Objectives	Program	1987–1991 in Million ECU
Quality of life	Programs concerned with health and the environment	Aim	375
Toward an information society	To provide basic information technologies to European industry	Esprit Race	2,275
New technologies in industry	Application of new technologies to existing industries	Brite Euram BCR	845
Biotechnology	Concert national efforts to develop community expertise in the area	Flair Eclair	280
Energy	Nuclear fusion, safety, waste management	Jet Net CCR	1,173
Science and technology for development	Promotion of scientific cooperation between EC countries		80
Seabed and marine development	Research on basic marine techniques and fishing	Mast	80
A Europe for research workers	Training and exchanges between scientists, researchers, and academics	Comett Fast	288
Total			5,396

Source: Office of the European Communities, 1989.

In addition to R&D, the EC also subsidizes agriculture.
Fair living standards for farmers and a secure food supply at
reasonable prices for consumers were the objectives for agriculture set down by the Treaty of Rome in 1957. The Common
Agricultural Policy (CAP) has achieved a reasonable degree of
success on both these points. Agriculture is the only area in
which the community assumes total responsibility for funding,

which perhaps goes a long way in explaining why CAP gobbled up more than 60 percent of the total EC budget in 1988. (Fraudulent claims from farmers abound, and national governments are far from stringent in their checks on local producers—again, national interest wins over community interest.)

If anything, CAP has been too successful. From the 1975 deficit in cereal production, the EC now produces a thirty-two-million-ton surplus. Similarly, advances in dairy farming have resulted in cows producing 26 percent more milk than they did twelve years ago. Demand has not increased accordingly, however, resulting in surpluses that are unreasonably expensive for the EC as a whole.

But the EC is not alone in excessive grain production (in 1987, for instance, the United States ran a 127-million-ton surplus). Table 2-4 shows the relative size of agricultural support in the United States, Japan, and the twelve countries of the European Community.

Of the three trading blocs, even though the amount of money given as agricultural subsidies is highest in the EC, per full-time farmer the EC gives considerably less than either Japan or the United States. Japan gives the largest amount of agricultural support in terms of hectares farmed and per full-time farmer, while the U.S. support per hectare farmed is clearly the smallest of the three. It must be stated, however, that subsidy per cultivated hectare is not the best way of comparing farm subsidies, as such a comparison favors the extensive agricultural plains of the United States (431 million hectares compared to 134 million for the EC and only 5 million for Japan) rather than

Table 2-4. Agricultural Subsidies.

Producer Subsidies	EC 12	United States	Japan
ECU (in billions)	61.5	40.0	30.7
ECU per hectare	726	114	7,900
ECU per full-time farmer	10,000	22,500	36,000

Source: Services of the Commission of the European Communities, 1989.

the intensive farming techniques practiced on small European farms or the family-run rice paddies of Japan.

Finally, EC countries support their national companies through direct protection of certain essential industries. The free trade directives do not yet apply to water and energy supply, or to transportation. The commission has issued proposals to extend the present rules to include these industries. Even if existing protection is eased to the extent that these industries are open to all firms from all EC countries, there might still be considerable obstacles in place for firms from outside the EC.

U.S. industrial policies match the European ones, although they are less direct. According to U.S. Senator Jeff Bingaman, the U.S. government spends a staggering $20 billion each year on civilian research. To this one must add another $3 billion from the defense budget spent on research, as well as additional sums offered as defense contracts or for improving existing technologies and/or developing new ones. There have been inevitable commercial spin-offs from these technologies, which are in fact an indirect method of subsidizing commercial products. For example, Boeing started its aircraft development program in order to supply military planes to the Pentagon. As Europeans point out, Boeing's lead in commercial aviation would not have been possible without the patronage of the Department of Defense. Europeans thus feel justified to a large extent when they claim that there is little difference between the indirect help given Boeing and the direct loans and subsidies bestowed upon Airbus Industries. Similar commercial spin-offs resulting from spending by the National Aeronautics and Space Administration (NASA) and many other government procurements, which provide commercial benefits to U.S. firms involved in research, developing new technologies, and providing components or final products, may also be considered indirect subsidies. Because of the huge budgets involved, the commercial benefits can be absolutely phenomenal and cannot be separated from those directly offered to military or space applications.

In addition to defense, NASA, grants provided by the office of naval research and several other military agencies, and government procurements, there are many research agencies providing direct grants for high-tech work. Considerable sums are available from the National Research Council and private foundations such as Ford, Carnegie, and Rockefeller. Moreover, U.S. tax laws favor donations to universities, a good proportion of which are used for research that brings about commercial spin-offs. Finally, there are also direct grants whose aim is to improve the competitive position of U.S. firms (for example, Sematech, the consortium created to develop the new generation of computer microchips, receives more than $100 million a year from the Pentagon). Thus, when aiding research, Europeans see themselves as emulating American practices rather than as providing unfair subsidies to their own firms.

Japan's industrial policy is more direct and much more effective than those of the EC and the United States. MITI (Ministry of International Trade and Industry) and STA (Science and Technology Agency) aim to help Japanese firms along the road to global competitive dominance. For instance, one of the major functions of MITI is to act as a market research organization monitoring consumer trends, spotting changes in consumer needs and preferences, and identifying new potentials. It also gathers marketing, demographic, and economic data throughout the world and can be used as a reference library and sounding board for Japanese companies looking for opportunities to expand abroad. On the other hand, the aim of the STA is to coordinate science and technology projects and help Japanese firms become world technological leaders (the Japanese are currently responsible for almost half of the patents being filed in the world).

Although the formal powers of MITI and the STA are limited, their effects on the development of Japanese industrial policy and technology are not. Through research grants (for example, in biotechnology, semiconductors, fifth-generation computers, solar energy, and new industrial material), they are able to influence the course that technological innovations take. Through their power of persuasion, they can bring Japanese firms to work together on certain projects, encourage the formation of strategic alliances, or incite outright mergers. Through their state-of-the-art knowledge in various research areas, they coordinate the overall research effort by bringing R&D know-how, human resource talent, and commercial capacities together. Advocates argue that the long-term outlook of MITI and the STA, the consistency of their objectives, and their highly motivated and extremely well-trained personnel are factors that have contributed significantly to Japan's current success. No European country, the EC offices in Brussels, or the United States even comes close to providing similar services to their firms. Moreover, European and U.S. firms are less inclined to cooperate with their competitors when developing new technologies or products than are their Japanese counterparts. Although Japanese firms are willing to cooperate during the development stage, it is understood and accepted that once the new technology or product has been developed fierce competition among the previous allies will occur.

Investment Spending. Investment spending in EC countries has lagged behind that of the United States and Japan since 1976; it was comparable with that of the United States before that date and well above Japan's during the 1960s and early 1970s. Figure 2-2 shows the evolution of gross capital formation from 1960 onward for the EC, the United States, and Japan, which demonstrates the inability of the twelve to keep up with their two major commercial rivals.

There are several explanations for the poor EC investment record since 1976. Wages and fringe benefits increased considerably faster in the 1970s in the EC countries than elsewhere. Moreover, higher labor costs were not compensated for by increased productivity. Thus, business firms found themselves unable to invest without borrowing heavily, which in turn created a problem because of the extremely high interest rates prevailing at the time (as high as 20 percent). Furthermore, government spending increased from less than 35 percent of GNP in 1960 to close to 50 percent in 1988 (compared with similar spending of around 30 percent in the United States and Japan). The effect of such high government spending has been to force governments to increase taxes, thus further depriving firms of available funds to invest and forcing interest rates to

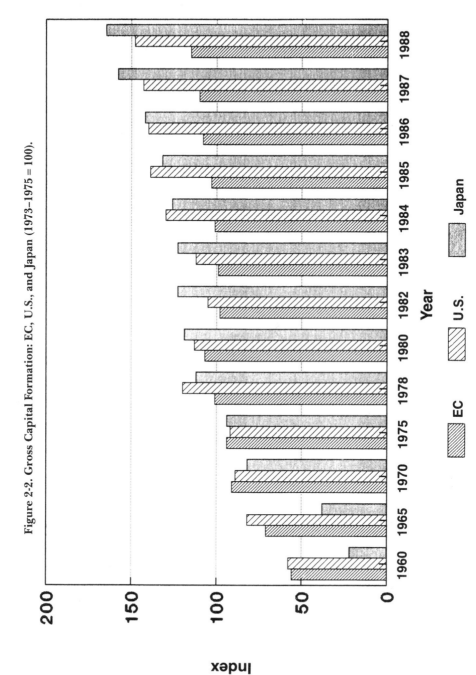

Figure 2-2. Gross Capital Formation: EC, U.S., and Japan (1973–1975 = 100).

Source: Services of the Commission of the European Communities, 1989.

**Table 2-5. Growth Rates in Gross Capital Formation of Selected EC
Countries, the United States, and Japan.**

	1969–1979	*1979–1987*	*1985–1988*
Italy	0.8	1.4	9.4
United Kingdom	0.8	1.4	9.1
Spain	2.2	1.0	31.2
Denmark	2.3	1.6	19.3
France	3.2	–0.1	7.7
Germany	1.9	0.2	4.7
Belgium	2.7	–1.4	0.3
Netherlands	0.7	0.8	10.1
Greece	3.4	–2.6	–4.1
Japan	4.9	3.8	23.7
United States	2.7	2.4	11.3
EC	1.9	.5	11.0

Source: Services of the Commission of the European Communities,
1989.

climb. In addition, EC governments started to interfere more in
the way businesses were run and in the borrowing they did
(state-owned banks were often the only available source of loans
in many of the EC countries). Finally, government budget deficits soared, fueling inflation. Under these conditions, EC capital
formation in 1984 was below its level of ten years earlier and
only increased slightly in 1987 to 11 percent above the 1984
level. The corresponding increase in the United States was 44
percent and that in Japan was 57 percent.

Investment spending, measured by capital formation, has
been uneven among the twelve EC members. A pattern of a
slowdown following 1976, however, has been common to all,
with the exception of Italy and the United Kingdom. At the same
time, it is interesting to note a considerable increase in growth
rates during and after 1985, when the Single European Act was
accepted. Although EC growth rates increased well above those
of the pre-1985 period, they are (with the exception of Spain and
Denmark) considerably lower than that of Japan. The growth
rate of the twelve EC countries as a whole is comparable to that
of the United States, but less than half that of Japan. Table 2-5

Table 2-6. Growth in GNP of the EC, the United States, and Japan.

	1969–1979	*1979–1988*
EC	3.1%	1.9%
United States	2.8	2.9
Japan	4.7	3.9

Source: Services of the Commission of the European Communities, 1989.

shows the growth in capital formation of the twelve EC countries, the United States, and Japan between 1969 and 1979, 1979 and 1987, and 1985 and 1988.

As investment spending is closely related to growth in GNP, relative economic wealth in the EC has lagged behind that of the United States and Japan. (The GNP growth rates of EC countries, the United States, and Japan between 1969 and 1979 and between 1979 and 1988 are provided in Table 2-6.) At the same time, even though the post-1985 GNP growth rates of the EC countries have matched that of the United States, they are still lagging behind Japan's.

Thus, a great many of the EC's economic ills have been directly related to its inability to invest as heavily as its two major trading rivals. In order to emphasize the direct link between investment and growth we have constructed Figure 2-3, which shows the relationship between capital formation and growth in GNP for the periods 1969 to 1979 (Figure 2-3a) and 1979 to 1988 (Figure 2-3b). It is obvious from these figures that European firms need to increase their investments in order to improve their competitive positions and contribution to a higher economic growth across the EC. The EC leaders are well aware of the need for higher investment and have started on the long road toward improving the business climate and stimulating business investments. The Single European Act and the rationalization of operations on a Europe-wide basis have further increased the level of investment. This level of investment can be seen in the last column of Table 2-5, which shows that, since 1984, investment spending has increased considerably in all EC countries

Figure 2-3. Rate of Gross Capital Formation and Growth in GNP.

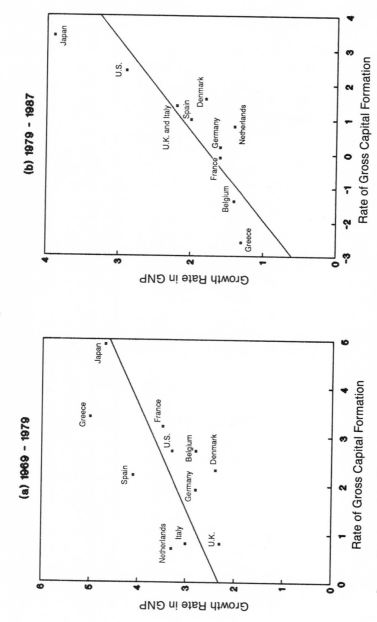

(a) 1969 – 1979

(b) 1979 – 1987

Source: Services of the Commission of the European Communities, 1989.

(with the exception of Greece), although it is still below the 23.7 percent growth rate Japan achieved during the same period.

Savings and Interest Rates. In the period 1980–1988, Japan's net savings amounted to about 20 percent of its GNP, while the corresponding percentage in EC countries was less than half that amount. The high rate of savings, coupled with cartel-type agreements between banks, has resulted in extremely low interest rates for individual Japanese depositors. Regular savings accounts, for instance, yield 0.75 percent in Japan while they yield more than seven times as much in the majority of EC countries. but this does not stop Japanese households from saving. In 1988 Japanese households saved an estimated 13.3 percent of their earnings, while the corresponding percentage in the EC countries was less than half this figure.

High savings rates coupled with low yields for depositors have meant extremely low interest rates for commercial loans. The differences, for instance, in the most recent prime lending rates are striking, as can be seen in Table 2-7.

The lowest lending rates in the EC countries are twice as high as Japan's, while the highest lending rates (in the United Kingdom and Spain) are three times as high as Japan's. Critics, therefore, claim that the high rate of spending in Japan is a direct consequence of the extremely low lending rate, which can

Table 2-7. Prime Lending Rate Comparisons.

Netherlands	10.25
West Germany	10.50
France	11.00
Belgium	12.75
Italy	14.00
United Kingdom	16.00
Spain	16.25
United States	10.00
Japan	4.88

Source: Services of the Commission of the European Communities, 1989.

be maintained at such a low level only because of the oligopolistic powers of the Japanese banks and the legal restrictions that prevent non-Japanese firms from entering and competing in the regulated banking sector. Thus, Japan indirectly subsidizes its companies by making available loans that are artificially low, providing Japanese firms with a considerable competitive advantage vis-à-vis their American and European counterparts (who have to borrow through banks operating in a free-market environment). At present there is strong pressure on the Japanese to deregulate their banking system and let market forces determine interest rates (obviously if Japanese people can place their savings in a bank abroad, interest rates in Japan will have to follow those of the rest of the world). Our predicition is that such pressures cannot be ignored and that Japan's low rates of interest will come closer to those found in Europe and the United States.

Education. Total spending on education, as a percentage of GNP, has been roughly equivalent in the EC countries, the United States, and Japan (around 5 percent). There are, however, considerable differences between the European educational systems and those of the other two countries. In Europe, most of the vocational training is provided at the high school level while in the United States and Japan it is provided after high school. In addition, in the United States a higher percentage of the population goes to college (university) than in Europe or Japan. The European curriculum tends to be more theoretical than is the case in either the United States or Japan. European educational institutions are also often considered more rigid and less able to adapt to the changing needs of business than are similar institutions in the other countries. Furthermore, there is less interaction between European educational institutions and industry than is the case in the United States and Japan. Thus, European students are sometimes taught skills that are not necessarily appropriate for the employment needs of European business and industry. This, in great part, explains the extremely high unemployment rates in the under-twenty-five age group in many regions of Europe.

Europeans lag behind the Americans and Japanese in technical education. For example, only 39 students per 100,000 graduate each year in technology-related areas, while in Japan and the United States this number rises to 76 and 77 students, respectively. Furthermore, in the United States and Japan more students graduate in engineering than in Europe, even though Europe graduates more scientists. Finally, European students study for the least number of days per year (Japanese students study the most hours — some 40 percent more than those of the United States and almost 50 percent more than those of most EC countries).

As Europe moves toward economic unification, facing the prospects of global competition and the need to modernize its education system and to standardize education across the twelve EC states becomes critical as, in our view, a well-trained labor force is more than ever going to be the key to industrial success.

Management education and master's degrees in business administration (M.B.A.s) are relatively novel in Europe and are concentrated in a few countries. Executive education programs are also somewhat limited. In some countries, such as Germany, business education does not really exist. The largest and best-known business school in Europe is Institut Européen d'Administration des Affaires (INSEAD), with an annual student population of about 420 candidates for M.B.A. diplomas. An additional 2,200 executives annually attend courses ranging in duration from one to seven weeks — that is, one-third of Harvard's or Wharton's student population. Compared with the 70,000 M.B.A.s graduating annually from U.S. business schools, Europe's 3,000 represent a rather meager group. There is practically no M.B.A. education in Japan, although it is common practice for Japanese companies to provide on-the-job training and sometimes to send employees to study for an M.B.A. in the United States or Europe.

Professional management is still a novelty for the vast majority of Europe's family-run firms. The lack of professional managers, coupled with cultural perceptions about the *role* of management itself, has created wide divergences in the efficiency and effectiveness of business practices and corporate success. As community-wide interaction becomes common-place, more professional management of a more equal quality will inevitably be required throughout Europe.

Professional managers are much more common in the United States, where the idea of professional management actu-ally originated more than fifty years ago. At the same time, America's professional management has often been criticized for its overreliance on analytical thinking and, in particular, its overemphasis on short-term profits. Japanese management, on the other hand, is rarely trained at business school but on the job through actual apprenticeship where a candidate follows around a seasoned manager for a long period of time to learn the job. Japanese managers are often said to be less concerned with hard, analytical tools than they are with soft, intuitive information, which they use to maximize long-term market share and profitability. Moreover, Japanese firms often benefit from their visionary founders, who still play the role of grand strategists in the large corporations they created.

Another striking difference to be found between EC coun-tries, the United States, and Japan is that of continuous educa-tion. Europeans seem less inclined to return to the classroom once they have started working. With the exception of Germany, neither in-company training schemes nor employee attendance at educational institutions is common in European countries. It is estimated that U.S. and Japanese employers spend about $2,500 a year per employee on continuing education, while European employers, on the average, spend five times less. Even in Germany, which spends more on continuous edcuation than the other EC countries, fewer than 10 percent of those employed receive in-company training, while the corresponding percent-age in the United States is 20 percent. In Japan, more than 80 percent of all companies include at least 30 percent of their employees in some form of training.

Japanese education is more practical and focused, with students specializing more than their European or American counterparts. Additionally, Japanese students spend more hours in school, are expected to study harder after school, and seem to exhibit a higher degree of classroom discipline. Their higher level of specialization and more disciplined studying habits seem to have contributed to an overall attitude that continues beyond their school years. Experts on Japan cite this practical and specialized training as a major contributing factor in Japan's industrial success. Working in small groups where they pull together their various specialities, the Japanese have been able to effectively cross-fertilize the knowledge they have gained at school. On the negative side, experts claim that the Japanese educational system encourages conformity rather than creativity, which translates in the workplace as lack of originality and entrepreneurship. Thus, the Japanese may well encounter problems when faced with the emerging challenges: the creativity and entrepreneurship the Japanese may lack are to become *the* critical determinants of success tomorrow.

The major challenge for European countries will be to modify their educational systems in order to make them more flexible, more practical and capable of adapting their teaching to meet the changing demands of industry. Moreover, much greater interaction must be developed between European universities and businesses. Finally, continuous education and in-company training must rapidly expand. Employees must be viewed as a strategic resource of the highest value that must be continually retrained if full advantage of such a work force is to be taken. Even though some progress has been made, much more needs to be done to raise education levels, particularly in the areas of computer science, high technology, and applied engineering, where notable scarcities exist at present. Finally, language training must be accelerated if all barriers to trade and the movement of people are really to be removed. Until Europeans are able to communicate successfully, integration or transnationalization can only be achieved partially.

Current Competitive Position: A Summary. Japan's competitive lead is indisputable. Its high productivity (particularly in some high-value industries such as those outlined in Table 2-1), its strong growth in GNP, its high rate of saving and investment, and its long-term outlook and focused educational system have all been fundamental elements contributing to its meteoric

Figure 2-4. World Competitiveness and Business Confidence Scoreboard.

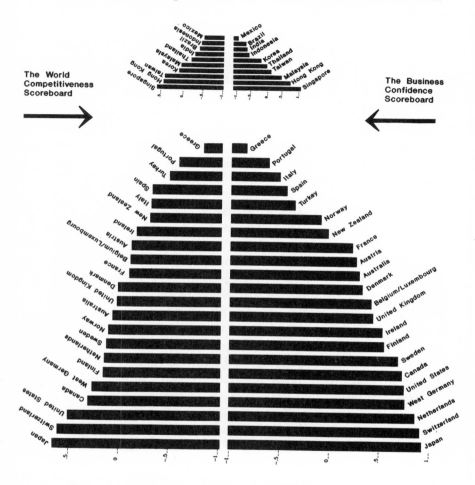

Source: Imede and the World Economic Forum, 1989.

rise during the last ten years. At the same time, Europeans and Americans are bound to catch up with the Japanese as cross-learning and imitation increase. How fast and in which specific areas the catching up will take place depend on the specific advantages and drawbacks of the EC countries, the United States, and Japan, and new technological and other developments, such as the emergence of large trading blocs.

There are attempts to measure the world competitiveness and business confidence of various countries, and Figure 2-4 and Table 2-8 present a summary of the results found in one such study. As could be expected, Japan leads in almost all individual criteria and rates highest overall.

Future Competitive Advantages and Drawbacks: EC, the United States, and Japan

The world's political and economic systems are in a state of flux. Neither the spectacular economic ascent of Germany and Japan from a point of total destruction following World War II nor the relative economic decline of the United States (both part of today's realities) could have been predicted twenty years ago. Similarly, the recent and unexpected democratic liberalization of the Eastern bloc countries, the Russian drive toward free-market institutions, and the internal pressures from its various peoples, reinforce the view that other unforeseen economic and political changes can and will occur in the future. In like manner, many technological innovations were not predicted even a couple of years before their widespread implementation (for example, computers), while other events that were predicted (for example, marine cities) failed to occur. Nevertheless, we cannot refrain from attempting to predict how the future economic, political, and technological environments might evolve and how forthcoming change will affect the competitive positions of various countries (or trading blocs) and different firms.

Figure 2-5 shows the proportion of the 500 largest firms in the world that are based in the EC, the United States, and Japan. We see that the actual number of such corporations is diminishing in the United States, increasing in Japan, and holding nearly

Table 2.8. World Competitive and Business Confidence Report (for Selected Countries).

Factor Country	Dynamism of the Economy	Industrial Efficiency	Dynamics of the Market	Financial Dynamism	Human Resources	State Interference	Natural Endowments	Outward Orientation	Innovative Forward Orientation	Socio-political Stability
Belgium/Luxembourg	15	9	14	16	14	15	11	5	16	10
Denmark	9	8	9	12	8	18	14	11	11	11
France	13	12	11	10	11	17	8	12	8	17
Germany	4	5	5	3	12	7	10	4	3	5
Greece	22	22	21	22	20	21	21	22	21	21
Ireland	10	16	20	20	17	6	16	7	9	14
Italy	19	13	17	17	19	20	19	17	18	16
Netherlands	14	6	13	5	10	16	7	3	10	4
Portugal	21	20	22	21	18	11	20	18	22	20
Spain	18	14	18	15	22	9	18	16	13	22
United Kingdom	11	10	12	8	15	8	5	6	12	15
Japan	1	1	3	2	3	5	13	2	1	2
United States	2	3	1	6	1	2	9	9	6	3

Source: Imede and the World Economic Forum, 1989.

steady within the EC (although there might have been a small increase since 1985, when the ideas included in the White Paper were accepted by the Council of Ministers). Although statistics such as those shown in Figure 2-5 might not reveal the whole story of industrial competitiveness, they point to the relative decline of the United States, the outstanding success of Japan, and the stagnation of EC countries. The fundamental question is to what extent this trend will continue in the future.

A major reason for Japan's phenomenal success has been the fact that the United States (and European executives) could not accept that the Japanese were capable of competing against them. Japanese companies were thought to be badly managed; they were considered copycats unable to develop new technologies of their own; their products were believed to be of an inferior quality; and they were thought to be completely lacking in even elementary marketing skills. The performance of Japan has reversed this view. The Japanese way of thinking and Japanese business practices are much better understood than was the case in the 1960s and 1970s (hundreds of books have been written on the topic) and are even greatly admired: they are considered major factors in the Japanese success story of which Westerners are so envious. Furthermore, Japanese manufacturing, R&D, and marketing skills are no longer underestimated. Europeans and Americans are learning from the Japanese as much as the Japanese learned from the West. In some instances U.S. know-how has found its way into the world at large through Japan — as was the case with Edward Deming, the American quality-control genius whose work was largely ignored in his own country, only to be "discovered" once the Japanese started using his ideas and methods to produce superior-quality products. Today, it is the Western countries that are attempting to imitate Japanese skills in human relations, manufacturing techniques, and management methods.

There is little doubt that Japanese competitive advantages will become more akin to those of European and U.S. companies as cross-learning takes place and successful techniques and practices are applied across the Pacific, as well as on both sides of the Atlantic. Moreover, as Europeans and Americans no

Figure 2-5. Number of the Largest Corporations in the World with Headquarters in Japan, the EC, and the United States.

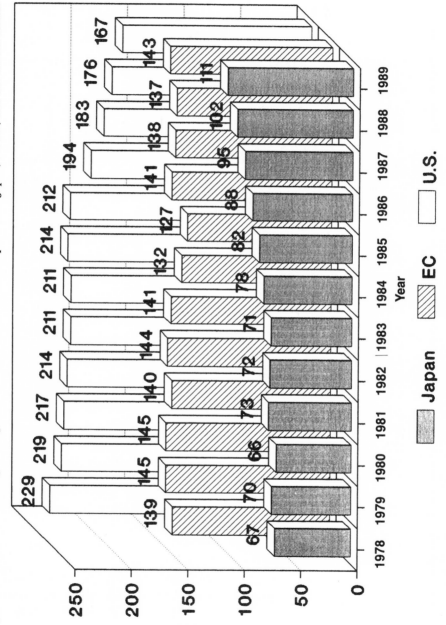

Source: Author's compilation from various issues of *Fortune*, 1978–1990.

longer underestimate the Japanese, it is unlikely that they will get caught by surprise or that they will overlook another major technological advancement from the Japanese. In addition, as standards of living rise in Japan, so will the wages and fringe benefits Japanese firms provide their employees. (Ten years ago, the average Japanese wage was two-thirds of the average American one, whereas today the two are practically equal.) The new generation of Japanese, growing up in a period of affluence, may not be as laborious as their parents or as willing to work longer hours than their European or American counterparts. Even now, the older generation complains about how the younger people do not work as hard as they did when they were young and no longer share the high motivation and discipline they as young people did. They cannot even understand how some of the younger generation are willing to spend their annual vacation period photographing remote capitals around the world when they could be working at home in Japan (the older generation seldom took their vacations even though they were entitled to two weeks' paid leave every year).

If Japanese workers (who at present work more than 50 hours per week, including overtime) adopt similar habits to those of European workers, and to a lesser extent American workers, Japanese firms will no longer have the kind of competitive advantages that have made them world leaders. Higher labor productivity in Japan may well become a thing of the past, as even official government attitudes are changing with an emphasis on improving people's everyday lives rather than the Japanese trade surplus. In addition, the role of hard labor and team spirit may well become less important in the future as new technologies and extended automation replace the skills that were once provided by the labor force. Different skills such as creativity may become the most important requisites for success. It is also very likely that as the European Community and North American trade associations become stronger, Japan will find itself increasingly left out (unless it adopts standards and policies more in line with those of the other two trading blocs). Japan will find it harder to export to the United States and Europe if it continues protecting its own market from imports.

Thus in all likelihood, the balance will be somewhat less in favor of Japan. Japan's trade surplus is expected to amount to merely half the level enjoyed five years earlier, and, as a percentage of GNP, less than that of Belgium, Norway, or Switzerland and three times smaller than that of Germany. Moreover, Japan's share of world trade was estimated at about 9 percent for 1990 (versus 14 percent for the United States and West Germany), whereas it was practically the same as Germany's five years earlier. Finally, the extent of Japan's trade surplus would have been less than half its present amount had it not been for the high yen value. Thus, Japan's share of world trade and its trade surpluses vis-à-vis other countries have already started to diminish. We predict that such trends will continue into the future.

Emerging Technologies. New technologies and changing market conditions might shift the game of competitive dominance to other fronts. It might even be that Japanese businessmen will feel as threatened by the rise of some other superpower as European and American businessmen have felt threatened by Japanese firms.

In the future, the extent of automation in both the factory and the office will increase, so that labor costs will be lower, representing a diminishing percentage of overall product or mass service costs. What will then become crucial are the technology needed to automate and the type of goods produced or services provided. Countries that will become technological leaders in industries such as semiconductors, microchips, microprocessors, computer software, lasers, and biotechnology might acquire the kinds of advantages that countries leading world production in steel, machine tools, automobiles, or tractors did thirty years ago. European and American firms have complained that Japan has had a three- to five-month lead in designing new products incorporating Japanese-made microchips. These complaints focus on the fact that Japanese firms have had access to the blueprints of forthcoming chips and thus have been able to design their products on the basis of the known characteristics of the new chips. The European and American firms cannot start the process of designing their own products until the new chips have been actually delivered, hence the three- to five-month delay.

European and American firms will have to catch up with the Japanese in such high-tech sectors. The Japanese have been producing more than half of the world's requirements in semiconductors and close to 80 percent of DRAM (dynamic random access memories), whereas Europe has been producing barely 10 percent of the world's semiconductors and only about 2 percent of DRAM; U.S. production amounts to around 40 percent and 20 percent, respectively, in these two areas. Given the high stakes involved and particularly the strategic importance, Europeans are focusing a great deal of effort on closing the gap between themselves and the Japanese. For example, Jessi (the cross-border collaboration project) is developing a 32 MB (megabyte) chip and hopes to commercialize it ahead of the Japanese. The Eureka program was initiated to stimulate research in high-technology areas (particularly in the flattening semiconductor industry), while Esprit aims at increasing research into the computer-related technologies with the hope of eliminating Japan's lead. Thus, Europeans believe that they will be able to match, or even surpass, Japan's technological capabilities between now and the beginning of the twenty-first century (see Chapter Fifteen).

In addition to technology, leadership and creativity are becoming of extreme importance. As automation reduces the numbers and importance of semiskilled and unskilled labor and technology becomes generally available to all who can afford it, competitive advantages transpire less easily from cheaper labor, higher labor productivity, or more efficiently utilized machines. Instead, the ability to sense consumer needs and preferences, creativity in coming up with new products and services, and R&D capabilities for developing new or better products will provide the highest value, endowing the countries or firms that have them with competitive advantages. The ability to learn from and adapt existing strategies to the changing environment (initiated and implemented by first-rate leadership) will become critical factors in gaining or maintaining competitive advantages, as will flexibility and longer-term commitments,

Japan is not therefore in a better position than the Europeans vis-à-vis creativity, R&D capabilities, leadership, or ability to learn. Thus, its successes of the 1980s will not, necessarily, continue. The European prestige in the high-fashion industry might extend to other areas where creativity will be the critical factor in determining success.

In order to develop the labor force of the future, countries and companies will have to invest heavily in education, as the new skills (technical competence in high-tech industries, creativity, flexibility, and strategic adaptablility) will require a higher level of education and possibly even unprecedented ways of teaching that emphasize creative thinking rather than rote memorization and problem formulation and solving rather than number-crunching skills. Following established techniques and existing procedures or espoused management theories without first questioning them will no longer suffice. Finally, we might see offshore operations, this time not of manufacturing facilities but rather R&D and other "brain-intensive" areas, in countries like India or Brazil, which profess to have an oversupply of well-trained Ph.D.s.

Larger Trading Blocs. As the cities and states of ancient Greece and the regions and nations of medieval Europe discovered, modern countries have come to realize that military, political, and economic objectives are better achieved in unison. The free-trade agreement between the United States and Canada, the EFTA trade association, Council for Mutual Economic Assistance (COMECON), and, of course, the EC aim to benefit the nations involved by creating larger markets, thus allowing for economies of scale and the harnessing of the advantages of specialization.

As the European Community becomes the largest Western market, fears of Fortress Europe abound. As the world's leading trading power, the EC has signed bilateral trade agreements with more than 120 countries and is party to more than 30 multilateral agreements. A major advantage of the community is its increased negotiating power: all negotiations in the areas of trade agreements with outside countries, customs barriers, and anti-dumping practices and regulations are now made at the community (rather than the national) level. In addition, the EC is extending its unified role in the political sphere, where it now speaks with a single voice on most of the major issues facing its member states. The trend toward increased economic and political union should continue well into the future.

As the EC's success becomes more apparent, the pressure will increase in neighboring nations to create economic or free-trade associations of their own. In North America, the idea of Mexico eventually joining the United States and Canada to create a North American Economic Community (NAEC) is not inconceivable. Across the Pacific, Japan, Korea, Taiwan, and Singapore could also form their own community, maybe even including Hong Kong (if politically feasible) and Macao and stretching as far as New Zealand and Australia in the distant future.

At the European end there is considerable demand to increase membership of the EC beyond its current twelve states. Turkey and Austria both applied for membership last year, and Norway, despite its initial rejection in 1972, still seeks closer ties with the EC. In addition, even though Sweden presently advocates strengthening EFTA, it may well change its stance — particularly if Austria and Norway join. In addition, several North African countries (for example, Morocco) would like to join. Finally, the EC and EFTA have agreed to abolish all customs duties between the two blocs (with the exception of services and agricultural produce). Thus, although EFTA is not a part of the European Community, it is frequently consulted and follows all the technical, health, and safety standards approved in Brussels. There is also very close cooperation between the two in several other areas, especially with regard to R&D programs such as Eureka (where all six EFTA members are involved) and programs such as Arianespace, ESA, Eumetsat, Apollo, and Cern (where a number of the EFTA countries participate). We can say that the community market actually includes more than 30 million EFTA consumers.

Even though the COMECON countries are still unable to negotiate with the community, recent events in Eastern Europe have increased the prospects of closer economic cooperation between the EC and countries such as Hungary, Czechoslovakia, Poland, Yugoslavia, and even Rumania (see Chapter Three). The combined population of these four ex-Communist countries and that of East Germany, which was quickly integrated within the EC once it united with West Germany, is close to 130 million people, while their total GNP is around $435 billion. Some EC leaders envision a close cooperation with the Eastern European countries, as France's president Mitterrand noted in his 1990 New Year's address: "During the 1990s I hope to see the birth of a European confederation — in the real sense of the word — which will associate all the states of our continent in a permanent single organization dedicated to peace, security, and exchange."

The EC, EFTA, and the six Eastern nations make up about half a billion people with a combined GNP of more than $5.5 trillion. This is the equivalent of the total combined GNP of the United States, Canada, and Mexico, and more than double that of the Pacific Rim countries.

As the power of trading blocs increases, their bargaining power to negotiate favorable bilateral agreements also increases. Thus, international trade may become less of a free-for-all and more and more based on reciprocity. It is likely that trading blocs will be less willing to accept substantial trade imbalances for long periods of time, in particular if some countries are perceived as practicing protectionism. In such cases, it is likely that governments will interfere: through direct or indirect means and various other forms of industrial policies, they may attempt to minimize the competitive disadvantages in their firms in order to reduce threatening trade deficits. Since it is practically impossible to know for sure that a certain country does not help its firms or indirectly subsidize them (or whole sectors of the economy), there will always be pressure in favor of protectionism and, invariably, new legislation working loopholes into existing free-trade agreements. Such was the case in 1987, when the EC extended previous antidumping regulations to prevent Japanese manufacturers from chiseling out market niches with their screwdriver plants in Europe. Reciprocity in trade, at least among countries that are of the same level of industrial development, will therefore become necessary to resolve conflict and allow for more specialization and advantages of scale. With such a scenario, the larger the trading bloc, the more powerful (and the more successful it will be in its demands for reciprocity). Thus, there might even be further pressure for enlarged free-trade zones or bigger economic communities as, in addition to bargaining power, their ability to set technical and other standards will depend upon the size of their market and their economic might.

Although Japanese successes have indeed contributed to the harboring of billions of dollars (see Figure 2-6) from trade surpluses, which they are wisely investing around the world, such success has promoted resentment, as is invariably the case. Today, concerted efforts to catch up and compete on equal terms with the Japanese have become the flavor of the day. As information flows freely and speedily, it is more difficult to hide success or avoid imitation. We therefore believe that the trend toward competitive equality will continue, bringing the Europeans, Americans, and Japanese to a standstill concerning accrued competitive advantages. Furthermore, we doubt that trading blocs will accept continuous deficits from single countries (or groups of them) without demanding and getting reciprocity. This means that countries will specialize more and gain competitive advantages in certain industries, so that there will be more positive trade balances and an absence of longer-term deficits or surpluses. We cannot see how any long-term equilibrium can be maintained without some form of equality, as the various big players will shift their alliances, create new patterns, and support critical industries until a balance of economic power among them is achieved.

The front line of the battle for competitive supremacy will probably be transferred to Third World countries, which will need advanced technologies and cheap industrial and consumer products. If these countries are not strong enough to demand reciprocity or if they are reliant on imported technologies or products to accelerate their economic growth, they will inevitably run up deficits. It remains to be seen how these deficits will be financed or, if loans have been provided, repaid. Thus, it might be necessary to find new, creative ways of helping

Figure 2-6. Japan's Trade Balance.

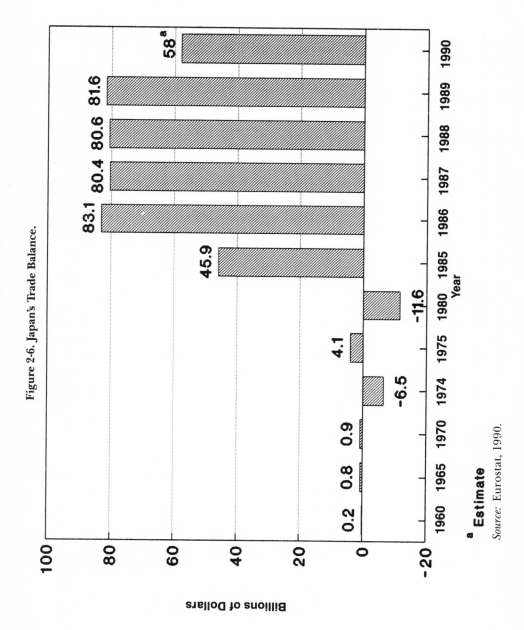

a Estimate

Source: Eurostat, 1990.

Third World countries improve their standard of living or finance their purchases of imports in order to ensure that the growth in industrialized countries continues—particularly as there will definitely be a serious slowdown in the growth of home markets, as population rates are dropping to zero (see Chapter Eleven) and consumer demand in many areas is reaching a plateau.

Conclusion

The EC countries, the United States, and Japan have different infrastructures, customs and habits, educational systems, human resources, and research capabilities that total up to different advantages and drawbacks for each of them. Moreover, there are differences in working conditions, productivity, business practices, and perceptions about profits, as well as in governmental attitudes toward businesses and the help provided them to improve their ability to compete globally. There is no doubt that Japan has gained an advantage over Europe and the United States as far as technological know-how, manufacturing capabilities, and successful managerial practices are concerned.

The Japanese challenge is well understood in both Europe and the United States. As argued on several occasions in this book, the rapid elaboration of the single European market has been to a large extent a direct response to the belated comprehension among European business and political leaders that no community country can successfully face the Japanese challenge single-handedly. Moreover, American businessmen fully understand the fact that, in order to survive, they must adapt their organizations in a way that will allow them to compete successfully with the Japanese. At the same time, internal Japanese changes will reduce the number of hours Japanese workers are willing to toil, increase their vacation time, and put a greater emphasis on spending and *yutori* (peace of mind) than on the accumulation of more wealth for the powerful Japanese corporations. Thus, the future will witness important changes as learning and imitation take place and strategic alliances are formed in order to achieve an equilibrium of forces. The stakes involved are too great to let any single country (or group of them) achieve superior technological or economic dominance. In the final analysis, the game will be one of maintaining some form of competitive equilibrium among the major economic players and demanding reciprocity when short-term imbalances threaten it. The major battleground will have to be Third World countries and the emerging population superpowers such as China, India, and Latin America. One cannot forget the U.S.S.R. and the role it will play in the future if *perestroika* succeeds (see Chapter Three).

References

Eurostat. Brussels: Statistical Office of the European Communities, 1990.

Imede and the World Economic Forum. *European Affairs*, Autumn 1989, pp. 14–17.

Liesner, T. *One Hundred Years of Economic Statistics.* London: Economist Publications, 1989.

CHAPTER 3

Politics and Economics

Prospects for Gorbachev's Common European Market

Jonathan Story

As the second millennium speeds to its conclusion, a variety of visions contend for the attention of Europeans. First into the field was the European Community's (EC) commission president Jacques Delors, who declared in June 1988 that "in ten years' time, 80 percent of economic legislation — and perhaps tax and social legislation — will be directed from the community." Former British prime minister Margaret Thatcher then sketched her view of Europe as a family of nation-states, incorporating the peoples of Eastern Europe and "that Atlantic Community — that Europe on both sides of the Atlantic — which is our greatest inheritance and our greatest strength." On October 1988, Pope John Paul II appealed to all the peoples of Europe to shake off their spiritual lethargy, by drawing on the "same faith and the same values that constitute their most precious heritage."

The following May, U.S. president George Bush saw the new century holding "the promise of a united Europe" tied to the United States in "a more mature partnership." In July, Soviet president Mikhail Gorbachev urged Western leaders to consider "future stages of progress towards a European Community of the twenty-first century." After the collapse of the European communist party-states in the course of 1989, West Germany's chancellor Helmut Kohl declared, "My goal, if the hour of history allows, is the unity of the nation." And in January 1990, French president François Mitterrand declared that "the main axis for us French, is the development of the community and the reinforcement of its structures."

New circumstances prompt this flurry of visions. In 1985, the main features of Europe were not too dissimilar from those of the early postwar years. In half a decade, the contrast is startling. The EC has moved well along the path to political and market integration. Germany has unified, and the Soviet Union is undergoing revolutionary changes. As the cold war recedes, the postwar alliances are either disintegrating or undergoing profound transformation. Europe is indeed living through momentous times.

Europe in 1985

In 1985, Europe's postwar inheritance was forty years old. The situation was characterized by the presence of the great powers, with their alliances. The United States, as the pillar of the Atlantic alliance, has been at the center of a network of military bases, strung around the periphery of the Soviet Union in support of the policy of containment. Political pluralism and market economies prevailed in Western Europe; monopoly party rule and centralized planning were clamped onto the Eastern satellite states. This enduring structure of world politics bound European affairs into the rhythm of global relations between the United States and the Soviet Union, after having provided the secure context within which Japan and West Germany could emerge as respectively the world's second and third economic power. The Soviet Union's achievement of nuclear parity ended the invulnerability of U.S. territory, but its record at home was one of political repression, a slide into economic stagnation, and social anemia. By the early 1980s, Moscow's main means of influence in Western Europe was to manipulate fears of war.

In the meantime, Western Europe had built a network of relations among its member countries, and with the rest of the world, unrivaled in density and scope. Traditional bilateral diplomatic ties were supplemented by a host of global or regional multilateral institutions. These forums had competing functions, overlapping competences, and variable membership. One cluster was formed around the Atlantic alliance, with its focus on political and military matters affecting the United States and the Western European allies. The North Atlantic Treaty Organization's (NATO) sixteen members were also in the twenty-four-nation Organization of Economic Cooperation and Development (OECD), which included Japan. Another cluster was formed around the twelve members of the European Community, with their complex political institutions and ambitious aims "to speak with one voice" in trade relations. The EC's foreign ministers engaged jointly in declaratory statements on world politics, while managing the charged agenda of community affairs with the commission, the EC's executive body. There were also the thirty-five states in the Helsinki conferences, including the United States and Canada, whose near permanent discussions enmeshed the party-states in Europe's diplomatic system.

A myriad of links had also been built up tying local and national markets into global ones. Competition in world markets was manifest in the struggle for technological leadership between corporations. A major determinant was the individual ability of states to harness human capital, innovation, information, and financial resources for the national pursuit of wealth and power. Yet the central thrust of postwar Western European history had been to downplay national differences through the promotion of complex political and economic interdependencies. A permanent tension had thus been created between the national exigency to stay ahead in world competition, and the effort to create a more interdependent Europe. Growth rates, at 5 percent in the 1960s, had fallen to 3 percent between 1974 and 1979, and to 1 percent in the first part of the 1980s. Unemployment edged steadily upward, reaching double-digit figures. The prevalent diagnosis of Europe's ailments identified national regulations as the source of the problem. In short, Europe's revival required a mixture of liberal and interventionist policies on a continental scale in order to escape the straitjacket of the national states.

The national states, though, were Western Europe's central political units. The principles of legitimacy for Western European states were national self-determination, constitutional pluralism, and human rights under the convention associated with the twenty-three-nation Council of Europe. Since the fall of the Iberian and Greek dictatorships in 1974 and 1975, this standard was shared by all states, either as a measure of actual policy or as an aspiration, as in the case of Turkey. Each state had its own configuration of political arrangements, economic policy institutions, and market structures. Each was responsible to domestic constituencies, and bound in different degrees into the three clusters of NATO, the EC, and the Helsinki conferences.

Western Europe's intricate polity had developed its own specificities with respect to the rest of the world, but remained highly differentiated within. Besides the disparities of geography, religion, and language, there were at least five political Europes in 1985. There was the Europe of Brussels, with the headquarters of NATO and the institutions of the EC. There was the Europe of the Soviet Union's satellite states, increasingly vulnerable to the pull of Western Europe. The neutral and nonaligned countries (including Switzerland, Austria, Scandinavia, and Finland), with their Western institutions and markets, straddled the diplomatic fence in East-West relations. European Russia, only one-fifth of the Soviet Union's geographic area, represented the bulk of the population and most of the economic resources. The United States, geographically isolated from Europe by the Atlantic Ocean, was nonetheless omnipresent in Europe, in military, economic, and cultural terms.

Europe and the World in 1990

By 1990, Europe had become the center of attention in the external policies of the Soviet Union, the United States, and Japan.

The paradox of Gorbachev is expressed in his popularity in Europe and the United States, in contrast to the disaffection with his policies in the Soviet Union itself. The concentration of powers with his election as head of state by the People's Congress in May 1989 represented one more step toward assuring his position. His aim was the restructuring of the inherited apparatus in order to create a "socialist state of law." But Gorbachev had to temporize between factions in introducing his policies, while lighter censorship had revealed a growing gulf between public expectations and present results. The main stumbling block was the party's "leading role," articulated in the Soviet Constitution's Article 6. It left ample space for threatened party leaders to block changes or to appeal to local resentments against Moscow. The stirring of national and religious demands in the multiethnic empire in turn fostered Russian chauvinism, threatening the union's cohesion. Tensions were aggravated by disastrous economic conditions, hidden inflation, and a surge in foreign debt. Only a legitimate government issuing from multiparty elections could make the necessary decisions. Hence, Gorbachev's success in early 1990 in suspending Article 6, ending the party's monopoly in power, was a major step toward reform. But the key decisions still lay ahead. The destination of the Soviet Union's internal restructuring, in short, remained uncertain.

Gorbachev's major successes relate to external affairs. Relief from the burden of military expenditures — estimated as equivalent to 18 percent of GNP — has necessitated a revision of foreign policy. "Sufficiency" and "defensive defense" describe the "new thinking." Gorbachev's disarmament offensive was launched in February 1986, with dramatic proposals to rid the world of nuclear weapons by the year 2000, to withdraw U.S. and Soviet fleets from the Mediterranean, and to denuclearize Europe, along with "the total withdrawal of foreign troops from the territory of other countries." While President Ronald Reagan showed U.S. determination to remain a Mediterranean power with the bombing of Libya in April, he lent a more ready ear to Gorbachev's acceptance of his earlier proposals to withdraw intermediate range missiles in Europe. Washington overrode objections from Bonn, Paris, and London that Western Europe was thereby more exposed to the deployment of Soviet military power, and the way was cleared for the Washington Treaty of December 8, 1987, between Gorbachev and Reagan, whereby all missiles with a range of between 500 and 5,500 kilometers were to be destroyed within three years. First among agreements of this kind, the treaty included extensive verification procedures. The resulting climate of confidence facilitated a spate of agreements on chemical weapons, and the resumption of discussions on strategic arms cuts and conventional forces, with talks between NATO and Warsaw Pact members opening in Vienna in March 1989. At Malta in December 1989, Presidents Bush and Gorbachev spoke of a new treaty limiting conventional arms in Europe, which was signed in November 1990.

The other arm of Gorbachev's peace program was also initiated in February 1986, under the slogan of a "common European house." Initially, the motive was to confirm the Soviet Union's status as a European power in the face of the EC's rapid progress toward integration, while underlining the divergence of interests of the Western Europeans and the United States. The major difference with the past was Gorbachev's readiness to lend credibility to the unity of Western Europe through reforms in Eastern Europe. At the Communist Party of the Soviet Union (CPSU) 27th Congress in February 1986, Gorbachev declared that "radical reform is necessary." Then in his book, *Perestroïka*, published in autumn 1987, he added that "we do not seek to impose our view on anybody" (p. 207). In his United Nations speech of December 1988, along with a renewed emphasis on the common interests uniting humanity, he announced a unilateral withdrawal of fifty thousand Red Army troops from the German Democratic Republic (GDR), Czechoslovakia, and Hungary. Finally, at Strasbourg in July 1989, he stated categorically that "any attempts to restrict the sovereignty of states, friends, allies and any others, are inadmissible" ("The Gorbachev Doctrine," 1989, p. 22). No Soviet troops stirred when the revolutions of November and December 1989 swept aside the "fraternal" regimes in the GDR, Czechoslovakia, Bulgaria, and Rumania. A breach was opened in the Berlin Wall on November 9, 1989. These momentous changes paved the way to the extension of pluralist democracies into Eastern Europe, including East Germany. Suddenly, the overriding issue in Germany is national unity.

The changes in the Soviet Union and Eastern Europe have highlighted Japan's situation. The foundations of the postwar U.S.-Japanese relationship were containment of the Soviet Union and interdependence. But the United States and the Soviet Union are declaring peace on each other, while Japanese corporations continue to compete ferociously with a view to victory against rival producers in Western markets. Japan's trade surpluses with the United States and the EC have piled up, as Japan has become the prime source of surplus capital to the world economy. Irritation at unequal access to Japan's markets has inspired the EC's bid to achieve a continental economy, as a basis from which European corporations can strike back at the Japanese. Economic relations between the EC and Japan are to be negotiated on reciprocal terms.

The new thinking is that Japan, rather than the Soviet Union, must be "contained." The argument is that little has been achieved in past trade negotiations in the way of Japan's developing a political and market system compatible with that in Western countries. A more effective method of dealing with Japan is thus for the United States and Western Europe to restructure world politics by seizing the olive branch tended by Gorbachev. Whereas Reagan's eight years saw an emphasis on military containment, switching later toward preferred relations with Japan, the focus of the Bush administration has been almost exclusively on Europe and the Soviet Union. An end to the cold war in Europe spells an opportunity to redeploy technological, financial, and human resources to meet Japan's challenge on world markets. It also spells a new goal for U.S. foreign policy: "the integration of the Soviet Union into the Community of nations." This is conditional on the extension of political, market, and individual freedoms into Eastern Europe, as well as steps toward political pluralism and human rights in the Soviet Union. Referring to Western Europe's emergence as "a partner in world leadership," President Bush has stated that "a resurgent Western

Europe is an economic magnet, drawing Eastern Europe closer toward the commonwealth of free nations." "New mechanisms of consultation and cooperation on political and global issues" are to be developed between the Atlantic allies in preparation for a world after the cold war (U.S. Information Service, 1989).

Europe's renewed centrality was betokened by the 1989 itineraries of world leaders. Gorbachev visited London, Bonn, Paris, and Rome prior to his meeting off Malta in December with Bush. Bush made visits to Brussels and Bonn in May, Paris in June, and Brussels in December. Partly in response to Gorbachev's active diplomacy, Bush also visited Poland and Hungary in July. And Japan's prime minister Kaifu made a ten-nation trip to Europe in January 1990.

Europe's position in world affairs has changed radically from the postwar period, and prospects are quite different. Progress on disarmament promises to demilitarize international relations, allowing for a significant redeployment of resources and pointing toward the elaboration of a pan-European security system. The United States seeks an intimate but more balanced relationship with the new Europe. The Central and Eastern European nations are embarking on the arduous task of creating pluralist states on communist ruins. Gorbachev has started the Soviet Union on a revolutionary path of restructuring. The declarations of peace between the United States and the Soviet Union leave Japan diplomatically isolated, and trapped in economic struggle with the EC and the United States. The union of the two Germanys, accelerated by the spread of pluralism into East Germany, is creating another Europe—the "real Europe," as Mitterrand wrote, "that of history and geography."

A Europe Without Frontiers

The vision of a "Europe without frontiers" was nurtured in a divided Europe, and designed as a means to overcome stagnation. It is a vision, and based on a set of newly agreed rules, a timetable, and the overall goal of achieving a more efficient internal EC market. The major change with the past is that

France has joined the Federal Republic in a determined drive for stronger EC institutions.

The new vision is above all a political program designed to harness the twelve national states of the EC to a common task for the future. European publics are offered wider horizons than national introversion. But the main target of the program is improved competitiveness in the world of business. As the commission states, a key condition of success is "the credibility of the process, the assurance that in the medium term the environment will undergo a tranformation that will oblige all firms to adopt a European strategy" (European Economy, 1988, p. 21). The process involves a combined effort to fashion business expectations by acting on political impediments to a more efficient continentwide economy. It is an experiment in levitation whereby businesses are invited to believe that even if the program is not implemented in all its legislative guises, competitors may assume that it will be, thereby requiring risks to be taken as if the internal market were a certainty. Not least, the whole program is a media phenomenon, with a date — 1992 — that holds the promise that something significant is going to happen by December 31 of that year. It thereby resurrects a community method of writing a detailed timetable, on which all manner of expectations may be pegged.

The origins of 1992 — the promoted date of integration — lie in a prolonged campaign by the commission to revive the community. Starting in 1979, the commission sought to harness the multiple motivations of the individual states in order to launch a determined attack on nontariff barriers, promote a series of EC-wide technology programs, and strengthen its negotiating position as the EC's representative in trade relations with outsiders. Its allies were European businesses, particularly those represented in the Roundtable of European Industrialists. The Federal Republic, drawing on the traditions of Chancellor Konrad Adenauer from the 1950s, applied its political weight in favor of the new democratic Spain's entry to the EC, to be accompanied by further moves to political and economic integration. The Benelux countries remained loyal to their traditional attachment to the ideal of European union. The British government saw an opportunity to promote free-market ideals as a positive contribution to the common enterprise. Italy looked for a more determined lead from Brussels as a means to promote reforms at home, while welcoming the culmination of Spain's lengthy entry negotiations to the EC as providing a new impetus to community affairs. But the major change in attitudes toward the EC was registered in France: whereas in the 1960s and the 1970s, French diplomacy and public opinion had been wary of any loss of national independence, the early 1980s revived a latent enthusiasm for European integration. The European Community came to be seen as the only effective means to achieve national goals of economic growth and partnership with Germany.

The actual relaunch of the EC got under way with the conclusion of Spain's lengthy entry negotiations in March 1985. In June, the Milan European Council voted by majority to hold an intergovernmental conference to modify and extend community powers written into the Rome Treaty of 1957. At the Luxembourg European Council in December, another majority vote was cast in favor of an international conference to modify the Treaty of Rome. The Single European Act (SEA), finally ratified by all member states' parliaments in June 1987, both amends the original treaties and incorporates into it the institutions and practice that have developed alongside. The key element here is the move to majority voting over a wider range of issues relating to the internal market. The SEA strengthens the commission, upgrades the role of the parliament, and reinforces the community as a negotiating partner for third parties. But the states retain their legislative power in council. The device of the intergovernmental conference is now available for further treaty revision and extension of EC competences. The act also enshrines in Article 8A a commitment of the states to achieve "a progressive establishment of the internal market by December 31, 1992." The specific aim is the reduction of nontariff barriers. The process is expedited by resort to the new procedures, referred to in the SEA and by the broad application of the principle of mutual recognition. This principle, derived from EC law, holds that goods may be freely exported to another member state when they have been produced and commercialized in accordance with the regulations of the exporting country. Thus the kernel of the internal market program is to facilitate competition among public policies, and in all possible areas of business activity. The new approach is based on the diversity of the European state system in that it seeks to use rather than be blocked by it. It represents a shift toward a policy for a federation of distinct states, rather than imposing harmony as a step toward a single state.

A driving force behind the new policy is France, formerly the champion of the states' veto right in EC affairs and of national independence within the Atlantic alliance. Germany's defeat and division offered France an ideal chance to take the political initiative as the central state in Western Europe. A constant preoccupation has been to bind the Federal Republic westward, accompanied by gusts of anxiety that West Germany was losing its Western moorings and edging closer to the Soviet Union. The counterpart has been acceptance of the Federal Republic as an equal and support for its constitutional commitment to achieve national unity. Policy has alternated between two formulas: federalist institutions within a tightly knit community; and a Europe of the states, allied to the United States, and open to cooperation with the party-states.

Over the past decade, France has placed renewed emphasis on EC integration. The domestic opponents of the EC were marginalized momentarily, while the move to majority voting has accompanied the EC's enlargement to twelve. Policy is based on the idea that it is better to promote the complex interdependencies of the Western alliance that have been built up over the past forty years than to allow the nationality principle to become triumphant in Germany. France's concerns have taken a number of forms. French security policy has moved closer to NATO, without sacrificing the principle of independence in the determination of nuclear weapons policy. The West European Union (WEU)—a somnolent appendage of the Atlantic alliance—has been revived, when its seven members produced a joint statement in October 1987 entitled "Platform on European Security Issues." A month after the Washington Treaty of December 1987, a Franco-German Security Council was agreed on. But little has come of it. As Mitterrand declared: "The mission of France is not to assure the protection of other European countries" (David, 1989, p. 317). Given the difficulties in creating closer defense links among the Europeans, successive French governments have promoted single market Europe as the best means to galvanize the French economy, reduce German mercantilism, and bind the Federal Republic westward. Above all, France champions the proposal for a European System of Central Banks. All of these policies hinge on West Germany, and are therefore conditional on the changing circumstances affecting its union with East Germany. German monetary union came into effect on July 2, 1990; political union followed on October 3. The first all-German elections since 1932 were held on December 2, and gave a clear victory to Chancellor Helmut Kohl's Christian Democrat and Liberal coalition.

As expressed in a contemporary foreign policy report, "European integration has become a sine qua non condition for a modus vivendi with the Germany question" (Kaiser and others, 1983, p. 59). Mitterrand announced France's renewed emphasis on EC integration in two key speeches early in 1984 at The Hague and Strasbourg. France's EC presidency of that year cleared the way for integration strategy by initiating reform of the EC's farm policies, setting the stage for Spain's entry, and patching up agreement on the EC budget. In parallel, the French government began to deregulate France's financial markets, in order to reduce corporate reliance on bank debt. The privatization of state properties then extended the capital base of French corporations and strengthened the ability to deploy and ally on an international scale.

Three of the key successes of the French EC presidency in late 1989 were further progress on the path to liberalization of EC financial markets, adoption of measures liberalizing the seventy-five billion ECU telecommunications markets between mid-1990 and 1993, the creation of a more effective EC competition law. From September 1990 on, the commission has sole power to block large community mergers, with a combined turnover of 5 billion ECU, of which 250 million ECU of each company must be in the EC. Commission powers in this crucial area are likely to be augmented in the future.

Finally, France has emerged as the main champion of a European central bank. The concept is simple: the best way to reduce policy dependence on the Bundesbank is to join it. The European monetary system (EMS), set up in 1978–1979, had helped to stabilize intra-EC exchange rates. But the plan to create a European central bank was shelved, leaving the Bundesbank free to set the parameters of policy for other currencies. German business benefited by the permanent undervaluation of the DM, a growing trade surplus, and low interest rates. Other EC economies were tied to the growth path of the German economy, with a 1 percent GNP average from 1981 to 1987.

In June 1988 a deal was cut at the European Council at Hanover, whereby France and Italy agreed conditionally to liberalize all capital movements by July 1, 1990; and Germany acquiesced in a mandate for a report to study the means for achieving monetary union. The report, presented at the Madrid European Council in June 1989, proposed monetary union in three stages, with a federal scheme for a European System of Central Banks (ESCB). At the Strasbourg European Council of December 1989, an accord was reached whereby the EC pledged support for the German people to "refind unity through self-determination," and the German government agreed that a new intergovernmental conference — in the manner of 1985 — be held prior to the German elections in 1990, with a view to incorporating monetary union into the treaties. That in turn means a reinforcement of the federal dimension in EC institutions.

France's championing of monetary union is an indication of Mitterand's determination to give the EC (and France) the means of its ambitions for a unified Europe. His horizons give an idea of his agenda. Relected in 1988 with a large majority, Mitterrand has a mandate until 1995, with general elections in 1993. The internal market, and the deregulatory policies accompanying it, are to remain the new imperative for France, along with the creation of a European "social space," environmental policies, and monetary union. The creation of a European pillar in the Atlantic alliance has been postponed. Only a more federalist EC, with strong central institutions, can contain a united Germany.

Germany and Europe

The three major policies for the 1990s—Gorbachev's *perestroika*, Bush's "new Atlanticism," and 1992—converged on Germany, altering its domestic political balances as well as its international context. Germany plays a key role in NATO and the EC, but is also particularly sensitive to changes in the national situation.

A prime concern of Moscow remains the prevention of a tightly structured Western European security community. Gorbachev's disarmament campaign, rising in crescendo as Paris, London, and Bonn in 1986 and 1987 edged toward organizing a European pillar in the Atlantic alliance, met with an enthusiastic reception in Washington. Pressure was brought to bear on the NATO allies, particularly Bonn, to agree. Kohl reluctantly conceded. Washington then had Bonn renounce part possession of short-range nuclear weapons based in Germany. As French and British nuclear weapons were for national use only, and it was clear that the United States' willingness to spread a nuclear umbrella over the Federal Republic in the event of a crisis was a fiction, the only way left for Bonn was to seek reassurance in a new relationship with Moscow. In July 1987 President Richard von Weizäcker visited Moscow; the East German leader, Secretary-General Erik Honecker, went to the Federal Republic in September; and by December, the Washington accords were signed, opening up the prospect of a Europe after the cold war.

The promise of disarmament, coupled with the first moves to decompression in Eastern Europe, found Germany particularly receptive. Ideas to move NATO to a defensive conventional strategy had come to be widely shared, given fears of Germany as a potential nuclear battlefield. Equally, it was noted that the Washington Treaty meant the removal of nuclear weapons, whose use spelled the devastation of Germany. Yet the British and Americans argued that their troops could not be expected to fight for German freedoms without nuclear cover, while the potential enemy enjoyed massive superiority in the European region: "no nukes, no troops," the argument ran. Germany, in short, was no longer defensible on conditions to which the allies could agree. The embarrassment was evident at the NATO summits of March 1988 and May 1989. Kohl conceded eventual modernization of NATO battlefield weapons, if progress was not recorded in the conventional arms talks at Vienna. With their rapid progress of the talks in the course of 1989, and the collapse of the East German regime in November, their modernization has been postponed indefinitely. The national question has moved to the forefront of Germany politics; NATO armies bunched on German soil have lost a clearly definable enemy, and run the risk of being perceived as occupation forces rather than as allies.

The Washington Treaty of December 1987 was followed by the Federal Republic's tenure of the EC's sixth-month rotating presidency. Here was a chance to reassure the community member states that the Federal Republic was firmly anchored to the West. As Western Europe's industrial powerhouse, the Federal Republic had much to gain. About 75 percent of its exports are with Western Europe, whence come about 95 percent of its trade surplus. The DM is Europe's leading currency. The Federal Republic had championed Spain's entry to the EC and the EC's internal market policy.

The German presidency of early 1988 proved decisive in the launching of Europe 1992. It marked the transition whereby Germany's political influence in Europe and in the world is coming to match its economic eminence. In February, Bonn was instrumental in negotiating a long-term EC budget package, satisfying the demands of Spain for more funds to the poorer regions. Bonn thereby increased its contributions to the EC budget by 40 to 50 percent, underlining its role as Europaymaster. It pushed through a spate of market-opening measures. In the meantime, the German standards institute (DIN) has become the main player in the EC's policy for harmonization of standards. The German trade union confederation (DGB) provides the principal support for the EC's "Social Charter," aimed to protect acquired worker rights in a more unified market, and the German public's sensitivity to environmental issues makes Bonn a champion of high standards in the EC as well as in other forums. The Bundesbank is Western Europe's de facto central bank.

The resurgent EC under the presidency of a more assertive Federal Republic burst onto the world's attention in June 1988: on June 13, the EC finance ministers decided to move to liberalization of capital movements; at the seven-power summit of advanced industrial states, held in Toronto on June 20, the EC resisted U.S. pressure to "eliminate" farm subsidies; and at the European Council of Hanover on June 27, the EC political leaders appointed a committee to study a move to monetary union.

The Federal Republic's EC presidency also recorded a triumph in securing mutual recognition of the EC and the Council for Mutual Economic Assistance (COMECON), set up in 1949 as an equivalent to Western European integration. The two bodies recognized each other, but the EC's status was underlined by allowing for COMECON member states to make bilateral trade deals with the EC. The Federal Republic (with Italy) is the country that stands to gain most from the arrangement. Kohl's October 1988 visit to Moscow highlighted the significance for the Soviet Union of economic relations with West Germany. For the Soviet Union, Germany and the EC provide 70 percent of hard currency earnings; Germany is seen as Moscow's key technology partner; its banks have the resources to help in the necessary economic restructuring of Eastern Europe and the Soviet Union. But historical resentments and revolutionary conditions in the East draw sharp limits around what the Federal Republic may do alone; the EC, not a solitary Federal Republic, has the moral authority to bind each newly formulated accord for trade concessions and aid packages to political reforms. The result is that the community's trade and aid functions have expanded extensively into Eastern Europe and the Soviet Union. They were reinforced at the Paris seven-power summit meeting in July 1989, in response to Kohl's requests, to give the commission the task of coordinating Western aid for Eastern Europe. The EC is also to establish a European Reconstruction and Development Bank (ERDB), to help in the reform of the Eastern European economies. Besides accords with Hungary and Poland, the EC signed a ten-year trade agreement with the Soviet Union that stipulated that all quotas on imports be removed by 1995. The broad aim is to open EC markets in order to allow the former party-states to earn hard currencies. But competition from neighbors with low labor costs will no doubt generate protectionist pressures in the member states.

The central novelty in Europe deriving from the changes in the world balance is the prospect of Germany unified. That means a nation of eighty million people with a dynamic economy equivalent to about 60 percent of Japan's, but right in the heart of the continent. German unity was endorsed in June 1989 by Bush's invitation to the Federal Republic to become a "partner in leadership" and by his expression of U.S. support for the right of the German people for self-determination. It is implicit in Gorbachev's "common European home," predicated on self-determination and nonintervention; in the Soviet leader's readiness to allow the collapse of the East German regime and hold free elections; and in the Soviet Union's longer-term interest in economic relations with the Federal Republic, as expressed in Gorbachev's June 1990 visit there. The right to German unification, etched into the United Nations Charter, is engraved in the Basic Law of the Federal Republic and has been reiterated by Western leaders as a promise at the heart of the Atlantic alliance. It was the central feature of Kohl's ten-point plan for German unification announced in the Bundestag on November 28, 1989. "The way is open," the chancellor declared, "for an overcoming of Europe's division and thereby that of our Fatherland."

Following the events of late 1989, the prospect of imminent union set off a competition among West German political parties that transcends the old divide between the two states, accelerating the advent of an all-German policy. One after another, West German political leaders have abandoned gradualism. Calls to patience were undermined by the speed of events, and by the scramble between the political parties to position themselves for the elections in East Germany, the four regional elections in West Germany, and the general elections of December 1990. The Soviet Union shifted from demanding in December 1989 that the two Germanies remain distinct entities to the January 1990 proposal for reunification against neutrality.

Germany's unity in 1990 fundamentally altered Europe's postwar security structures, which have been based on Europe's division, with Germany as the major stake in the struggle. The key question is how to incorporate Germany into an all-European peace order. One answer is for the two alliances to remain in place, while negotiating and verifying foreign troop reductions or maneuvers. Such a process inevitably raises the problem of the role of German armed forces in a nation that has recovered its right to self-determination. It touches on the security of Germany's many neighbors, and therefore involves the stability of Europe. The Helsinki conferences provide one forum for discussions, but they lack any power of enforcement. Another proposal is for Germany to be incorporated in a minimalist NATO, and in a federally strenghtened EC: NATO keeps its command structures, but few troops are positioned on German soil and nuclear weapons are reduced in number. Such a low profile for Western defense facilitates a minimalist defense for Poland and the Soviet Union. A united Germany is bound into the EC, where it is large, but one among many. The EC extends its foreign policy reach into the "political and economic" domains of security policy, as outlined in the Single European Act. Not least, such an EC — in a new form of relation with the United States — incorporates Germany, and forms the cornerstone of a wider Europe that in the longer run includes the Soviet Union. A variant of such a minimalist NATO would be to transfer many of its present functions to the West European Union, which would stand independently of the EC, but cooperate closely with it through the EC foreign policy cooperation.

The EC as a Pole of Attraction

The paradox of EC moves to create an internal market, strengthening the commission's trade negotiating powers with third parties, is that they generate outsider concern at the goings-on in Brussels. Outsiders take preemptive action by accelerating inward investment, seeking EC insiders to act on their behalf, or by changing the geopolitical context within which the EC integration process unfolds.

Germany's EC presidency generated anxiety in Washington and Tokyo about "Fortress Europe." An EC united front, corresponding to the tough retaliatory powers granted the U.S. administration under the new Trade Act, heralded severe transatlantic trade clashes. But Washington's redefinition of relations with Europe has altered the terms of the debate, based on the realization that the EC is twice as large an export market for the United States as Japan is. U.S. corporations within the EC stand to benefit from the EC's internal market policy and Western Europe has become a crucial partner in opening Eastern Europe, and eventually the Soviet Union, to pluralist politics and freer markets. In this scheme, the U.S. institutional vision of Atlantic relations — Bush's "new Atlanticism" — is of a NATO serving as a forum to develop and implement arms agreements, and of an EC reinforced through the signing of a treaty with the United States.

For Japan, a resurgent Europe is altogether more problematic. With an economy twice the size of the Federal Republic's, Japan has presented German corporations with their most severe challenge. The constant revaluation of the yen and massive investment in capital equipment have moved Japanese manufacturers into headlong rivalry with their German competitors. Hence, one source of German industrial support for a European economic space from which to strike back at Japanese rivals, and a de facto interest in the opening up of Eastern Europe as a source of cheap and skilled labor. German, Dutch, and French corporations have prompted the community to develop a more effective armory of trade policy instruments, such as antidumping procedures and local content regulations. That in turn has generated preemptive inward investment by Japanese corporations, especially into the United Kingdom, whose industrial base has been gravely weakened since entry to the EC. The promise is of a Japanese-British industrial alliance that will regenerate British-based manufacturing through the expansion of Japanese-owned plants. But the prospect of a U.S.-EC treaty, and of Western Europe's central role in Eastern Europe, has lent new urgency for Japan to define relations on a more assured basis. Kaifu's ten-nation visit to Europe in early 1990 provided a first step: Japan is to be a major supplier of financial resources to the emerging pluralist states of Eastern Europe. But the success of its engagement depends on cooperative relations with the EC.

The Scandinavian countries and Finland, as well as Switzerland and Austria, are closely tied into the European economic space by industrial, trade, and currency relationships. They, too, are pulled toward the community by the dynamics driving a single market Europe. The EC is their major market. They have impeccable credentials for membership: They are European and pluralist, and they have market economies. They enjoy close institutional relations with the community. They participate in the EC technology projects and in the EC standards organizations. But they have tended to shy away from membership. One reason is that domestic regulations have formed an essential part of political bargains struck in the early twentieth century between national producer interests, on consensual management of the economy. Alignment on EC regulations spells their unraveling. Only Austria has opted in July 1989 to lodge its candidacy for the EC. But commission policy has been to postpone prospective EC candidacies until after 1993. Another reason is that in the past Moscow opposed having the neutral countries in EFTA seek to join the EC, with its ambitions to develop into a tightly knit political and even military entity. But with Moscow's grip on Eastern Europe loosened and the Warsaw Pact and COMECON mere ghosts of their former selves, the veto has lifted. Indeed, the former party-states are lining up to join Western European institutions such as the Council of Europe, and anticipate associate status, or even membership in the community. With such a perspective, the EFTA countries have pressed for an EC-EFTA Treaty. The hope was to create a European Economic Space (EES) composed of eighteen sovereign states with compatible domestic regulations, and comprising 350 million people. But the commission insisted on keeping the EFTA countries at arm's length. The talks failed. Sweden followed Austria in lodging its EC candidacy. Failure of the talks means that the EC faces a spate of further membership candidacies.

Other states, too, were concerned by the new configuration on the European continent. Turkey and Morocco both applied for EC membership in 1987; Morocco was politely turned down, and Turkey's candidacy is postponed until the first decade of the next millennium. African, Middle Eastern, and Latin American countries fear that Western Europe's trade and aid may go first to the countries of Eastern Europe and the Soviet Union. Yet any closure of European product markets to the population-rich countries on its southern borders will certainly stimulate a further rise in immigration. A major trend toward a growing conflict between a post-Christian Western European civilization and Moslem revivalism would thus be confirmed. The accumulation of weaponry in the Middle East and the Persian Gulf, combined with religious, ethnic, and interstate tensions, makes the whole area a potential powder keg. The Western European economies remain vulnerable to a politically motivated rise in world oil prices.

The Soviet Union's policy affecting a single market Europe has been to alter the geopolitical context within which it was elaborated. With German unification, the prospect is opened of a wider Europe of democratic sovereign states cooperating together. That Europe, in Gorbachev's words, is to be a "community of democratic sovereign states with a high level of interdependence, of frontiers easily accessible and open to the exchange of technologies and ideas, to contacts on a grand scale between the peoples" ("Mr. Gorbachev. . . ," 1989, p. 3). It is expressed in the lengthening list of countries with guest status, attached to the twenty-four-nation Council of Europe, following Hungary's admission in 1990; the discussions in the community about trade and aid consessions to former party-states as they acquire political and market freedoms; and in general support for Gorbachev's idea of a Helsinki conference to start thinking about a European Community of the twenty-first century.

The prospect of such a Europe, following the revolutionary events in Eastern Europe in late 1989, has revealed the differences among the EC member states about Germany. The Federal Republic's demands for East Germany's association with, or entry to, the EC met with frank reserve. France and the Benelux countries used East Germany as a pretext to pospone indefinitely the 1985 Schengen accord with the Federal Republic on the free cross-frontier movement of people. The hitch was that they were unwilling to grant the Federal Republic that East Germany was not another foreign country. On the EC issue, Bonn pushed for East Germany to be treated as another candidate or member state. Holland objected to bringing East Germany into the EC ahead of Austria, whereas Belgium switched to championing Austria's early entry. Britain's prime minister was for no enlargement before 1993, and the French were muted. The change in the Soviet position for German unity in January 1990 implied that the former East Germany entered the EC as regions in an extended Federal Republic, which meant that the deutschmark (DM) became the official currency for all Germany and that five new regions were added to the Federal Republic. The former East Germany came under EC internal market legislation, so that non-German firms could benefit by access to business there. But a single Germany is more than ever the hub not of the EC only, so much as of the nascent pan-European polity and market.

Conclusion

The two visions of a single market Europe 1992 and a common European home launched simultaneously in 1986 entail two competing strategies for Germany and Europe. France seeks to bind the Federal Republic into a strengthened community; the Soviet Union aims to prevent a tightly structured Western European defense organization. This means allowing political pluralism and market mechanisms to be built on the ruins of the communist party-states in Eastern Europe. The West is deprived of a unifying enemy, but the resultant symbiosis between the two Germanys is creating a new Europe, the contours of which may be only dimly perceived.

Part of that new Europe is the territory covered by the former party-states, and where the future must be built on a pre-1945 history, ridden by national and ethnic rivalries, and on a post-1945 nightmare of police states and monopoly party power. Another unknown is the Soviet Union itself, whose leaders must invent a new legitimacy if they are to hold together the tsarist empire, after the collapse of "real scientific socialism."

European affairs are laden with official or proposed timetables that stretch into the future. Most of the major leaders' terms of office last to 1992 or 1993, with Mitterrand sailing through to 1995. After his December 1990 election victory, Kohl has four years to imprint his policies on Germany and Europe. In East-West relations, a 1990 treaty on conventional arms at Vienna sets the stage for a redefinition of NATO's role as the Western forum for disarmament talks and verification procedures. The Warsaw Pact, like COMECON, is now a ghost, though a banquet was laid in the Paris November 1990 conference for the thirty-five signatory states of the Helsinki Final Act to discuss the principles of security, trade, and human rights affecting the future of Europe. This rapid evolution in the "common European home" has prompted France to start EC talks on monetary union during December 1990. Kohl seeks an increase in the federal powers of the EC institutions in counterpart for any loss of the Bundesbank's sovereignty. The date for the next move to monetary union has been earmarked as January 1, 1994, after near completion of the detailed agendas for the internal market. But before then, the EFTA states, jointly or separately, will seek to sign a treaty with the EC. A U.S.-EC treaty would have to be in place for the Republicans to take political credit in the 1992 presidential elections.

The political impetus behind a single market Europe is now considerable. The force driving it forward has been the changing world structure, evidenced by the rise of Japan and Germany. Japan provides the EC with a continued inspiration to build a continental economy, whereas its competitiveness is one factor prompting the United States to reach a settlement in

Europe, thereby releasing resources for nonmilitary use. An end to the cold war opened the way to a single Germany. The supporters of a more federal EC maintain that it is only through the equal curtailment of national sovereignties in a strengthened EC that the Western continental neighbors of a united Germany would feel comfortable. This aspiration may draw on the trends of the past decade, which has seen the federal dimension of the community reinforced, as evidenced in the EC's practice since the updating of its constitution with the Single European Act. Much political capital was invested in the successful outcome of the 1990 intergovernmental conference to extend the EC's federal powers, as well as in the completion of a single market Europe. Business expectations have been aroused, and may not be deceived with impunity.

The EC's bid for unity exerts an ever more powerful pull on neighbors in EFTA and the developing countries. The U.S. proposal for a treaty with the EC only strengthens the trend. Japan seeks to establish relations on a more enduring basis. A uniting EC acts as a magnet on Eastern European countries, which also feel more comfortable dealing with a Germany that is firmly embedded in the community. But outsider fears of an exclusive EC drive to union have engendered a scramble to influence insiders. France represents the French-speaking African countries, and Spain speaks in the EC for Latin America. Britain is building an industrial alliance with Japan. Germany is the main interlocutor for the Soviet Union and Eastern European countries. Fearing joint dominion by France and Germany in the EC, Italy joins Britain and the Benelux countries in keeping the United States tied into Europe. These multiple gateways into Europe are duplicated by market interdependencies with the rest of the world.

There is no certainty that such powerful trends toward a more united EC will win out. The EC stays differentiated within, and in relations between its component states and outsiders. National institutions, traditions, and interests remain vigorous, as exemplified by the states' resistance to abandon powers in education, labor markets, tax, money, or defense. Differences among the member states plague the development of foreign and commercial policies toward the rest of the world. Global economic interdependence ensures that each state is affected in particular ways by oil price movements, or by speculative shifts affecting exchange rate alignments. A multitude of problems attend the elaboration of a pan-European peace system, to replace Europe's security framework inherited from World War II.

The proponents of a Europe of the states insist that the national states alone have democratic legitimacy and international standing. The community, for former prime minister Thatcher, is a practical means to "achieve international cooperation between independent sovereign states." Her arguments appeal to the strong currents of resistance in each one of the EC member states, which are manifest in the concern about Brussels's centralizing ambitions within the EC and the commission's alleged propensity to trade protectionism. Resistance is also evident in the demands for a widening of the EC to include Austria and the countries of EFTA. Such a vision of a wider Europe, composed of sovereign states cooperating together, stretches out eventually to include the former party-states, once their political and market reforms have been implemented. It is to be achieved through negotiations in the Helsinki conferences to create a European order beyond the cold war.

But the probabilities are higher for a Western European union, clustered around the EC, than for a looser and wider association of states, concerned to ensure peace and to promote trade. Gorbachev's vision of a common European home is at once too vague and too rigid. It must remain vague, pending the complete transition to political pluralism and market mechanisms in Eastern Europe, let alone in the Soviet Union. It is too rigid because the most the thirty-five states could debate in the European security conference in 1990 was how best to ensure the international status quo, while political transitions proceed. The transition of greatest significance to the whole of Europe is the one in Germany.

The risk for the Western allies was that they sacrifice the German right for self-determination on the altar of European stability. Yet the Western European nightmare is of nationalism as a liberating force sweeping into Germany from Eastern Europe, in combination with the example of Japan, to re-create an assertive Germany, with hegemonic ambitions, in the heart of Europe. A Europe of the states, relying on cooperation alone, does not answer these fears. A closer European union, to be elaborated in the EC intergovernmental conference starting at the end of 1990, does. As the December 1989 Strasbourg European Council statement declared, German self-determination is to proceed "in the perspective of Community integration." Such a union is likely to have five dimensions: a strengthening of parliamentary and commission powers; a move to monetary union, and perhaps some agreement on a European System of Central Banks (ESCB); the internal market policy; a European pillar in an Atlantic alliance, where the military dimension has lost its former salience; and an EC that extends its foreign policy and security functions, in conjunction with NATO or the Western European Union (WEU), as the cornerstone for a wider Europe. The proponents of a federal Europe urge that the condition for a stronger EC is more parliamentary control to lend greater authority to EC decisions. A united Germany in such an EC would be central, but not dominant.

The timing was spelled out in Mitterrand's 1990 New Year's message. The new Europe should be achieved in two stages: In the first stage, the EC would be the "pole of attraction" around which the twelve, and then a future, wider Europe are to gather. The second stage would see the emergence of a "European confederation in the real sense of the term, which will associate all the States of our continent in a common and permanent organization of exchanges, of peace and security." The United States would be allied to the first on a new basis; the Soviet Union will be included in the second sometime in the mid- to late 1990s, depending on, of course, the unpredictable outcome of Russia's second revolution.

References

David, D. (ed.). *The Politics of Defense: Texts and Documents*. Paris: Foundation for the Study of National Defense, 1989.

European Economy, Commission of the European Community, 1992. *The New European Economy*, 1988, *35*, 21.

Gorbachev, M. *Perestroïka*. Paris: Flammarion, 1987.

"The Gorbachev Doctrine." *The Economist*, July 15, 1989, p. 22.

Kaiser, K., and others. *The European Community: Decline or Renewal*. Paris: IFRI, 1983.

"Mr. Gorbachev Understands the Opinions of Mr. Bush." *Le Monde*, Dec. 1989, pp. 3–4.

U.S. Information Service. President George Bush's five key foreign policy speeches, on Poland, Apr. 17, 1989; on the Americas, May 2; on welcoming a reformed U.S.S.R. into the world order, May 12; on the emergence of a united Europe; on the eclipse of communism, May 24. Washington, D.C.: U.S. Information Service, 1989.

PART TWO

Strategic Challenges
of the Single Market

CHAPTER 4

Pan-European Marketing
Combining Product Strength and Geographical Coverage

Robert Gogel, Jean-Claude Larréché

The preparation of a single European market has created a state of strategic turbulence in several industries. There is a potential danger that misunderstanding the strategic aspects related to the single market may lead to unsuitable actions. A crucial aspect of international marketing strategy is to achieve a balanced development of product strength and geographical coverage. The lowering of the internal barriers to entry among the twelve EC countries has made the development of geographical coverage of the entire European market more attractive. The effectiveness of investments made for geographical expansion depends on the product strength of a corporation, as geographical expansion based on inappropriate product strength may lead to the weakening of a company's competitive posture. This chapter presents the International Competitive Posture Matrix, a framework that provides an integrated perspective on the

Note: A version of this chapter was published in the *European Management Journal*, 1989, 7, 132–140.

product strength and geographical coverage dimensions of international marketing strategy. The framework is illustrated using the European food industry as an example. It is clear that, over the next few years, appropriate marketing strategies will be needed in order to better exploit the opportunities created by a pan-European orientation. We believe that the crucial strategic marketing issues will concentrate on developing product strength *and* geographical coverage.

The single market will offer corporations new opportunities and challenges. Whereas certain industries now fall under protective national legislation favoring local production, such regulations will no longer exist. For example, Italian regulation currently prevents low-alcohol beers being produced in Italy, although they can be imported with major administrative restrictions (Colby, 1988). The market opportunity for a company like BSN (the largest French food/beverage manufacturer) is significant, but for the moment BSN has chosen not to attack the Italian market with its low-alcohol beer because of the administrative barriers. (Rather, it has chosen to focus on the French market.) Given a single market Europe, BSN should be able to introduce its low-alcohol beer in Italy and take advantage of a much larger market base on which to amortize its R&D, production, and marketing costs.

There are hundreds of similar types of regulations in each member state of the European Community that currently protect local products from outside competition (see Chapter Five). The single market will eliminate customs and all other barriers that prevent the free flow of goods and services and allow a larger geographical coverage if a company so desires and has the necessary resources. It will also allow greater economies of scale, lower costs, increased efficiencies, cheaper products, and, ultimately and consequently, more variety and more satisfied customers.

Getting Ready for a Single Market: Which Stage Are We In?

Europe 1992 was announced in 1985, thus providing a specific target date well in advance and giving corporations time to consider the implications and prepare themselves for the event, and some corporations made preemptive competitive moves.

Such a major event is exceptional in business history. Not many similar situations are available for reference. Thus there is great uncertainty and consequent risk in formulating appropriate strategic responses. The deregulation of the U.S. airline industry, although more limited in scope, provides at least one example of a somewhat similar major planned event. Airline deregulation has dramatically changed the competitive dynamics of the industry, including the creation of new airlines, acquisitions, mergers, and very intense marketing activities. Some companies, both new (People Express) and old (Braniff), were forced into bankruptcy or mergers, while others consolidated their poisitions. One of the lessons to be gained from this experience is that inaction and overly ambitious expansion can be equally troublesome and can become the cause of sometimes fatal strategic mistakes. Drawing on the U.S. airline deregulation experience, we believe that it is valuable to consider the responses to such major events in four separate stages: mobilization, strategic turbulence, competitive struggle, and competitive equilibrium.

Stage 1: Mobilization. In stage 1, the external event's anticipated arrival often causes more anxiety than action. This behavioral pattern is visible around the single European market event. Although some corporations are gathering information on the possible implications of a single market and are trying to identify the opportunities and threats, others have adopted a wait-and-see attitude and are not preparing a clear strategic plan.

Stage 2: Strategic Turbulence. The confused state of affairs typical of stage 1 is followed by strategic turbulence, during which some firms emerge ahead of their competitors because they recognized the opportunity presented by the event early enough, and are taking advantage of it. Some early moves have been made even before actual regulatory changes take place. Others have been well prepared and are put into action at the time the change occurs. Such moves and actions include acquisitions, alliances, and internal expansion. Successful executives are those who are able to get their organizations to recognize the opportunity and act faster than their competitors, while at the same time being able to appreciate and control the risks involved. Such early preemptive moves represent a potential high-risk/high-return approach. They are high-risk because specific elements of the event are not yet well understood. They are high-return because of the benefits acquired from the first-mover's competitive advantages.

Stage 3: Competitive Struggle. Stage 3 typically involves an intense competitive struggle during which companies, now fully aware of the external event and its implications, attempt to exploit the new regulatory context in order to strengthen their competitive position within the market. The uncertainties of the new environment are minimal compared to stage 2, as the event has already occurred (or, in some instances, its implications are well known). This is the time when moves to obtain substantial competitive advantages are most likely to take place. During this stage, however, competitive reactions should be expected to promptly follow strategic actions.

The intense competitive struggle of a single market has not yet begun. In fact, two schools of thought have emerged. One holds that the struggle will never take place, as those corporations that are strong today will continue to be strong in the future. They are expected to use their force to discourage newcomers and restrict the freedom of choice of established players. The opposite view suggests that the struggle will be quite intense: such a major change will destabilize the existing competitive equilibrium and leave the door wide open to new entrants or major realignments among existing firms. These two perspectives correspond to different perceptions of the implications of a single market, or else they might be applicable in certain industries but not in others.

Stage 4: Competitive Equilibrium. Stage 4 is reached when the competitive struggle created by the external event slows down and competitive activities return to a reasonable level as a new competitive equilibrium is established.

One can only speculate about what the competitive equilibrium will be like in specific industries, but it is possible to anticipate that strategic thinking will become more refined as companies and industries pass through the four stages described above. Although some industries have already entered stage 2 (for example, financial services and the food industry), the turbulence is likely to continue and spread to other industries. Moreover, we believe that it is extremely important to have a broad strategic perspective on the challenges created by the single market, in particular the intense competition that will probably develop during stage 3.

Entry and Mobility Barriers

The move toward a single market represents an important environmental change that has numerous implications. During stage 1 (mobilization), the uncertainties involved can create both anxiety and confusion. Anxiety and confusion might, at one end, result in immobility, or lack of actions due to an inability to accept uncertainty and the risks associated with it. At the other end overly aggressive, rash, and expensive moves might take place in order to overcompensate for the perceived uncertainties. In this stage of high uncertainty, it is extremely important to identify the strategic implications of the single market and be able to separate the important issues, problems, and/or opportunities from the large number of unimportant ones.

In our view, the most important strategic implication is the impact on barriers to entry. Furthermore, as shown in Figure 4-1, it is essential to distinguish between external barriers to entry and internal ones. External barriers refer to the cost of penetrating the European market from the outside (that is, the cost of entry for a non-European firm without an established presence in Europe). The impact on these external barriers to entry is uncertain. In fact, U.S. and Japanese executives' and political leaders' fears about building a Fortress Europe reflect their anticipation of increased barriers to entry (Tigner, 1988).

Figure 4-1. Strategic Challenges of 1992.

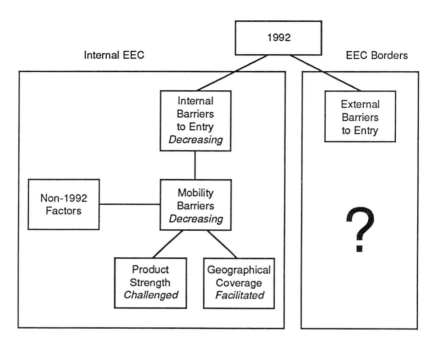

A recent study indicates that French executives feel that both Americans and Asians will be losers in the single market (Kahn, 1988). Other European leaders expect stronger non-EC competition as the result of decreased barriers to entry. We suspect that both attitudes are widely held across Europe, reflecting current uncertainty about the cost to business of maintaining these external barriers.

On the other hand, the impact of a single market on internal barriers to entry (that is, the cost for a firm from an EC country to enter the market of another EC country) is much clearer, as the lowering of internal costs is in fact its major raison d'être. Actually, the notion of a single European market makes the concept of internal barriers to entry obsolete. If the EC truly becomes a single market, there must not be internal barriers to entry. In this case the strategic region of reference is not an individual country but all twelve together. Internal barriers to entry would then be replaced by the softer concept of mobility barriers — that is, obstacles decreasing strategic mobility within the EC.

At the same time as nontariff trade barriers are dismantled through the creation of a single European market, other types of barriers also need to be modified in order to achieve a truly unified common market as follows:

Decreases in cross-national differences in consumption patterns

Development of distribution networks across Europe

Development of Europe-wide communication media (press, radio, television)

Mobility barriers within Europe might never disappear completely. A "Euroconsumer" does not exist at present. There are linguistic, cultural, and environmental differences among European countries that might require the adapting of corporate strategies for some time to come. Specific investments in R&D, factories, offices, salesforces, and advertising might be necessary at the local level to better satisfy the needs of particular groups of customers in single countries. Even in an open geographical market such market segmentation strategies are found, and they are actually used to exploit the existence of mobility barriers. However, the creation of a single European market, the emergence of new technologies, and competitive pressures from the United States and Japan are currently contributing to decreasing these mobility barriers within Europe.

The reduction of mobility barriers generates a higher level of competition, as it becomes less expensive and more convenient for corporations to invade their respective territories and markets. Consequently, broader geographical coverage and a higher level of competition produce economies of scale, greater efficiences, and lower prices. In his book *The European Challenge: 1992*, based on *The Cost of Non-Europe* reports funded by the commission, Paolo Cecchini explicitly recognized the

Table 4.1. Expected Gains from the Single Market as a Percentage of GDP.

	Lowest Estimate	Highest Estimate	Average Estimate
Removal of trade and production barriers	2.2%	2.7%	2.4%
Economies of scale and increased competition	2.1	3.7	2.9
Total gains	4.3	6.4	5.3

Source: Cecchini, 1988.

gains obtained through economies of scale and increased competition (see Table 4-1). These "indirect" benefits of the single European market are actually estimated to be higher than the "direct" gains obtained from the removal of trade and production barriers. At the macroeconomic level, they contribute to the welfare of individual consumers and to higher growth rates for GNP, while at the same time reducing the risk of higher inflation as increased competition results in a downward pressure on prices.

One should not underestimate the implications of declining mobility barriers at the level of the individual firm. In addition to opportunities for greater geographical expansion, there would also be greater competitive threats and greater pressures on the effecitve use of resources. At the corporate level, a firm manages a dual portfolio of products and geographical markets (Larréché, 1980). Its two main axes for allocating strategic sources are the development of product strength and geographical coverage. These two axes have to be managed in a balanced way. Focusing too much attention on product investments at the expense of geographical coverage may result in missed international opportunities. On the other hand, focusing on geographical expansion may result in underinvestment in products, weakening the competitive position of the firm. The creation of the single European market is making the geographical dimension of corporate expansion much more important than the product one. Consequently, corporate strategies will have to be systematically reassessed in order to avoid the danger of the two extreme positions: strategic immobility resulting in missed opportunities, and strategic overreaction leading to excessive geographical dispersion. To this end, the International Competitive Posture Matrix can be used to integrate the two strategic axes.

The International Competitive Posture Matrix

Consider the case of a corporation that produces and markets in five product categories in eight out of twelve EC countries. The strength of presence is not the same across these eight countries, as in some countries the corporation markets all five of its products while in others it markets only one or two. A total of sixty product-market possibilities (five products multiplied by twelve countries) represent the "chessboard" of global potentials for this company. If we assume that the firm is currently present in only twenty-four of the product markets, it is obvious that one possible axis of development for the firm is to increase its geographical coverage by investing in some, or even all, of the remaining thirty-six product markets.

The firm in question, however, is not equally strong in all the twenty-four product markets in which it is currently present. For instance, there are significant differences in the market shares of its various products in each of the eight markets. Specifically, the company has the leading market share in only eight of the twenty-four product markets it currently covers; moreover, in some product markets its presence is rather weak. Thus the second possible axis of development is not to increase its geographical coverage but to strengthen its market position in selected countries where its presence is already established.

The relative emphasis to be placed on developing product strength or geographical coverage depends on the current position of the firm relative to its competitors. If it is already strong on the product-strength axis, geographical coverage is likely to create more shareholder value than a further strengthening of its products (which is likely to hit decreasing marginal benefits). If, on the other hand, the existing product-market strength is weak, investing in improving in this area may be a more valuable strategy than expanding geographical coverage. In order to optimize long-term benefits, however, a balanced, systematic approach is required in order to exploit selectively the best opportunities on both axes of strategic development.

The two dimensions need to be explored to provide a clear perspective on international competition. They can be defined at different levels of detail. At the simplest level, one may use a numerical definition based on a crude but convenient index. A weighted definition taking into account the relative size of different markets will provide a more complete perspective. Finally, a composite definition integrating several quantitative and qualitative elements is even more complete. As more completeness is gained by adding more elements, however, there is an increase in complexity that also increases the risk of making mistakes. Below we provide an example of the three alternative definitions covering both the product strength and geographical coverage dimensions.

Product Strength

1. *Numerical definition:* Proportion of the company's product markets where it has a leading market share. For instance, since the firm is the leader in eight out of the twenty-four product markets in which it operates, its product strength would be measured as 33 percent.

2. *Weighted definition:* Average market share in all product markets in which the firm is present, weighted by the size of the corresponding markets. In such cases operating in a small market (say, Ireland) should be given less "weight" than in a larger one (say, France).

3. *Composite definition:* A subjective measure on an arbitrary scale integrating additional elements of product strength to that of the weighted definition of market share. These additional elements could include profitability, brand

awareness, technological leadership, and distribution power.

Geographical Coverage

1. *Numerical definition:* For a given geographical area and a set of product categories, proportion of all possible product markets where the firm currently operates. In the above example, geographical coverage would be measured as 40 percent (twenty-four product markets divided by sixty possibilities).

2. *Weighted definition:* Same as above, but weighted by the relative importance (size) of each product market.

3. *Composite definition:* A subjective measure on an arbitrary scale integrating several elements of geographical coverage, including number of product markets served, as well as their relative size, expected growth, competitiveness, and stability.

Having selected a definition for the two dimensions of product strength and geographical coverage, the International

Figure 4-2. The International Competitive Posture Matrix.

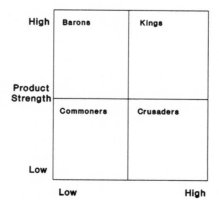

Competitive Posture Matrix can be constructed, as illustrated in Figure 4-2.

Different competitors in a given industry can be plotted on the competitive posture matrix and categorized in four groups: kings, barons, crusaders, and commoners. Kings are those companies in the strongest position. They have broad geographical coverage and their whole product portfolio is in a strong competitive position. They have been able effectively to expand geographically and have not wasted their resources on weak products. If they selectively expand their product portfolio through internal development or acquisition, they can obtain important leverage because of their geographical coverage. In the context of a single market, they are in the best position to apply a "Euromarketing" strategy.

Barons are those companies with strong products in a limited number of countries. They are in a good position to expand selectively either in other countries or in new product areas. The creation of a single European market makes geographical expansion more attractive to them. It also makes them targets to be bought by other companies that may consider reinforcing their own product strength or geographical coverage through acquisitions.

Crusaders are those companies that have been driven to expand geographically. They have what the barons do not—geographical coverage—but they lack strong products across several markets. Crusaders are vulnerable to an increasingly higher level of competition. Their challenge is to consolidate their product position, which may involve internal product development, acquisition, or making selective divestments, in order to concentrate their efforts on a narrower product portfolio consisting of leaders.

Commoners are those companies that have a relatively weak product portfolio and narrow geographical coverage. These companies usually benefit from strong mobility barriers that have protected them from intense competition in the past. They are the most vulnerable as the creation of a single European market progresses. Before considering any geographical expansion, they must strengthen their products. This is likely to require divesting some of their activities to free resources needed to build the position of selected products. If that is not feasible, they should be developing niche strategies such as supplying distribution chains with private label products. Expanding geographically on the basis of a weak product portfolio would probably be a fatal strategic mistake, as the environment is becoming increasingly competitive. These companies are likely to be acquisition candidates but, given their vulnerable position, at prices substantially lower than those of barons or crusaders.

The key point underlying the International Competitive Posture Matrix is that two strategic-development axes are competing for resources: product strength and geographical coverage. The four categories of firms corresponding to each quadrant of the matrix reflect different trade-offs made, implicitly or explicitly, between these two strategic-development axes. Furthermore, the posture of a given firm on the matrix also reflects how harmoniously it has been able to balance its resources between consolidation and expansion on both the product and the geographical fronts. Barons are the best at concentrating their resources: they do not cover a wide geographical area and probably achieved product strength by also avoiding dispersion into too many product categories. Barons may actually be missing some opportunities to increase shareholder value by over-concentrating on too few product markets. Crusaders are diagonally opposed to barons, both on the matrix and in their allocation of resources. They have expanded geographically, and it is also likely that their lack of product strength is due, at least in part, to an expansion into several product categories. Commoners may concentrate on one of a few geographical areas but have probably dispersed their resources over many product categories. Kings, on the diagonal above, concentrate their resources on a limited number of products but have expanded geographically.

While product strength and geographical coverage compete for resources, they also support each other: a strong product portfolio is a great asset for product expansion. Each dimension provides synergy with the other. However, product strength is the dimension that deserves the highest priority. It not only provides the required basis for expansion, but also represents the best defense against increasing competition. Nevertheless, as the decline of mobility barriers makes geographical coverage less expensive, it will be increasingly important to consider its strategic implications alongside those of product strength.

The road from commoner to king is certainly a long and indirect one. It requires both consolidation of product strength and an expansion of geographical coverage. Overemphasis on one of these two dimensions will make a firm more of a baron or more of a crusader. On the other hand, overexpansion on the geographical front may weaken the product base, while on the other, overconcentration on the product front may result in missed geographical opportunities. In the context of the single European market, acquisitions might offer the best opportunity to correct possible imbalances in the international competitive posture of some firms. The alternative of internal development is slow and requires learning about markets in new countries.

The Example of the European Food Industry

A recent study conducted for the European Commission investigated the issues of product strength and geographical coverage in the food industry. For many reasons, the food industry is expected to be particularly affected by the creation of a single European market. One reason is current protection provided by national regulations. Another, probably more important reason is the fact that a crucial strategic aspect of competition in this industry is distribution.

In no industrial sector is the shift in value added toward distribution more dramatic than the food industry. Over the last ten years, all major European countries have experienced a drastic concentration of food retailers. Figure 4-3 shows the market share of the five largest chains in selected countries in 1985 compared with 1967.

This concentration has provided increased power to the distributors in their negotiations with the food manufacturers, representing a major change from the past. Nowadays the dis-

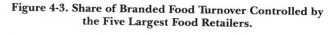

Figure 4-3. Share of Branded Food Turnover Controlled by
the Five Largest Food Retailers.

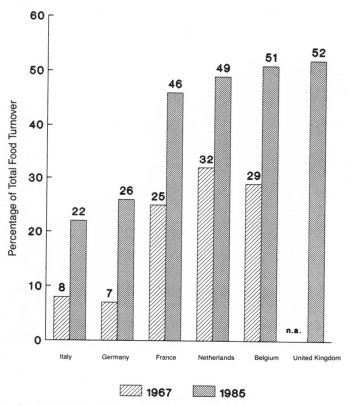

Source: Adapted from figures from Frisa, 1987, and MAC Group,
1988.

tributors have greater power in choosing brands and tend only
to stock brand leaders, which provide the greatest turnover. The
shift in power toward distribution is putting pressure on manufacturers to protect their component of the value-added chain
through product innovation as well as economies of scale in
manufacturing and marketing.

New developments such as international media and the
single European market itself provide opportunities for food
manufacturers to become more effective. Early in the nineties,

for instance, nine television satellites will be transmitting 113 channels across Europe, which will relay the same program in several languages simultaneously, allowing more effective Europe-wide communications.

Some distributors are already expanding their cross-border networks within Europe, and will continue to do so with the creation of a single European market. The best example here is the French retailers' attack on the Spanish market, where Promodes, Auchan, and Carrefour have developed significant market shares.

On the production front, the single European market will allow food manufacturers to capitalize on economies of scale and rationalization of distribution. For example, there are now over 1,100 breweries in West Germany and few have scale-efficient plants. Yet, Heineken and BSN are within a few hundred kilometers of German markets, and they both have large scale-efficient plants. Now that the German beer purity law has been repealed, the German market provides an excellent market opportunity for such scale-efficient firms.

Another key reason that distribution is gaining importance is the increase in sales of private label goods. New technologies and distribution methods are being developed, further enhancing the distributor's power. Scanner technology is being installed in many chains, allowing the retailer to have information on stock rotation — in some cases, better than the manufacturer. Distributors are also integrating the logisitics functions and shifting away from in-store deliveries to centralized platforms. This reduces store inventory and distribution costs, improves the accuracy of purchasing information, and provides increased flexibility and diversification of sourcing.

In order to face the distribution challenge effectively and to exploit new international opportunities, it is essential for food manufacturers to have an adequate posture in product strength and geographical coverage. In Exhibit 4-1, forty of the largest processed food companies in Europe have been plotted on the International Competitive Posture Matrix. The product strength and geographical coverage indexes are based on the numerical definition described in the previous section, and

Exhibit 4-1. Food Companies in Survey.

Code	Name	Country of Origin	Number of Products
ALY	Allied-Lyons	U.K.	9
ABF	Associated British Food	U.K.	7
BHL	Bahlsen Gruppe	Germany	3
BAR	Barilla	Italy	3
BAS	Bass	U.K.	3
BSN	BSN	France	13
BUI	Buitoni	Italy	7
CAD	Cadbury Schweppes	U.K.	2
COC	Coca-Cola	U.S.	2
CPC	CPC International	U.S.	5
OET	Dr August Oetker	Germany	7
DUB	DUB Schultheiss Konzern	Germany	3
FER	Ferrero	Italy	3
GN	General Foods	U.S.	4
GRM	Grand Metropolitan	U.K.	6
GUI	Guinness	U.K.	2
HAN	Hanson Trust	U.K.	4
HEI	Heineken	Netherlands	3
HNZ	Heinz	U.S.	7
JBS	Jacobs-Suchard	Switzerland	2
KEL	Kellogg's	U.S.	1
DKT	Kraft	U.S.	5
MAR	Mars	U.S.	4
NAB	Nabisco	U.S.	6
NES	Nestlé	Switzerland	15
NOR	Northern Foods	U.K.	5
MIK	Ortiz-Miko	France	2
PEP	Pepsi-Cola	U.S.	2
PRI	Pernod-Ricard	France	2
PER	Perrier	France	3
QUA	Quaker Oats	U.S.	4
RHM	Ranks Hovis McDougall	U.K.	7
REE	Reemtsma	Germany	3
ROW	Rowntree Mackintosh	U.K.	2
SLL	Saint Louis Lesieur	France	2
SAL	Sara Lee Corp	U.S.	2
SCO	Scottish-Newcastle	U.K.	1
UNL	Unilever	Netherlands	8
UB	United Biscuits	U.K.	1
UBG	United Breweries Group	Other EC	2

geographical coverage refers only to the five largest European countries (Germany, France, the United Kingdom, Italy, and Spain).

One can readily observe that the 50 percent mark on the product strength index is a tough one to reach, with only a small number of firms exceeding this mark. Of course, the position of the dividing line is subjective and several firms, including Nestlé and BSN, rate between 30 percent and 40 percent on the index, which corresponds to being the leader in one out of three product markets.

It may also seem surprising that, on the basis of the five largest European countries only, so few companies rate above the 50 percent mark on geographical coverage. Many of the companies do indeed operate in all five countries, but they fail to be present in a majority of their product categories in all five. This reflects an ad hoc geographical expansion across the product portfolio, with different offerings in different countries.

Interestingly enough, the two companies that have achieved product dominance combined with pan-European coverage are American: Kellogg's and Coca-Cola. They have both concentrated on a very narrow product portfolio and are leaders or coleaders in all five major European countries. Unilever (Anglo-Dutch) and Mars (U.S.) are not far behind, with broader product portfolios.

Apart from Unilever, the other three European companies with 1986 EC food sales in excess of three billion dollars are Nestlé (Swiss), BSN (French), and Allied-Lyons (British). They all have diversified product portfolios, but only Nestlé has achieved wide geographical coverage. The operations of Allied-Lyons and BSN are still concentrated on their home markets. At the opposite end of the spectrum, Jacobs-Suchard (Swiss) has concentrated on only two product categories (chocolate and coffee) and is present in all five major EC countries.

Product strength affects the capability of a firm to generate cash flows and is hence an important requirement for expansion. With the decline of mobility barriers within Europe, the importance of increased geographical coverage will provide economies of scale and other cost advantages that will eventually have an impact on product strength. The firms in the best strategic position will be those that effectively combine product strength and geographical coverage. A number of firms are moving in this direction through acquisitions, like Nestlé (with its acquisition of Buitoni of Italy and Rowntree in the United Kingdom) and BSN (pasta in Italy, mineral water in Italy and Spain, and sauces in the United Kingdom). While definitely enabling companies to shift their international competitive position faster, acquisitions should only be part of a comprehensive product strength/geographical coverage strategy.

Conclusion

In this chapter we have argued the following three main points:

1. The single market movement has created a progressively turbulent competitive environment with different strategic challenges that can be classified in four stages, each posing its own problems and opportunities. It is important to have a broad strategic perspective on these challenges in order to avoid immobilization and overreaction.
2. The key strategic structural change underlying a single market is the decline of mobility barriers within Europe. This evolution will facilitate geographical expansion, while presenting greater challenges to the existing positions of many products as competitive pressures increase.
3. The two main axes of strategic development — product strength and geographical coverage — must therefore be balanced in the formulation of an international strategy. The International Competitive Posture Matrix is a convenient tool for visualizing the relative strategic positions of different firms. More important, it focuses attention on the necessary trade-offs and complementarities involved when investing to further develop product strength in existing market areas or, alternatively, to expand geographical coverage by entering new markets in EC countries that are not already being served.

References

Cecchini, P. *The European Challenge: 1992, The Benefits of a Single Market.* Aldershot, England: Wildwood House, 1988.

Colby, L. "The Road to European Unity: 1992." *Wall Street Journal,* Sept. 19, 1988, pp. 1–2.

Frisa, M. T. "The Evolution of the Grocery Supermarket." *Largo consumo,* Dec. 1987, pp. 110–111.

Kahn, A. "Conditional Enthusiasm." *Le Monde,* Enterprises 93, Oct. 15, 1988, pp. 4–7.

Larréché, J.-C. "The International Product-Market Portfolio." In H. Thorelli and H. Becker (eds.), *International Marketing Strategy.* New York: Pergamon Press, 1980.

MAC Group, Commission of the European Communities. *The Cost of Non-Europe,* vol. 12b. Luxembourg: Official Publications of the European Community, 1988.

Tigner, B. "Fortress Europe." *International Management,* Dec. 1988, pp. 24–30.

CHAPTER 5

New Manufacturing Strategies

Taking Advantage of
Uniform Standards and
Alternative Technologies

Arnoud De Meyer

The Philips manufacturing plant in Brugge, Belgium, employs seventy engineers whose only task is to adjust the seven different types of television sets rolling off the assembly lines to meet widely differing reception (and other) technical standards throughout the European Community. These adjustments cost Philips around twenty million dollars a year — with the different electrical plugs alone accounting for an amazing two million. Eventually, Philips hopes that two or three different television models will meet all the national standards. If all goes well, by the mid 1990s, pan-European standards will require but one.

For many years car manufacturers have had to comply with a variety of technical and safety standards in order to sell cars in each country of the EC. These differences resulted in additional design, development, and production expenses, forcing manufacturers to concentrate their efforts on smaller, less economical production runs. The extra costs they incurred were inevitably translated into higher prices for European cars — putting them at a severe disadvantage compared with their

119

American and Japanese counterparts, who were selling cars in homogeneous home markets. In addition, European car manufacturers often wasted resources and energy coping with the whole spectrum of regulations present in each country instead of concentrating on designing and producing better-looking and higher-quality cars. Moreover, consumers were paying a higher price, which, in turn, put the brakes on the demand for cars.

Non-European companies have faced similar difficulties when operating in Europe. For years 3M's European plants turned out different versions of the same products for the various European countries and in so doing incurred higher costs. At present, 3M manufacturing plants produce goods for *all* of Europe. The pan-European view has helped 3M realize important cost savings, improve the attractiveness and quality of its products, and increase potential demand, thereby reducing selling prices.

Pharmaceutical and food manufacturers, responding to protectionist national regulations, were also forced to create assembly and packaging lines in many different countries of Europe, a phenomenon that has been not only costly, but also a severe drain on resources. The situation is changing rapidly today, as operating across borders has been considerably facilitated.

Large fashion producers in Europe, on the other hand, have not suffered as much from European fragmentation. As early as the late 1960s the use of information networks and sophisticated process technologies has been common, enabling fashion producers to develop unified production and distribution networks spanning the whole of Europe. At present they can supply the fashion-sensitive European market with six or seven different collections a year. Pan-European operations have opened up a large market where fashion producers have been able to harness enormous economies of scale. These economies have made it possible for companies such as Benetton to compete very favorably with the low labor cost countries. Producing high-quality, low-cost garments in a flexible way has made Benetton a world player in a market where buying habits and consumer tastes change at a phenomenally fast pace.

Whereas the majority of industries have suffered from fragmentation caused by obstacles to real pan-European operations, fashion producers have thrived in a difficult, highly competitive market because national governments never tried to protect their local industries (probably the relatively small amounts of money involved implied a lesser threat). Single market Europe promises to offer manufacturers similar or even larger benefits than those enjoyed by fashion houses today.

Product standards have not been the only factor adding to manufacturing costs, however. Before 1988, there were as many as seventy-five documents truck drivers needed to carry when crossing European borders. According to Wisse Dekker, chairman of Philips, the cost of completing these documents and the delays involved while they were verified at the various borders increased the journey time by a factor of three to five and cost up to 3 percent of the value of the sales involved. On January 1, 1988, this plethora of documents was replaced by the Single Administrative Document (SAD), limiting paperwork to a single (albeit complicated) form, which reduced the waiting time at custom checkpoints to a minimum.

In single market Europe, there will be no border checks, as truck drivers should be able to pass from one EC country to another as easily and freely as their American counterparts do when they travel from one state to another. The cost savings involved and the manifold implications are bound to create enormous challenges as well as dangers for manufacturers.

The outlook for manufacturing in a single market Europe will be influenced by two major types of changes. First, there are those changes caused by political and economic factors that will duly follow the creation of a truly common market. A reduction in customs and noncustoms barriers, for example, will lead to significant economies of scale, as manufacturers will have access to a market of 325 million people—the largest in the industrialized world. Moreover, standardization of security norms and other regulations across Europe will lead to a higher interchangeablity of components and subassemblies, which in turn will allow for a wider variety of products for the consumer (while at the same time permitting lower production costs).

Due to the sheer size of the European consumer market the effects of the political and economic changes will not be confined to the countries of the European Community. Just as manufacturers in the EFTA countries chose to adopt community-regulated standards, American and Japanese firms will also be forced to comply if they are to compete effectively in the largest Western consumer market.

In addition, the freedom of movement of capital and labor will contribute to the redesign of the map of Europe in terms of localization of factories, specialization of various plants, and distribution and after-sales service networks. The end result will be further reductions in the costs of manufacturing and distribution, which will eventually lead to an increase in demand as the prices of goods sold fall. Similar effects will be observed in the after-sales services.

Political and economic changes will be complemented by huge technological changes affecting European firms: the extension of computerized manufacturing and the superautomation of factories. Such changes will create challenges for European executives in their effort to stay competitive within the European market as well as in global ones.

The Business Environment

Manufacturing in Europe Before 1990

European industry has been operating at overcapacity or at a capacity level ill-adapted to demand. In the automobile sector, for example, capacity is in excess of demand by about 20 percent, or, put another way, by more than the equivalent of the total production capacity of one of the big six European auto makers. The capacity in most sectors of the chemical industry is equally abundant, although for some specific products (such as plastics and fine chemicals) there have been periodic shortages. For nationalized companies or when governments are, or have been, major customers, overcapacity is even greater. Locomotive production in Europe is presently spread among sixteen different manufacturers, each with an idle capacity between 20 and 50 percent. Traditionally, governments have tended to encourage overcapacity by indulgent support of preferred suppliers, particularly in such sensitive areas as telecommunications or military equipment, claiming justification for reasons of national independence or conservation of regional employment.

Consumers and Standards Across Europe

The removal of trade and other barriers and the harmonization of standards and regulations will not lead instantaneously to a homogeneous European market. Differences in tastes and preferences will prevail among European consumers (see Chapter Ten). Thus, consumers who prefer top-loading washing machines will continue to choose them over front-loading ones, and the French tradition of high-temperature cooking will continue to necessitate self-cleaning ovens to eliminate the grease splattered over the inside of the oven, while the Germans, who cook at lower temperatures, will probably not request such an option. Furthermore, local conditions will require the design and manufacturing necessary to meet those conditions. This means that detergents must be adapted to the local hardness or chalk content of the water whether or not there is a single market. Similarly, car designers cannot ignore the differences in income between Northern and Southern Europeans (usually lower in the south), road conditions (usually narrower and more crowded—particularly in inner-city areas—in the south), and temperatures (hotter in the south).

Established standards in different countries cannot and will not disappear overnight. The fact that British electrical plugs are different from those in France or Germany will continue to hinder the process of standardization. The installation of a single type of electrical system from Aberdeen (northern Scotland) to Zakros (southern Crete), for example, is far too expensive a project to be achieved in short order. Even though companies such as Philips have begun to standardize the plugs they attach to electrical appliances, they will have to accept existing differences and incompatibilities in the short and maybe even medium terms.

The potential for standardization will vary depending upon the specific product, established practices, and local conditions. Thus, standardization of the electricity systems installed in the various countries of Europe will change only gradually, consumer tastes and preferences will probably change even more slowly, and some local conditions, such as temperature differences, cannot change at all. The majority of product differences are not unique to Europe, however. American manufacturers have to provide for a variety of consumer tastes varying widely between the Northeast and the Midwest, or the South and the West. Moreover, they also have to adapt their products to local conditions. Their main advantage over their European counterparts is that standards are unique and there are no customs or other barriers to moving products from one region to another.

Product prices will be the major leverage point in ironing out or eliminating differences in tastes, established practices and preferences, and the effect of local conditions. As the price of goods produced using the common European standards becomes cheaper (because of economies of scale), consumers will be faced with the choice between something familiar and more expensive or something different but cheaper. We believe that economic realities will prevail over tastes and preferences (for example, in top- versus front-loading washing machines) when the utilities are identical and one choice the obviously better value. The huge success of fast-food restaurants (for instance, McDonald's) in France is an excellent reminder of the fact that where extra benefits are provided (lower costs, faster service, reasonable quality) consumers do indeed change tastes and preferences that they have had for a long time, sometimes even quickly.

Standards adapted to local conditions will also diminish, maybe even considerably, if prices become substantially lower for products with a common standard. Again, consumers will use personal economic criteria to decide whether the savings from lower prices make it worthwhile to switch to the new standard (although manufacturers might have to accommodate some local conditions by adapting their products accordingly).

Perfect market harmonization might not be achieved quickly. Nevertheless, basic economic reasons will provide the impetus toward a harmonized single European market not different from that existing in the United States today, by the end of this century. In this light, the unified market of 1993 can be considered an important landmark rather than the final stage of European integration.

Economies of Scale

A single market of 325 million consumers will be created when the 1992 deadline is implemented. The greatest advantage to manufacturers will come from the sheer size of such a market and the unique opportunities it will provide for harnessing economies of scale. The following areas are singled out for discussion as being particularly influenced by economies of scale.

R&D Expenditure. R&D has played a critical role in gaining and maintaining competitive advantage and will continue to do so. At the same time, the cost of R&D increases faster than inflation as qualified personnel become harder to find and the cost of the laboratories and equipment involved increases. This is particularly true in the high-tech areas, where R&D costs are increasing at an even faster pace than those in other areas.

High R&D costs can best be depreciated by large volumes of goods produced and sold. Obviously, companies will budget larger amounts for R&D if they anticipate a large market and high sales. High R&D expenditure will increase the chances of developing new products and/or improving existing ones, thereby generating extra revenues, which will compensate for their high costs, provide additional profits, and in turn motivate even higher spending for expanded R&D work. R&D spending is becoming, therefore, a pivotal factor in gaining and maintaining competitive advantages in today's fast-changing world. But high costs mean that big companies operating in homogeneous markets are favored. Such companies must be capable of affording the costs involved, assuming the risk that their R&D output may produce no returns, and being patient enough to wait the several years that may elapse between the conception and funding of an idea and its completion as a commercially successful product.

European firms have not been as large as their North American and Japanese competitors (of the 1,000 largest companies in the world, only about 200 are from EC countries while there are about 350 North American ones and 350 Japanese). Moreover, European firms have operated at a disadvantage vis-à-vis R&D spending: as the European market is fragmented, a good part of R&D money is wasted meeting local standards and coming up with product designs and manufacturing modifications aimed at meeting the requirements of each country. On the other hand, U.S. and Japanese companies have operated in homogeneous home markets that provide an efficient base on which to develop and test new products, a base that can consequently be used as the springboard to global operations. It has been estimated, for instance, that European manufacturers are currently spending $30 billion to develop digital switches, compared with $9 billion in the United States and only $6 billion in Japan. The end result of such huge inefficiencies is much higher costs for consumers, as can be seen by, say, the price of a personal computer modem card: $250 in the United Kingdom while only $25 in the United States. A major benefit of the single European market will therefore come from not only higher but also more efficient R&D spending, which will facilitate higher rates of return.

Product Design. As the success of the single market increases, so will the need to design products based on standardized components. Such products will decrease production costs as components will be mass produced; they will also be of higher quality due to the specialization of component suppliers. Lower component costs and improved quality will, in turn, result in lower product costs and higher quality and greater value for the end customer, effectively increasing demand and permitting European manufacturers to compete more equally on a global basis.

Delayed Differentiation. Mass production and standardized components can be maintained even when production has to be tailored to some local conditions through what is called differentiation. This means that a product is designed in such a way that its manufacturing is exactly the same for all countries or regions until as late in the assembly process as possible. Only in the final stages does differentiation take place by introducing specific components and particular features. Delayed differentiation allows for the harnessing of as many economies of scale as possible while at the same time permitting product differentiation in order to meet local conditions.

Rationalizing Operations and Strategies

Pan-European manufacturing has been severely constrained by customs delays, excessive bureaucratic procedures, the lack of mobility of people and capital, language problems, and delays in relaying information. Although improvements have been made, optimal geographical rationalization on a European scale—that is, without any customs or other restrictive barriers—has not been achieved. The manufacturing rationalization that began in the early 1980s will continue to accelerate. Philips, Thomson, Electrolux, Alcatel, and Ford are examples of companies that are in the process of creating pan-European networks of factories (producing both components and finished goods) and distribution/after-sales services. For example, the Philips television factory located in Brugge, Belgium, uses tubes supplied from a factory in Germany, transistors from France, plastics from Italy, and electronic components from a different factory in Belgium. Even in the area of military equipment and telecommunications similar rationalization is taking place through intergovernmental agreements or cross-border mergers and acquisitions. In 1984 in the telecommunications sector, there were ten digital switch makers competing for market share, which situation has devolved to just three manufacturers.

Factory Location. Apart from a few exceptions, the location of factories in Europe has been influenced mostly by political, legislative, and import duty considerations. In the single market, economic factors override all others. Concerns such as taxes, political incentives, and uniform product standards force manufacturers to strive to locate their factories in such places as to minimize production and transportation costs and ensure an uninterrupted and adequate supply of products.

Distribution and After-Sales Service. Language and bureaucratic barriers have obliged companies to organize their distribution and after-sales servicing on a country-by-country basis. Such an organization is costly inasmuch as some European countries are small and major cities of one country can often be served much more efficiently from another. For example, in after-sales servicing there is no reason the northern French city of Lille could not be better served from Brussels (or vice versa) than from Paris (Brussels is about 100 km from Lille, while Paris is about 220 km away). Similarly, Nice is closer to Milan than to Lyon or Paris and could therefore be best served by Milan. Alternatively, a distribution/after-sales service center located in Liege could serve Belgium, Holland, Luxembourg, Northern France, and a good part of industrial Germany much faster and more efficiently than individual centers in each of the five countries.

Mergers, Acquisitions, and Strategic Alliances. Another, often complementary approach to rationalizing manufacturing, distribution, and after-sales servicing across Europe has been through mergers and acquisitions of related companies in various European countries. Moreover, where mergers and/or acquisitions are not possible, alliances and joint ventures have been concluded to allow better integration and improve the ability to operate throughout Europe. Manufacturers have accelerated their efforts to establish themselves in the entire European market, which further increases the number of cross-border mergers, acquisitions, and strategic alliances, resulting in economies of scale and in efficient and cost-effective distribution and after-sales networks.

Consequences of a Single European Market on Manufacturing

The creation of unified European standards will be a great benefit for European manufacturers in both inter-European and world operations. The sheer size of the European market (the largest among industrialized countries) and the value that will come from the adoption of one standard throughout that market will force suppliers from Japan, the United States, and the Eastern bloc to adopt the standard; otherwise their competitive advantages will be reduced by being excluded from the European market. In this context, it is interesting to see that the Soviet Union has decided to adopt the German industry standards (DIN) used in West Germany for all its international economic activities. Apart from the political choice that such an option entails, it also indicates the Soviet Union's attitude toward the relevance of the German standard: it will eventually become the European standard. Another example is that of high-definition television (HDTV). The hidden commercial battle between Japanese and European producers about HDTV is really a question of who will be able to gain the competitive edge in world markets. The fact that this conflict exists is due to a common European position and the size of the European market, which the Japanese cannot ignore. Had a single country or an individual company in Europe tried to engage in negotiations with Japan, they would not have been successful, as they would have been easily ignored by the powerful Japanese.

The homogenization of the European market and the uniformization of standards are not necessarily good news for all European companies. The market for pharmaceuticals in the European community is both highly fragmented and highly regulated. Against this backdrop of controls, regulations, and national differences, many local companies have thrived, and the bureaucratic complexities of the national markets favor those companies that know the system. Changes such as the harmonization of the regulatory requirements, product information, patent legislation, pricing transparency, and a European system of registration might favor those companies that have learned to work in large homogeneous markets. And it is not necessarily Europe's national companies that can most successfully operate within the single market. The chairman of Volkswagen once expressed his doubts about the single market by saying that it will take away one of the few competitive advantages European companies had over their non-European competitors: knowing how to work in a highly complex and fragmented market.

Manufacturing Technologies in the 1990s

Existing and emerging technological innovations will greatly modify the way manufacturing is carried on in Europe, the United States, and the more industrialized countries of the Pacific Rim, with serious implications for European manufacturers and their global competitiveness. This section describes these technologies and discusses their implications.

Existing and Emerging Technologies

The computer has indisputably become *the* tool for manufacturing. First, computer-aided design (CAD) and later computer-aided manufacturing (CAM) systems have provided us with the tools to reduce product life cycles and improve the effectiveness and efficiency of manufacturing systems. Moreover, flexible manufacturing systems (FMS) are rapidly spreading throughout industry, making it economically feasible to produce small runs and provide a wider variety of products. The biggest change in manufacturing technologies came when mechanical technologies were substituted and/or supplemented by electronic and software technologies.

The shift from hardware to software is transforming what was essentially rigid mechanical production into a more versatile and general-purpose one. As time passes, the shift toward making machinery more rapid, more highly automated, and more cost-efficient will become increasingly apparent. This shift can be seen in the percentage of electronics and software in new machinery: A heavy press consists of about 50 percent mechanical parts and 50 percent electronic ones and software. In the near future, these same percentages are expected to account for the composition of a car.

In some industries (for example, the newspaper printing industry), computers, telecommunication equipment, and software programs already make up close to two-thirds of the total value of the printing investment. Electronics and software included in machines will gradually allow them to become multifunctional, replacing complex, general-purpose machines that cost much more and are difficult to operate. New programming languages, special-purpose computers, and improvements in robots (increased precision of their sensors and grippers and higher speeds) will move manufacturing toward a new era by bringing superautomation to even those industries that have been difficult to automate (for instance, the garment industry, where the variablity of raw cloth restricts automation).

At present, software-based manufacturing technologies (like electronic ones) are still being hindered by problems ranging from difficulties in implementation to incompatibility of equipment and programs. Organizational changes are important. Top management must realize the importance of any desired change and work to persuade middle and lower management, as well as engineering and production personnel, why and how things have to change. If implementation is not smoothly managed not much can be expected, as the new technology will require even greater commitment than the old one did.

On the software side, major problems exist because various types of equipment, computers, and programs are not compatible. Integration requires compatible computer architecture and unified communication standards so that information from the various production centers of a factory and suppliers or customers can be freely exchanged. Incompatibility reduces their ability to communicate (and may even make it impossible) and consequently hinders efficient integration. Thus, computer-integrated manufacturing (CIM) often becomes an unattainable dream.

The most sensational attempt toward integrated manufacturing is that of General Motors' MAP (manufacturing automation protocol) system. It is not clear whether such a unilateral attempt to impose unified standards for equipment/computers and software talking different languages will succeed. The MAP system is complex and expensive. Already some manufacturers of production equipment have abandoned the idea of a MAP-type system, as empirical evidence has not substantiated claims of superior performance at a lower cost. However, the concept of MAP has focused attention on connectivity and the huge benefits it could produce. Thus, even if GM's system fails, other solutions will probably emerge utilizing the lesson learned from MAP's pioneering work. There is no doubt that more connectivity in the jungle of software, computers, and communication equipment will be needed to harness the full advantages of automation effectively.

An important technical evolution in manufacturing has been the rapid increase in the reliability of the hardware and software components used in production equipment. As Jaikumar (1986) emphasized in his comparison of large U.S. and Japanese installations, the key to successful implementation is reliable machines combining hardware and software technologies. If high reliability exists, installations can run unattended, reducing costs while improving quality. Unattended factories, however, require that every component of the manufacturing system exhibit a very high degree of reliability. It can be easily demonstrated that a system consisting of a hundred subsystems has an overall reliability of only 60 percent even when each of its subsystems has 99.5 percent reliability. Obviously, 60 percent overall reliability is not acceptable, making the widespread use of unattended factories unrealistic at present.

Manufacturing experts believe that if the additional resources required were made available it would be possible to develop systems with overall reliability approaching 99.9 percent, an investment that, in their opinion, would prove to be highly cost-efficient. Thus, efforts to attain superautomation resulting in unattended factories, with increased and improved production flexibility and reduced manufacturing costs, are continuing at full steam. It is highly likely that before the end of this century superautomated, unattended factories will be an economically viable alternative to the factories of today, at least in a good number of industries. European (as well as non-European) manufacturers will therefore have to consider ways of implementing superautomation in their factories and focus on the strategic and competitive consequences of superautomation for their firms.

The Consequences of Technology for Manufacturing Management

If the efforts to implement connectivity are successful, standardization of software modules, cheaper products, and fewer barriers to entry for newcomers will become a reality. In addition, this will allow for the creation of specialized systems architectures, or, as Ranta (1989) puts it, increased flexibility in the systems development process, which will reflect positively on flexible manufacturing systems: barriers to entry for newcomers will be reduced even more, application areas will be extended, and the concept of flexibility itself will broaden with respect to whole families of parts of subassembled components.

Trade-Offs Between Cost, Quality, Flexibility, and Reliability. Traditionally, low cost, high quality, high flexibility, and good reliability were considered mutually exclusive goals for manufacturers. In the past, a high-quality manufacturer could not also be a low-cost manufacturer, and flexibility of design could only be implemented at a higher cost and with lower reliability. The fallacy of the quality/cost and flexibility/cost/reliability trade-offs has been demonstrated by many successful Japanese and Western manufacturers. In the future, few manufacturers will be competitive if they still believe in the traditional trade-offs, making no attempt to reduce costs while increasing quality and reliability.

Production Runs. From as early as the late 1970s the size requirement for production batches to remain economically viable has been greatly reduced. This trend is expected to continue until (theoretically, at least) a batch size of one can be produced while maintaining economic feasibility. For example, Electrolux offers more than 1,000 different refrigerators in Europe with an economically feasible batch size of sixteen for their assembly. The car models offered by the Ford Motor Company reveal 100,000 different types and/or variations. This is an extremely high number for a company that sells 1,700,000 cars a year in Europe. Thus, the average car "run" is seventeen cars — a small number in an industry where mass production and economies of scale have been very much the Holy Grail.

Increased variation at the level of the end product is not a contradiction with the scale advantages we attributed to the creation of a single European market. By offering a large variety of end products through the countless combinations of standardized components, it becomes economically viable to offer customized products at low costs, precisely through the larger-scale production of components.

Product Life Cycles. Computer-integrated manufacturing systems and the availability of information will help manufacturers to drastically shorten the development cycle and the time it takes to market new products. At present, many electronic products have a product life of just a few months. Different models of videorecorders follow one another at a pace of two sequential models per year. The same can be observed in the specialty chemical industry. Courtaulds can provide its customers almost instantaneously with any one of seven thousand different types of dye — and that without keeping inventory. The conception, design, and manufacturing cycle for a car has been reduced from a period of between five to eight years to a development cycle of three to five years (Clark and Fujimoto, 1989). Honda plans to slash this time to one to two years in the near future and to reduce the cycle to less than a year.

Time as a Resource. The cutting edge for attaining and maintaining competitive advantage is time. Beyond the shorter product cycles, the importance of reducing the time span in delivery, product adaptation, and even innovation will become critical. Thus, fast and reliable information and its timely and effective use will become the backbone of all efforts to introduce new products or adapt existing ones in order to satisfy changing consumer needs.

Challenges for European Manufacturers

Manufacturers in Europe will be confronted with important challenges—political, economic, and technological. The factory will have to become more open to outside fluctuations and will therefore expose itself to the uncertainty of the environment. Moreover, manufacturing managers will be confronted with the increasing globalization of their manufacturing base and will have to learn how to think in terms of a network of production plants. Inside the plant, manufacturers will have to introduce simplicity, reduce the buffers of physical goods and time, increase the flexibility not only of machines but also of people and procedures, and reappraise their priorities in terms of improving productivity and the quality and acceptability of the goods they produce.

Eliminating Buffers. The traditional manufacturing plant buffers itself from the environment in order to reduce uncertainty. It uses forecasts developed by marketing departments to decide on manufacturing targets and determine production plans and schedules. It does not manufacture new products before they have been thoroughly tested by engineers outside the factory. And it handles the uncertainty due to suppliers and vendors by using stocks of raw materials and components. Direct contact with the workers is avoided by having a union to negotiate with management. The existence of competitors is ignored at the manufacturing level and is only considered at the corporate level, where overall corporate strategies are developed. Although many manufacturing executives will be quick to refute such claims, a large number of manufacturing concerns, many of them in Europe, do indeed buffer themselves from their customers, suppliers, workers and competitors, and concentrate all their efforts on manufacturing as if nothing else matters.

To be effective, factories will gradually have to reduce (and eventually eliminate) the different sorts of buffers that are used widely today. For instance, customers should be given the possibility to intervene directly in the factory's planning system; in this way their orders are automatically incorporated into the production schedule. Such a practice already exists, permitting manufacturers to pass orders via electronic links directly to subcontractors, avoiding all intermediaries. Component buffers can be avoided by having direct deliveries to the production line, as is done in just-in-time systems. The same suppliers can have a long-standing relationship with the factory, which would enable them to develop new components or to improve the quality of existing ones. Moreover, manufacturers will have to get to know their customers better so as to improve the quality and value of their products or to develop new ones that are more in tune with customer needs.

Increasing collaboration at the factory level is possible even among competitors, as various firms of the same region could agree to share production capacity and scarce resources, in a battle against competition from other countries and/or regions. Factories will also require different human resource management policies as the annual negotiations between management and unions will prove insufficient. Japanese companies have been very successful in their labor relations by treating workers as collaborators working toward the achievement of a common objective rather than as adversaries.

Reducing and eventually eliminating buffers is not something to be achieved overnight. An abrupt exposure of the factory to the unpredictability of outside forces and the uncertainties involved might destabilize operations and bring chaos. Gradual exposure, with a parallel review of procedures and methods, would be a more appropriate response. In the same way as just-in-time production eliminated inventory buffers, it will be possible to conceive of and implement effective new approaches to reduce or eliminate the remaining buffers.

Network of Plants. Manufacturing strategy will continue to develop an international network of plants. Plant localization is traditionally determined by three factors: access to cheap labor, availability of raw materials, and proximity to markets. The importance of cheap labor is of diminishing value, especially for those industries where superautomation requires little or no unskilled or semiskilled labor. The reverse is true for software R&D departments, whose personnel cannot be replaced by computers and whose costs are rising. At present, communication links allow scientists and technologists to communicate effectively over long distances. Thus, it is possible for a European company to install its software and R&D activities in India, for example, where engineers with Ph.D.s are easily found and cost little. Through electronic mail, faxes, and satellite links, it is economically feasible to transmit to the European factory the daily output of such R&D work for immediate use. Some large European chemical companies have already transferred a part of their R&D functions to India and others are in the process of following suit. In other words, the heavier physical goods that used to be produced in low-labor-cost countries might be produced within the large consumer markets in order to reduce delivery time and minimize transportation costs. R&D or software developments might be better achieved in countries where salaries of qualified scientists are negligible in comparison with those in the countries of the EC. Daily details concerning work requests from the factory and feedback from the R&D facilities could be transferred back and forth electronically through satellite links.

In determining a plant's location, access to technology will become as important a factor as proximity to technologically sophisticated competitors, suppliers, or customers, or access to a pool of engineers and scientific institutions. It is interesting to note that Japanese investment in Europe follows two different patterns. Larger, labor-intensive screwdriver plants for assembly of consumer products tend to be located in the United Kingdom, while smaller, more sophisticated outlets in the machining industry go to West Germany in order to have

better access to the German network of technologically advanced suppliers and customers.

Implementation. New technological developments including software for manufacturing purposes do not guarantee
flexibility or reduced costs. Describing the successful implementation of new manufacturing technologies, Jaikumar (1986),
Voss (1986), and Tyre (1989) stress the need to complement
technology with appropriate changes in the systems and procedures of the factory, coupled with the education and training
of both management and operators of the factory. Flexible
manufacturing technology will not help companies become
flexible if their workforce is not retrained, if procurement policies do not change, and if production planning favors long lead
times and large lot sizes. Jaikumar (1986) describes how the
successful implementation of flexible manufacturing systems in
Japan was usually carried out by small groups of engineers who
worked in self-organized teams, the members of which come
from different backgrounds representing different functions.
Before attempting any large-scale implementation, these teams
installed the new methods in experimental factories in order to
eliminate bugs and iron out the initial problems associated with
the application of any new technology.

Integration of the different functions in the organization
is another internal challenge, underscoring the need for inter-
disciplinary teams whose aim is to shorten development cycle
times (Imai, Nonaka, and Takeuchi, 1985; Hayes, Wheelwright,
and Clark, 1988). Technology can help in the integration process by making available well-designed relational databases that
provide a unified set of data to all parties in the company. In a
scenario of what postindustrial manufacturing could become,
Jaikumar goes as far as to envision a world in which manufacturing would be reduced to a staff function, supporting engineering (which would become the real line function), coming up
constantly with new products, new variations and adaptations,
and new manufacturing processes.

Manufacturing Strategy. Manufacturing strategy will not
and cannot remain static. Increased automation will shift the

quest for competitive advantage to new areas. Without a doubt, low production costs or higher-quality goods will not by themselves suffice, as a large number of manufacturers will be capable of achieving both. The technology involved in both cases can be bought, so implementation is only a question of money and time. Thus, the competitive battle will have to move to new ground. In the previous sections we have outlined some major challenges facing manufacturers. We would now like to envisage the consequences of a large number of manufacturers having the same highly automated technology, meaning flexibility, low costs, and high quality for all. How will they be able to differentiate themselves from their competitors? Competition will be stronger — probably as severe as it is among agricultural firms today — and succeeding will require different types of skills from those needed today. Creativity, effective problem solving, and efficient management of internal resources (most notably people) will become the new conditions of success. In addition, manufacturing operations will have to be better integrated with marketing functions so as to interpret incoming information as quickly as possible and take appropriate action to adapt to ever-changing market conditions. Manufacturing strategy will become of critical importance and will be in the forefront of any effort to succeed.

Conclusions

Manufacturing is a vital function whose importance has increased in the face of global competition. Mass production and the ability to produce goods at low cost are no longer the cornerstones of manufacturing strategies. In order to gain and/or maintain competitive advantage, other considerations such as quality, flexibility, and responsiveness have become of critical importance. Moreover, low cost, high quality, reliability, increased flexibility, and quick responsiveness are no longer exclusive of one another. As a matter of fact, successful manufacturers are those who will be able to achieve all of these at the same time.

Unification will provide European manufacturers with a unique opportunity: a single market of 325 million people. A single market will open up huge possibilities for economies of scale and rationalization of operations across the continent. At the same time, the single market will also multiply the dangers, as it will attract outside competition and intensify internal battles. In the end, successful manufacturers will be those who can operate across Europe as if it were a single market, and master new technologies and implement them within their organizations effectively, while at the same time accepting and efficiently dealing with new challenges appearing on the horizon.

References

Clark, K. B., and Fujimoto, T. "Overlapping Problem Solving in Product Development." In K. Ferdows (ed.), *Managing International Manufacturing*. Amsterdam: Elsevier Science Publishers, 1989.

Hayes, R., Wheelwright, S. G., and Clark, K. B. *Dynamic Manufacturing*. New York: Wiley, 1988.

Imai, K., Nonaka, K., and Takeuchi, H. "Managing the New Product Development." In K. B. Clark and R. Hayes (eds.), *The Uneasy Alliance*. Boston: Harvard Business School Press, 1985.

Jaikumar, R. "Postindustrial Manufacturing." *Harvard Business Review*, 1986, *64* (6), 69–76.

Ranta, J. "The Impact of Electronics and Information Technology on the Future Trends and Applications of CIM Technologies." *Technological Forecasting and Social Change*, 1989, *35* (2/3).

Tyre, M. J. "Managing the Introduction of New Process Technology: An International Comparison." Proceedings of the Second International Production Conference, INSEAD, Fontainebleau, 1989.

Voss, C. *Managing New Manufacturing Technologies*. East Lansing: Michigan State University, 1986.

CHAPTER 6

Aligning Strategic Demands and Corporate Capabilities

Yves Doz

The move toward a European single market will increase the intensity of competition in Europe, not decrease it. The most direct consequence of the single market for corporate strategies is to enlarge the arena for competition from national to pan-European dimensions. To some extent, this shift from national to pan-European competition has been already taking place for some time; in the future, the single market will be extended to sectors where national procurement policies, cultural preferences, and protectionist regulations had sheltered national champions from international competition.

The changes will allow national companies to break free of their domestic markets. But they will also make them more vulnerable to competitors who already operate on a pan-European basis. The single market is predicated on a Darwinian

Note: The author is most grateful to Professor C. K. Prahalad of the University of Michigan, with whom many of the ideas and analyses summarized in this chapter were first developed, researched, and published.

141

selection process in which the fittest survive and excel and in which national champions that do not adapt to new competitive demands are bound to represent an endangered species.

National companies have been preparing themselves to survive the coming battles by reducing the variety of their business portfolios and internationalizing their remaining businesses. The impossibility of competing with the whole portfolio of services or products on a European level is forcing clearer managerial choices between businesses that can develop internationally and others, which become candidates for divestitures. The acceleration of mergers and acquisitions in Europe over the last few years testifies to this. The battle actually started in the 1960s, when American multinational companies (MNCs) began to rationalize their industrial activities in Europe into integrated networks of specialized plants, focusing their R&D centers on different but complementary technologies and products (Doz 1978, 1986). During the same period European companies began their international mergers and acquisitions. This drive ranged from usually unsuccessful mega-mergers (for example, Dunlop-Pirelli) to more incremental ones aimed at operational rationalization (for example, the restructuring of the petrochemical industry in the late 1970s and early 1980s) including quasi-rationalization through partnerships and consortia in politically sensitive sectors (for example, Airbus, Panavia, Euromissiles, and other collaborative projects in the aerospace industry).

Yet, viewing the strategic consequences of a single market as only Europeanization is both too restrictive and too broad—too restrictive insofar as competition in Europe cannot be dissociated from competition elsewhere. Obviously, a Europe open to both European and outside firms could become the battleground for American and Japanese companies should the American and Japanese markets be protected or European companies not expand their presence beyond Europe. The single market of 1992 may thus become a spur for European companies to become competitive worldwide, or it may, on the contrary, result in European companies being at such a disadvantage vis-à-vis their global rivals that they are threatened with extinction. Ironically, American multinationals, and to a lesser extent Japanese corporations, are better placed than their European competitors to take advantage of a single market Europe, as American companies already have for the most part networks of partially integrated operations throughout Europe, and the Japanese start from scratch but with large resources.

Viewing the strategic consequences of a single European market as merely the needed internationalization of European companies is too broad insofar as sources of international competitive advantage are shifting in parallel with the evolution toward Europeanization. The issue for European companies is therefore to anticipate and be in a position to intercept future sources of competitive advantage rather than to meet current ones — that is, to start developing the capabilities that will be most critical in the future.

This chapter starts by discussing the changing sources of competitive advantage in Europe in the 1990s, and what demands these changes have placed on competitors in the European industry. Considering six key elements of international competitive advantage — factor cost; productivity; foreign exchange; market prices; distribution and brand strength; and product families and life cycles, influencing price and margin advantages — this section concludes that competitive advantage will shift from structural, often locational advantages, to firm-specific advantages that are less dependent on location, at least within Europe.

A second section discusses how companies should deploy and manage their resources Europe-wide, to benefit from these new sources of competitive advantage. This section argues that more than resource deployment, the key to future competitive success is how companies make trade-offs between often conflicting priorities of operational integration across borders, responsiveness to local market conditions, and strategic coordination in the face of other Europe-wide or global competitors.

A third section argues that communication and learning processes are key to the ability to improve the quality of the strategic trade-offs over time, and thus the competitiveness of the companies operating in Europe.

Shifting Sources of Competitive Advantage

Definitions of *competitive advantage* are often elusive. Competitive advantage means some form of superiority over adversaries of a sustainable nature. Measuring superiority, and its consequences for performance over time, can be difficult. In order to simplify the approach, we can equate competitive advantage with the sustained ability to generate larger cash flows than those of competitors. Ultimately, cash flow is both the consequence of the current competitiveness of a business and a basis for a continuation. Cost and revenue streams determine cash flow over time. In the following analysis we will focus on cash flow as a proxy for competitive advantage. In a simple fashion one can consider cash flow as the result of cost reduction and revenue maximization. Cost reduction can be achieved by factor cost reduction (for example, moving to a country where labor costs are lower or where capital investments are subsidized), by productivity increases (for example, better-trained work forces, more efficient plants), and by the structural advantage that currency over- or undervaluation may provide to companies exporting from countries with weak currencies toward countries with stronger currencies. Revenue maximization is more complex, but the experience of the companies we researched suggests three main axes: exploiting the pricing structure differences that still exist between countries within Europe for the same products; getting better margins through strength in distribution and brand image; and gaining competitive strength through a wide enough, rapidly enough renewed product range. The likely impact of a single market on these six main sources of cash flow is reviewed below.

Factor Costs. Economists have traditionally conceived of production factors as raw materials, labor, energy, and capital. Several key changes affect these factors. First, although differences in labor costs are still great in Europe, the realization of a single European market is likely to accelerate the convergence of labor costs between Northern and Southern European countries. Second, labor costs for which differences are greatest (typically direct manufacturing labor) are contributing less and less to total value added. In addition, research and development costs, engineering costs, indirect manufacturing costs, and marketing sales and service costs are increasing. While factories can often be located so as to minimize labor costs, downstream activities such as marketing, sales, and service usually have to be located close to customers. In R&D, the supply of competent scientists and technical personnel is often a stronger determinant of location than relative wages or other considerations.

Factor cost competition has been shifting from capital equipment, raw materials, and blue-collar workers to strategic expenses (R&D, marketing), intellectual property, and highly skilled labor, such as software development engineers. Intra-European differences in labor costs for these scarce, highly skilled employees are likely to be smaller (and to converge more rapidly) than for traditional unskilled or semiskilled labor. Further, European integration will probably result in a convergence of social costs and employment taxes that will make total labor costs (not just wages) increasingly similar throughout Europe.

As these shifts take place, traditional differences in factor costs will become less and less important; other, "softer" dimensions such as educational levels, professional training, and the ability to work in an international context will prevail. To a large extent the flexibility of these highly skilled workers to work in teams, to build collective know-how, and to interact successfully across tasks and functions in a creative unplanned way will be key.

Productivity. As with labor costs, the concept of productivity is inherited from an industrial tradition, epitomized by a Taylorist view of scientific management and plant organization. This view is obsolete for at least two reasons. First, as argued above, R&D, services, marketing, software, and other "knowledge" functions now often overwhelm direct manufacturing costs in the total value added of most products, systems, and services. The productivity of these less immediately tangible tasks, and the systemic productivity that stems from their effective execution, depend much more on the quality of interfaces among various functions than on the productivity achieved in performing individual tasks. For instance, the ability to design for manufacturability and to successfully incorporate market-driven functionalities into products becomes a much more significant source of cost reduction than marginal improvements in industrial productivity. Second, even in the manufacturing tasks, productivity stems increasingly from workers' involvement, constant attention to learning, and mobilizing the collective experience of all employees rather than from mandated improvements in efficiency.

Productivity is thus shifting from a "hard" basis such as the age and design of plants to "soft," less easily measured, systemic coordination capabilities. Although national cultures and national educational systems have been the source of productivity differences in Europe in the past and will remain critical, firm-specific capabilities are likely to play an increasing role in the future, based on different managerial approaches and organizational capabilities to mobilize and focus efforts across functions and across units.

European integration will increase the potential for competitive advantage from system-based productivity gains. Improvements in telecommunication infrastructures will make integrated R&D management across Europe feasible and decrease its cost, by allowing engineers in different countries to use software interactively in order to obtain real-time, three-dimensional visualization of new product designs. In the final analysis, however, the true harnessing of the potential provided by European integration will depend on the capabilities of individual companies: The actualization process will only make it easier for companies with the appropriate competencies, organizational capabilities, and strategies to exploit the potential for increasing the productivity of knowledge workers on a pan-European basis.

Foreign Exchange. Gaining competitive advantage by exporting from countries whose currencies are undervalued to countries with overvalued ones has been a frequent practice of managers in international companies. For years, supplying the German market from production bases in Southern Europe carried such attraction. Yet, this is a risky game. In the longer term, sustained differences in the strength of various currencies are likely to reflect differences in economic structure and policy that also affect manufacturing costs (for example, higher rates of inflation and wage increases in Southern Europe than in Germany). Thus, trying to take advantage of temporary differences in exchange rates usually locks the firm into a pattern of sourcing and manufacturing that may no longer be appropriate in a few years. The anticipated gains may thus not be worth the costs incurred and the risks involved.

Further, the European monetary system (EMS) (see Chapters Twelve and Thirteen) has already encouraged the convergence of exchange rates in Europe. The EMS leads European governments to adopt increasingly similar economic and fiscal policies, resulting in almost fixed exchange rates between European currencies. The likely adoption of a single European currency would make exploiting currency differences in a united Europe completely impossible.

Taking into consideration the three dimensions of cost differentials outlined above (factor costs, productivity gains, and exchange rate differentials), built-in differences in competitiveness are likely to be severely eroded within Europe but also to some extent outside of Europe. Even between Europe and the rest of the world, cross investments make locational differences in factor costs, productivity, and currency valuation less and less relevant.

As firms become more aware of global competition, they more carefully monitor their approaches and compare themselves with one another, making major lags in products and processes unlikely. For instance, in the 1990s European car manufacturers would not let a major technological improvement in Japan, or elsewhere, go unnoticed, and would not make the wrong choice, as in the 1960s and 1970s, of relying on cheap—but nearly illiterate—immigrant labor. Sensitivity to workers' skills as key assets is now much higher. While the more complex processes, such as the accelerated product development cycles that allow Japanese producers to offer product variety at low cost, may still be difficult to understand and imitate, major shifts in competitive advantage based on surprises are unlikely.

In summary, if we consider the cost and productivity dimensions of competitiveness we can conclude that built-in advantages or disadvantages are going to erode. We may also expect that company-specific capabilities, in particular for learning and for technology development and exploitation, are likely to play the most critical role, as the competitiveness based on these capabilities is likely to override the more traditional benefits derived from lower labor cost and more modern facilities. Even more than in the 1970s and 1980s, firm-specific systemic learning capabilities will drive cost reduction.

Revenue maximization, the other face of competitive advantage, is being affected by similar transitions. First and foremost, the single market is likely to put an end to the very wide price differences observed in a variety of products among national markets in Europe (see Chapter Two). Second, integration is likely to place a premium on marketing strength, both in distribution and in brand franchises (see Chapter Four). Third, an integrated European market is going to require a stronger product and service development policy on the part of many European companies and also to justify it. Let us consider these three transitions next.

Market Prices. In the past, prices were set to allow the survival of inefficient national champions. Key trends such as product standardization, external competitive challenges, and growing intra-European competition through the opening of public markets are affecting most industries, including services. They spell the end of protected markets and national profit sanctuaries.

Up until the late 1970s, for example, IBM imposed a price "umbrella" on the international computer markets at a high level. The prices set by IBM reflected the lesser efficiency of smaller national competitors; such prices allowed IBM to be quite profitable and the smaller competitors to survive. More recently, faced with growing Japanese competition and no longer confronted with antitrust action in Europe and the United States, IBM shifted to lower prices. The company now no longer maintains an artificially high price and competes actively.

European computer suppliers can no longer enjoy the profit sanctuary provided by national customers served by proprietary systems. All smaller European computer suppliers suffer, therefore, despite their attempts to provide value through services and system integration. In summary, price competition across Europe is likely to become much more intense. The wide price differences and the relatively high overall level of prices, which characterize European markets, are not going to survive easily, and the advantage of just selling in protected, fragmented markets where prices were artificially high will disappear.

Distribution and Brand Strength. Companies that benefit from a strong brand image can obtain better distribution coverage, higher end-user prices, and lower distributors' margins, hence a larger volume and better margins than their competitors. In the current European situation of high distributors' clout and bargaining power, and increasingly concentrated distribution, a well-regarded brand may become, more than ever, a key source of competitive advantage. The current wave of pan-European and transatlantic mergers and acquisitions in branded consumer goods (food, beverages, drinks, hotels and restaurants, and so forth), and the high premiums paid for consumer good companies, testifies to the importance of brands. Thus, brands and their reputation constitute the strong "invisible assets" for major companies.

Brands and reputation are vulnerable to product mispositioning, changes in distribution structures (for instance, Philips' share of consumer electronics in some European countries was anchored to a dense network of relatively small "main street" specialist shops that found it difficult to survive competition from big chains; Matsushita is facing the same problem in Japan), and poor quality or functionality of the products. Developing a strong brand image is thus a long-term goal in which new products and emerging channels have to be screened for their fit with the image and reputation of the brand. Besides prestige names like Mercedes and Porsche and a handful of mass market brands such as Philips, European companies do not fare very well among European consumers in either awareness or positive image. On the other hand, some Japanese companies, particularly Sony, Honda, and Canon, have relentlessly built up the images of their brands within Europe as well as worldwide and have developed a tightly managed approach to brand image.

A consistent brand image does not necessarily mean, though, that the same brand and product positioning is appropriate across all geographical markets—for example, Heineken is a premium beer everywhere except in the Netherlands, its home country. The same Canon camera models have been positioned quite differently from one market to the next depending on existing attitudes toward photography and on the age and type of cameras Canon was trying to replace (Takeuchi and Porter, 1986). This led the same camera to be positioned as a Leica replacement in Germany and as a way to upgrade from the Kodak Instamatic to a full-feature camera in other markets. Yet, these quite different positionings of the same basic products, with different add-on features, were marketed in a way consistent with the image Canon was trying to promote for its single corporate brand across a wide range of products, industries, and geographical markets.

The current European location for Japanese car manufacturers whose design activities have traditionally been centralized in Japan is no coincidence; it denotes a growing sensitivity to the need to customize mass-manufactured products. Here, too, the basis for competitive advantage is shifting from "hard" efficiency to "soft" effectiveness, to market intelligence and micromarketing, to anticipating customer needs and reducing product development cycles. The next competitive battle is going to be fought around market understanding, consumer needs anticipation, and most effective leveraging of brand reputations, Europe-wide. The paramount factor in corporate adaptation will be intelligence-related, as there will soon be more flexibility in manufacturing than companies know how to exploit successfully.

Product Family and Product Life Cycle. It is a well-known fact that product life cycles are becoming shorter, but the full implications of shorter product life cycles are not always well understood. First, the time it takes for a new product to reach the market becomes essential. In a growing number of businesses, a six-month delay makes the difference between substantial profits or serious losses. Speed in bringing technologies to market is therefore essential. It allows the manufacturer to incorporate the latest component or subsystem technologies and minimizes the risks of shifting market preferences. Whereas in the past European suppliers often shrugged away the need for faster product renewal rates as Japanese gimmickry, they now recognize that shorter product cycles are indispensable. The adoption of more powerful software design tools allows faster product development by shifting to parallel rather than sequential development steps and reducing the cost of each step. Computer simulation technologies in such diverse fields as pharmaceuticals (with "designer's molecules") and computers (where the old "breadboard" prototypes are replaced by virtual simulated computers on other computers) are now widely used, further reducing the time to market and decreasing the costs of product development.

It is also becoming increasingly important not only to have rapidly renewed products, but also a wide enough range of related products across which brand image, advertising expenditures, and other distribution support costs can be leveraged. Broad product range companies can also cross-subsidize their entries into further product lines more easily (Hamel and Prahalad, 1985). Developing coordinated product development, market presence, and distribution strategies across multiple product lines thus becomes essential.

In summary, as we consider the determinants of revenues for international companies operating in Europe, we observe that they are shifting from built-in locational advantages to firm-specific learning and mobilizing advantages—that is, how to exploit both the opportunities for integration and the need for local market adaptation. Thus, the underlying competitive logic shifts progressively from better efficiency to faster and better learning.

Deploying Corporate Resources in Europe: Trade-Offs Between Responsiveness and Integration

The changes in the sources of competitive advantage analyzed above create new demands for multinational corporations (MNCs) operating in Europe. Traditionally, the fragmented European markets led MNCs to develop autonomous, full-fledged subsidiaries in each national market. As trade barriers, economic policies, and government purchasing preferences kept these markets separate, having autonomous affiliates in the various national markets allowed the MNCs to transfer technological skills and marketing and management know-how from headquarters to affiliates relatively easily. Patterns of internationalization were replications—that is, a full copy of the parent company, albeit usually smaller, was established independently in each country. As affiliates grew and became more varied in order to adjust to their local market conditions, the value of what headquarters could still contribute decreased and with it the dependence of affiliates on headquarters (Prahalad and Doz, 1981). As European integration proceeds, this repetitive form of growth and the resulting decentralized, autonomous management of the MNC affiliates are becoming increasingly unsuited. Only in government-controlled markets, in which preferential national purchasing maintains market fragmentation, does the replications mode of internationalization remain appropriate (Doz, 1979).

U.S. MNCs have often been among the first to take advantage of the opportunities presented by freer trade in Europe. Companies such as Ford, Otis, and IBM rationalized their activities in Europe in the 1960s and 1970s, with Ford evolving into a Europe-wide network of efficiently sized, focused factories located in some half a dozen countries (Doz, 1979). European companies were, by and large, slower to react. Integrating operations across Europe was often delayed by the fact that national fragmentation did not make the emergence of global competition easily visible. The separation of management along national lines, with strong affiliates not intensely preoccupied with activities outside their borders, did not facilitate the identification of new international competitors, in particular the Japanese, as a threat to their profitability. Further, many European companies were active in a range of businesses, many of which remained government-protected or locally oriented. Many European companies' top managers, often coming from businesses under government protection, applied the logic of protected industries to businesses exposed to open competition, making the adjustment of their firms even more difficult.

The very process of responding to the new competitive reality called for a major reallocation of decision-making power in companies, in particular from the country managers, who used to be "kings in their countries" to the international product managers running Europe-wide or worldwide businesses along product lines. Such a transition has been slow and painful, in particular when top management is concerned with not killing the entrepreneurship of the local affiliates, which is often a key strength of the company. Finally, rationalization efforts were usually resisted, at least initially, by the unions and often by the host governments, both of which hoped that tough stances against plant closures would lead other countries to bear the social cost of rationalization.

The process of pan-European rationalization went on through the entire 1970s and 1980s and is still continuing, in particular in businesses for which local market differences and national protection were the strongest. For example, in appliances, Electrolux has been driving the process of rationalization by acquiring and integrating local companies into a Europe-wide network of plants and coordinating the policies of the various brands. Consumer nondurable goods companies, such as Procter & Gamble and Unilever, are going through a similar process. Integration is only starting in the hitherto most fragmented government-controlled industries such as electrical equipment, as witnessed by the 1988–1989 web of agreements among CGE (Compagnie Générale d'Electricité) in France, GEC (General Electric Company) in the United Kingdom, and Siemens in Germany. Such an agreement is likely to result in consolidation of many of the three companies' businesses. For example, GEC and Siemens will manufacture telecommunications equipment, CGE and GEC will cooperate on electrical equipment, and CGE and Siemens will be partners for nuclear engineering.

Yet this mode of rationalization is increasingly counterbalanced by the growing pressures discussed in the first section of this chapter, that is, the need to remain responsive to local markets to exploit manufacturing flexibility and brand strength. The need for national responsiveness is less and less a result of policy-induced market fragmentation; it increasingly stems from the desire to exploit opportunities for market and product differentiation. Closeness to customers becomes the key factor in identifying changes in demand quickly, developing micromarketing approaches, and strengthening one's brand and distribution positions.

Companies thus need to manage several priorities at once:

- The *integration priority*, that is, the need to keep increasing their geographical integration into efficient development, manufacturing, and logistic networks.
- The *responsiveness priority*, that is, the need to remain responsive to local markets, but on the basis of active closeness to customers and orientation toward differentiating markets.
- The *strategic coordination priority*, that is, the need to coordinate competitive interaction between markets and product groups, as the same competitors are found in multiple markets and in multiple product lines. This coordination issue is further complicated by the fact that the same company

can be a competitor in one business and a partner in another, as, for example, GEC to CGE.

The above three priorities cannot all be fully achieved simultaneously. Integration pushed to its extreme eliminates national responsiveness unless an extremely effective market intelligence and feedback process is put in place. Responsiveness makes integration complex. And it is difficult to keep a high level of integration, while at the same time being sensitive to the more subtle differences between markets. Japanese companies that have maintained an export orientation, developing all their products and producing most of them in Japan, have compensated for their extreme form of integration with very intensive communication and information channels with their most important markets (Bartlett and Ghoshal, 1989).

In order to be successful in the unified but differentiated market found in Europe, companies will thus need to make trade-offs between integration opportunities and the need for market adaptation. While in theory such trade-offs could be made centrally, their sheer number across countries, functions, and businesses is likely to call for a process of decentralized choice. Before analyzing the organizational basis for such a process, we shall make a brief overview of how priorities for integration, responsiveness, and coordination are likely to affect various functions and tasks.

Priority Areas for Operational Integration. Manufacturing is likely to remain a priority area for integration as it has been in the past (Doz, 1978). While the absolute size of operations of many companies in Europe is beyond the minimum efficient scale, increasing product variety and shorter product life cycles are likely to counterbalance the effect of flexible manufacturing on minimum scale. Except where fundamental changes in process technology reduce minimum efficient scale — potentially in some areas of the chemical industry, for example — one can expect continued pressures for integration of manufacturing. The improvements in the speed and reliability of European cross-border transportation that will result from integration will also make pan-European manufacturing integration easier. This, in turn, will allow more effective management of logistics, reduced inventories, quicker deliveries to customers, and overall greater flexibility in developing and managing a manufacturing system over time. The variety of products available on short notice can be increased by the reduction of supply and storage points.

Priority Areas for Local Responsiveness. Sales are usually local (except for major projects, such as transportation infrastructure or major capital equipment goods such as aircraft), and they require an extensive understanding of customers' needs and their decision-making processes for purchasing goods and services. While similar market segments may exist in different countries, their relative size varies considerably. Distribution channel structures and relative efficiency also vary from country to country, calling for brand positioning and channel differentiation policies that may be very different. Traditional local brands are often stronger than multinational executives would sometimes like to believe.

Channel and brand management are other tasks that benefit from local responsiveness rather than integration. Customer service and feedback from the marketplace are also tasks usually best performed locally, and these tasks are often essential to product development policies and the customer orientation of manufacturing.

Areas for Strategic Coordination. Global competition is increasingly intense in more and more industries. Coordinated competition across European markets thus becomes progressively more important for major European companies. Home bases are no longer protected, as even national champions interpenetrate one another's markets. Beyond integration, such competitive interdependence across European markets will become even stronger than it is today. Hence, the need to coordinate competitive strategies across Europe will increase. Such coordination will encompass the most obvious operating dimensions, such as pricing policies and the management of corporate brands, as well as the more clearly strategic issues such as new business entries, new business development, and acquisitions.

Beyond actions in various countries in the same business, the coordination of interbusiness strategic interdependencies is also becoming critical (Prahalad and Doz, 1987). It is no longer unusual for companies to be competitors, collaborators, and customers or suppliers of one another in different business areas at the same time. Although there may not be a general rule as to how to manage these multiple forms of relationship, it is essential to recognize the potential for conflict among them and the need for a coordination of choices in resolving these conflicts in the context of a common set of strategic priorities.

Resource deployment in MNCs in Europe will thus continue to become increasingly complex as pressures for Europe-wide integration and local market and country responsiveness increase at the same time as national responsiveness and integration of operations become more and more interdependent. In order to deal with such complexity, the roles of headquarters and affiliates will have to be redefined in terms of the contribution of each toward the deployment of corporate resources with the aim of exploiting market opportunities.

As competitive advantage becomes more firm-specific than ever, organizational learning becomes the key to corporate success. Companies operating in Europe, a set of differentiated but highly interdependent markets, may take advantage of the opportunities for learning offered by various markets as long as that learning can be adapted and transferred from one country to another. The process of learning and its effective diffusion across organizational units within Europe are bound to become the most critical capabilities for long-term competitive success. Learning creates the ability to make finer and finer trade-offs between responsiveness and integration. It allows one to find creative solutions that increase both responsiveness and integration by selectively exploiting interdependencies.

Organizational Capabilities for Flexibility and Learning

The subtle trade-offs mentioned above cannot be managed in the context of the traditional unidimensional product, geographical, or functional structures. Each of these is likely to privilege one dimension to the detriment of the others with all decisions being made according to one single dominant logic.

A structural view of organizations does not allow differentiation, except through the multiplication of overlay structures and coordinating staffs, both of which tend to become sources of confusion and introduce delays in decision making (Doz, Bartlett, and Prahalad, 1981). A different view is needed whereby organizations are not considered as structures, but rather as processes providing a context in which to perceive and analyze the environment, make trade-offs and reach decisions, and mobilize resources for competitive action. In order to capture the various key dimensions of the post-integration European environment, a single perspective is not sufficient. Multiple perspectives must thus be presented in decision-making processes to allow creative trade-offs to be made. Chosen strategic trade-offs need to be followed by actions. This also requires the corporate organization to distribute the power to act and to balance forces for autonomy and cooperation in ways consistent with the strategic priorities.

The MNCs best prepared to take advantage of integration are likely to have an understanding of their own organization that transcends simple structural dimensions of products, geography, and functions, and allows for multiple perspectives in perceiving of the environment, in decision making, and in resource mobilization.

A Shift of Concept on Multinational Organizations

Perception and Analysis. The market, as well as the competitive, political, and technological environment in Europe, needs to be perceived and debated in terms of multiple perspectives. Contradictory demands will put a premium on capabilities to gather diverse information, to avoid strategic "dogmas," and to be thorough and analytical in information gathering.

Strategic Choices. The more open postintegration European competitive environment will probably call for a reexamination of the strategic management premises of many companies in Europe. The main stumbling block is not likely to be the inability to develop "smart" strategies, but rather the difficulties faced in mobilizing human resources and performing operational improvements in order to achieve strategic objectives. Rather than the strategic planning of past decades, "strategy deployment" (the mobilization of the entire company in order to accomplish a common strategic intent) is likely to be the main issue facing the corporate strategists of tomorrow (Hamel and Prahalad, 1989). While strategic intent fixes the corporate objectives, a more rapidly changing competitive environment and the need to mobilize the whole organization call for a more opportunistic and participatory strategy deployment process.

Flexibility will thus also become a major source of competitive advantage. The strategies of companies will need to be better prepared to seize new opportunities, and willing to make creative compromises between short-term performance and longer-term potential. In practical terms, this requires consensus on the broad strategic goals of the company and commitment toward programs of action that contribute to the achievement of these goals.

The concept of strategic intent requires companies operating in Europe to develop clear, ambitious, long-term goals, and promote internal consensus and commitment to achieving them and the values they embody. In this approach we are far from the traditional distinction between strategy and operations. Indeed, operations are made strategic, and the collective intelligence of the organization is mobilized for strategic accomplishment. Such mobilization requires room for interpretation of, and influence upon, strategic choices, and thus flexibility; at the same time, a clear intent that establishes direction must also exist.

Power to Act

For multiple perspectives to be legitimate and for consensus on strategic goals and flexibility in means and commitment to action to take root, the power to act must exceed the power to veto. The traditional bureaucratic hierarchical organizations of past decades are unlikely to be suited to the new competitive demands of a postintegration Europe. Here again, a unidimensional power allocation, driven by a unidimensional hierarchy, is not effective. Operating managers must be able to draw on resources along multiple paths, depending on the nature of the issue at hand.

Yet the sharing of power over resource allocation need not be equally balanced between priorities. It may vary over time as a function of the relative importance of various priorities. Executives who manage key dependencies between the corporation and its environment are likely to evolve toward greater influence in decision making, and to gain power in the organization.

Adopting this more fluid approach to strategy development requires a major cultural evolution on the part of many companies operating in Europe—away from a traditionally static and hierarchical mode of organizing and toward one that is both dynamic and more achievement-oriented. Companies that to some extent already have this culture, such as DEC in the computer industry or ICI in chemicals, are better positioned to take full advantage of integration than companies with more rigidly hierarchical processes. The current efforts at decentralization and flexibility on the part of Siemens and, less visibly, of many other traditional companies in Europe witness the extent of change and evolution required to adopt a more flexible response to new competitive demands in Europe.

In sum, there are multiple perspectives of how contradictory environmental demands are perceived. Flexibility, opportunism and mobilization in strategic action, and empowerment within the organization are likely to be key priorities on the management agenda of European CEOs.

Research on the management of MNCs in Europe suggests that at least three approaches can contribute to meeting these priorities: communication, dualities, and learning processes. These are analyzed below.

Communication

Richer, more flexible, more effective combinations of responsiveness and integration and more agile use of strategic coordination opportunities are called for. Effective communications, however, do not develop on their own.

In the international companies we have observed, communication was a result of interdependence and complementarity between the units performing tasks whose primary orientation was toward national responsiveness and those performing tasks whose primary orientation was pan-European integration. Complementarity can be explicitly structured with, for instance, product-oriented executives developing Europe-wide product plans and national affiliates' marketing and sales managers developing key account plans country by country. Developing a complete, realistic business plan called for product executives and marketing and sales managers to communicate intensely and work together. Sensitivity to the value of complementarity can be fostered by career paths that alternate product and geographical responsibilities in the careers of general managers. Moreover, management development can be explicitly used to encourage cross-functional interactions and alternation between product and geographical responsibilities.

In European companies, interactions between key market areas, such as the United States and Japan, and centers of competence mainly located in Europe are critical. They provide invaluable inputs into product policy, product development, and strategic coordination discussions (insofar as key non-European markets are also usually the home bases of key competitors). Companies that have the richest communications, notably within Europe, but also between Europe and Japan and North America, are likely to be best placed to take advantage of integration, not only in Europe but also worldwide (Ghoshal and Nohria, 1989).

Speed and integrity of communications will also be increasingly important as timeliness becomes more than ever a source of competitive advantage. Response times of major companies in Europe will have to be cut. A strong internal culture may accelerate response time and also facilitate communication integrity by providing clearer sense-making maps.

The desire for speed, integrity, and intensity of communication is likely to lead more and more companies to be organized internally as networks. Practically speaking, this will involve more direct contacts and exchanges between subsidiaries without passing through headquarters. In addition, national subsidiaries will increasingly be given supranational corporate responsibilities (for example, a subsidiary being responsible for a product Europe-wide, or for serving a particular customer group). International project teams will also tend to become a routine way of managing the development and launching of new activities, making the various affiliates stakeholders in the success of new projects. The common objective of these approaches is to blend local and Europe-wide responsibilities for key executives and to put organization units in different countries in a position of being both the providers of support and the receivers of assistance. Thus, the mobilization of corporate competencies can take place flexibly, and independently from central headquarters.

While most companies operating in Europe are still far from this network approach, many are evolving toward encouraging lateral communication, distributing corporate responsibilities among affiliates, and deemphasizing the vertical relationship between subsidiaries and headquarters.

Dualities

To encourage cognitive variety, strategic flexibility, and power fluidity, companies operating in Europe need to recognize the need for dualities—that is, the existence of multiple perspectives on single issues. For strategy development, for example, we observe that:

- Dissent must be tolerated, even encouraged, when representing in good faith a different point of view. Dissent can be more easily seen as legitimate when the motives of members of the organization are clear and their loyalty to corporate interests is above doubt.
- Open debate is a necessity, but it must be structured and controlled. This means a beginning and an end to such a

debate, rather than constant questioning of existing commitments.

- Collective discipline in managing the debate must be exercised to avoid politicization and the pursuance of self-interests.

Such dualities in strategy are unlikely to be achieved, however, without corresponding dualities in the management of people. Managers in European companies also need to shift to dualistic norms to assess people, their behavior, and the effectiveness of their decisions (Evans and Doz, 1989). Our evaluation of individuals tends to be binary: we judge people as "good" or "bad." Some personal qualities are desirable, others are not. Yet we cannot manage complex adaptive organizations with such a simplistic framework. For example, the observation that a person is decisive is not by itself adequate for a positive evaluation. When does decisive turn into impulsive? Moreover, is decisiveness complementary to the quality of reflectiveness? Beyond explicitly fostering dualities in managing, the way in which corporate cultures evolve may or may not favor dualities.

In many companies, such as DEC, Shell, and several Swedish multinationals operating in Europe, managers have developed an informal culture of "buy-in." This means that they possess an implicit understanding of who the key person(s) are within the organization to consult, secure approval from, obtain commitment from, and so on, which helps them speed up decision making and implement decisions without major difficulties. There are no formal rules, but divergent perspectives are consistently reconciled through buy-in norms. In the course of these "reconciliations," the strategic intent of the company, its operating principles, and its key priorities are constantly, but indirectly, reasserted and communicated to new members of the management group.

Contrary to strong unidimensional cultural perceptions, which often turn into blind dogmas and compliant orthodoxy, organizational cultures that recognize diversity and duality make the company more adaptive to its environment. Such corporate cultures are necessary in postintegration Europe.

Learning

In the postintegration environment, with the emphasis we have described on firm-specific advantages often drawn from collective know-how within the firm, organizational learning will play a major role in determining success. A company can learn through scanning, trial and error, or by observation of the experiences of other companies. These forms of learning are likely to become increasingly important.

Learning from scanning and analyzing the competitive and technological environment will be used to achieve strategic direction and flexibility. Without such scanning, it will be difficult for European companies to identify changes in the environment and quickly respond to them. Active learning through actual experimentation will be important as well. For example, some European markets can be used as test grounds not only for the remaining European markets, but also for the American and Japanese ones. As changes will be more rapid, the ability to test and benchmark new products or services and consequently to improve them through customer feedback becomes the central factor leading to successful products or services. Companies that can experiment and learn are likely to enjoy competitive advantages over those that do not develop this experimental capability. Finally, identifying best practice and learning from competitors (that is, vicarious learning) are also likely to become increasingly important.

Conclusion

The three sections of this chapter can be seen as corresponding to three successive layers of competitive advantage for European companies.

First, the shift away from differences in competitive advantage from merely operating in different countries to company-specific capabilities calls for a more focused infrastructure, blending operations and tasks to achieve heightened national responsiveness in some cases and increased international integration in others. The key challenge for European companies is to increase responsiveness to market demands on selected dimensions (such as service quality) and international integration on some others (such as manufacturing and research and development).

Second, putting in place the relevant infrastructure would be useless without proper coordination. This clearly requires that particular attention be given to logistics and communication. A single European market will offer tremendous opportunities for both cost saving and revenue maximizing, but only for companies that can use pan-European logistics effectively and develop intense and effective communications around key processes in a way that will allow them to mobilize and exploit their resources to the fullest extent.

Third, as stressed at various points of the chapter, the ultimate basis for competitive advantage is likely to be organizational learning. Learning will be promoted by multiple perspectives and the effort to reach consensus within the firm on strategic priorities, an attitude that allows for experimentation and risk taking and a strong external orientation (toward both customers and competitors), which encourages vicarious learning and exposes managers to quick feedback from their markets. In the fast-changing environment of tomorrow such feedback will provide the means of quick responsiveness to new consumer and market needs.

These three aspects—a focused and mobilized infrastructure, intense physical and informational interdependence among geographical units, and collective learning in the organization—constitute an agenda for gaining competitive advantage in postintegration Europe.

References

Bartlett, C. A., and Ghoshal, S. *Managing Across Borders: The Transnational Solution*. Boston: Harvard Business School Press, 1989.

Doz, Y. "Managing Manufacturing Rationalization Within Multinational Companies." *Columbia Journal of World Business*, 1978, *13*, 3.

Doz, Y. *Government Control and Multinational Management; Power Systems and Telecommunications Equipment*. New York: Praeger, 1979.

Doz, Y. *Strategic Management in Multinational Companies*. Oxford, England: Pergamon Press, 1986.

Doz, Y., Bartlett, C. A., and Prahalad, C. K. "Global Competitive Pressures vs. Host Country Demands: Managing Tensions in Multinational Corporations." *California Management Review*, 1981, *23*, 3.

Evans, P., and Doz, Y. "The Dualistic Organisation." In P. Evans, Y. Doz, and A. Laurent (eds.), *Human Resource Management in International Firms*. London: Macmillan, 1989.

Ghoshal, S., and Nohria, N. "Internal Differentiation Within Multinational Corporations." *Strategic Management Journal*, 1989, *10*, 323–337.

Hamel, G., and Prahalad, C. K. "Do You Really Have a Global Strategy?" *Harvard Business Review*, 1985, *63* (4), 139–148.

Hamel, G., and Prahalad, C. K. "Strategic Intent." *Harvard Business Review*, 1989, *67* (3), 139–148.

Haspeslagh, P., and Jemison, D. *Managing Acquisitions*. New York: Free Press, 1990.

Prahalad, C. K., and Doz, Y. "An Approach to Strategic Control in Multinational Companies" and "Headquarter Influence and Strategic Control in Multinational Companies." *Sloan Management Review*, 1981, *22* (4), 5–13; *23* (1), 15–25.

Prahalad, C. K., and Doz, Y. *The Multinational Mission: Balancing Local Demand and Global Vision*. New York: Free Press, 1987.

Takeuchi, H., and Porter, M. "Three Roles of International Marketing in Global Strategy." In M. Porter (ed.), *Competition in Global Industries*. Boston: Harvard Business School Press, 1986.

CHAPTER 7

Seizing Opportunities

The Changing Role of Strategy in European Companies

Dominique Héau

Much has been said about the single market movement and its implications for European competitiveness. The importance of this movement is that it has accelerated a process of change in which many existing situations are challenged and established industry structures placed under increasingly severe pressure. The Europeanization of firms has been taking place in many sectors and industries over the past twenty years. Therefore, rather than focusing on integration as a single event, we need to understand the forces at work and reflect the changes they are likely to bring to the competitive environment.

This chapter is divided into three main parts: First, we present the evolution of strategic thinking from the 1960s and the tools and concepts available to strategists. Second, we deal with the strategic challenges of the 1990s. Third, we discuss the changing role of strategy and the implications of such changes. Our argument is that future strategy will have to be fundamentally different from that of the past, which will require that

European firms radically rethink the basis of competition if they are to survive.

Strategic Planning from the 1960s Through the 1980s

The Golden Sixties

The 1960s were essentially characterized by steady economic growth coupled with low rates of inflation and unemployment in most industrialized countries. Except for a few goods, markets remained largely domestic and were dominated by a few local producers. Money was easily available and at affordable rates. Competitors maintained rather gentlemanly rivalry among themselves—what the French called *"la drôle de guerre"* (the phony war).

During that period, properly managed companies were able to increase their turnover, retain their market share, and generate healthy profits and steady cash flows. Strategic dilemmas during such a "peacetime" environment were few (Lorange, Scott, and Ghoshal, 1986). Top management's role and the essence of strategy were focused on short-term performance, as there was little concern about long-term success. One might compare the "golden sixties" metaphorically to a surfer riding the crest of a wave, where his most important preoccupation is to maintain his equilibrium at every moment: The long term will "take care of itself" as it is a natural extension of the short term.

In the 1960s top management's major concern was to ensure short-term efficiency by deploying existing assets and resources in as optimal a manner as possible. Pricing, product, inventory manufacturing, and other decisions were determined by considering various alternatives during the budgetary process and selected those that maximized short-term profits. Complex, diversified corporations were organized along profit centers in order to identify and maximize high profit potentials (Dyas and Thanheiser, 1974). Moreover, profit centers competed with one another for investment funds.

The emphasis on short-term profits, demonstrated by Harold Geneen in his management of ITT, was further reinforced by the stock market, where the value of shares most often depended on the quarterly earnings performance of the given firm. Many firms at that time were also engaged in some form of long-range planning, but such planning became a number-crunching task that did not influence decisions in any significant way. Long-range planning was a normative exercise with no value for operational managers, as the prevailing short-term focus relegated planning to the level of a ritual, demanded by headquarters but having little practical consequence.

The More Competitive Environment of the 1970s

Business conditions abruptly changed toward the middle of the 1970s. Under the impact of the quadrupling of oil prices and increased competition, economic growth stalled, inflation soared, and unemployment reached unheard-of levels. While the economic situation improved in the United States (except for budgetary and trade deficits) and in Japan, European countries and European companies found it difficult to adapt to the new and more competitive environment.

Increased competition was due to a combination of factors. First, lower economic growth meant lower overall demand; many markets were in severe decline, and existing firms were forced to compete more fiercely. Second, technological innovation rapidly brought substitute products and services that increased supply and provided better and cheaper alternatives. Third, due to deregulation, many markets opened up to competition and transactions became far more efficient as the power of cartels was gradually dissolved. This was especially true of such sectors as financial services, communications, and transportation, where customers enjoyed a greater choice, thereby driving profit margins down. Fourth, customers themselves became more knowledgeable and more sophisticated. Finally, greater access to capital and technology coupled with lower tariff barriers allowed new competitors to emerge, turning the marketplace into a "global village" where needs and tastes were increasingly convergent and technological innovation was speedily diffused worldwide.

The Battle for Competitive Advantages in the 1980s

In the late 1970s and 1980s, managerial concern shifted. As profit margins were under severe pressure from substitutes and customers were buying cheaper imports rather than locally manufactured products, many companies were unable to remain profitable. Managers started wondering whether they were following the right strategy, as firms, failing to anticipate market and competitive changes, saw their profit margins disappear. EMI Medicals (the inventor of the CAT-scanner) went from a 50 percent market share to exit in less than four years. Michelin, the inventor of radial tires, a highly profitable firm of the 1970s, lost ten billion French francs (about two billion dollars) between 1982 and 1985.

As competition increased, firms suddenly realized that they had no inherent competitive advantage to help them to survive. At the same time, governments were less willing to subsidize failing enterprises. Thus, management began to understand that short-term profitability was by no means a guarantee of long-term survival. Short-term profits were obviously necessary, but in such a competitive environment corporate survival depended on the ability to secure long-term benefits. Management's concern shifted toward the concept of competitive strategy—that is, a conceptual framework helping to identify sources of long-term competitive advantage (where competitive advantage was defined as something unique to a firm, valued by its customers and not easily replicated by its competitors).

In the 1980s, strategy became synonymous with the pursuit of competitive advantage, which included the following: deciding in which business to compete by dividing the market and/or industry into different segments; selecting those segments where, based on its capabilities, the firm possessed or could achieve a competitive advantage; and establishing or strengthening such an advantage by dissuading competitors to enter those selected segments. This was best achieved by investing over time in assets and skills that could not easily be replicated by competitors (Cool and Diericks, 1989).

It was commonly agreed during this period that there were two essential types of competitive advantage. First, a firm could strive to become the low-cost producer either through economies of scale or by increasing efficiency through value engineering and learning. The second type of strategic advantage came from offering a unique product or service, which provided added value to some category of customers, thereby justifying a premium price, which would compensate for the higher costs of manufacturing and/or delivering the differentiated product or service.

Strategically speaking, a firm could therefore either be the low-cost producer (in most cases through market leadership) or focus on some profitable niche by offering clearly differentiated products. The worst position would be to get stuck in the middle with neither of the two distinctive advantages (Porter, 1985). Thus an automobile manufacturer could succeed as Fiat did (low-cost producer) or as BMW did (market niche), but not with a middle-of-the-road strategy like Saab's.

As the 1980s progressed, markets and competition became increasingly global. Aggressive firms began formulating their strategies in terms of country portfolios. Globalization was aided by faster and cheaper air transportation, electronic mail, fax, and video conferencing, which contributed to shrinking the barriers to communication and diminishing the importance of geographical distances. Significant scale economies in R&D, manufacturing, or distribution encouraged companies to expand their operations worldwide. The emergence of financial instruments allowed firms to protect themselves from currency fluctuations and increased their motivation to operate abroad (Hamel and Prahalad, 1985).

Multinational companies had to choose between two types of strategies. Some firms focused on efficiency and geographical rationalization (Hoechst, Volvo, and Nixdorf). Such a strategy was appropriate for products or services that corresponded to universal needs and were similarly distributed, or where manufacturing and research were subject to substantial scale economies. The organizational structure best suited for such a strategic approach was the highly centralized corporation, where key decisions were made at the top and uniformly implemented through the various subsidiaries. The alternative strategy emphasized local responsiveness (Doz and Prahalad, 1987) and sacrificed global efficiency to local flexibility in order to serve domestic markets (Unilever, L'Air Liquide, and ABN Bank). Many key decisions were made by autonomous local subsidiaries. This second approach was congruent with heterogeneous market needs, dissimilar distribution channels, high transportation costs, and/or protectionist public policies.

Strategists in pursuit of sustainable advantages were searching both for strategic principles (derived from a rigorous evaluation of competitive dynamics) and for analytical tools that could help formulate a successful competitive strategy (Porter, 1985). Still widely used today, such principles and tools include those discussed below.

Industry Analysis. Derived from microeconomies, the structure-conduct-performance paradigm was adapted to business situations where industry profitability and hence attractiveness were said to be determined by the intensity of competition. Competitive intensity was itself the result of various factors, in particular substitute products, customer and supplier relationships, potential newcomers, and internal rivalry among incumbents (Porter, 1985). Establishing and maintaining entry barriers (against potential competitors) or mobility barriers (across strategic groups) constituted the core of strategic investments. Understanding the likely evolution of such competitive pressures over time was a prerequisite for strategy formulation.

Value-Chain Analysis. Even though industry analysis remains a useful framework for understanding "how competitive forces shape strategy," it falls short of guiding specific strategic actions (Porter, 1979). Various consultant groups such as McKinsey, the Boston Consulting Group, and Braxton Associates thus came up with what became known as the "value-added process," which consists of identifying the managerial activities required to achieve competitive efficiency within each business. For instance: Was it scale-sensitive, and if so at which level (regional, national)? Was it learning-sensitive (reputation, production, marketing), and if so, which one? Which were the activities that corresponded to the firm's basic capabilities? Should a given activity be produced or subcontracted? Was product diversification in related fields providing economies of scope? By identifying specific activities, the value-chain analysis provided a fairly operational tool for selecting businesses and focusing investment. However, the detailed analysis required was rather difficult to make because relevant information was lacking and because what has happened in the past could not always be used to predict the future as customers, suppliers, competitors, technology, and markets could and were constantly changing.

Strategic Segmentation

If competitive advantage is concerned with superior performance, the obvious questions become: How do we define the proper competitive arena? How do we define a "business" in such a way that lasting competitive advantage can be associated to such business? How do we segment the market in the most meaningful way and build appropriate strategic business units (SBUs)? A strategic business unit corresponds to a given product/market segment with specific key success factors. Therefore, the key to successful strategic segmentations is identifying different SBUs with specific competitive requirements.

In deciding how specific competitive advantages can be gained, the strategist needs to realize that SBUs tend to vary over time as technology and/or market changes have an impact on the value-chain configuration, and thereby influence the boundaries of SBUs. Furthermore, SBUs are not identical to profit centers (SBUs are concerned with the best allocation of investment to establish a competitive advantage, while profit centers are concerned with the best utilization of existing assets). At Thorn EMI, for instance, kitchen mixers were a separate profit center with a separate budget and income statement. All small electrical appliances, however, constituted a single SBU, as competitive success largely depended on low unit cost (achieved through commonality of components), reputation (common name for all such appliances), and shelf space (breadth of product range). Some companies, in fact, developed a dual organizational structure: an operational structure around budgets and profit centers and a strategic structure around business plans and investments (Haspeslagh, 1982). Thus, strategic segmentation and SBU definition go right to the heart of strategy. In many ways they often become synonymous with success. Unfortunately, existing theories (and consultants) have not provided much help on how to segment the market or find the best way to define an SBU.

Competitive Assessment

Competitive advantage is a relative concept. Once a strategic business and the various key success factors have been identified, it becomes important to assess where the firm stands vis-à-vis its various competitors. Successful firms tend to establish sophisticated competitive intelligence systems, where information is collected from various sources (suppliers, salesmen, bankers, public speeches, and so on), and analyzed centrally. Moreover, they prepare "competitive profiles" for their business by ranking various competitors on a series of key factors. Some companies go even further and assess each of their competitors through quantitative scores and weights. Yet, information about competition is not easy to obtain. Competitors can provide false signals to mislead the competitive assessment of their opponents. In addition, new competitors can enter the market and old ones can change their strategies, invalidating prevailing competitive behavior or signaling patterns.

Having defined a given business, assessed its attractiveness (growth, concentration, capital intensity, profitability) and the respective strengths and weaknesses of various competitors, Figure 7-1 can be drawn. According to the principles advocated by competitive strategy, businesses that fall into square 1 are clear candidates for divestment; those in square 2 ought to be strengthened through additional investments; businesses in square 3 either might provide investment opportunities, if it is

Figure 7-1. Competitive Positioning of Businesses.

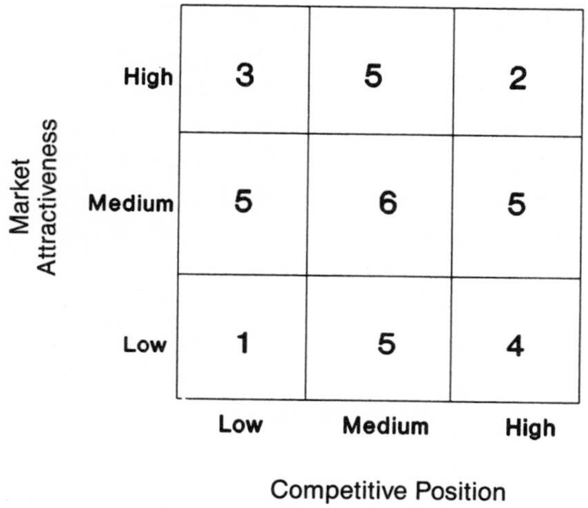

	Low	Medium	High
High	3	5	2
Medium	5	6	5
Low	1	5	4

Market Attractiveness

Competitive Position

judged that competitors can be overcome, or should be divested, if competition cannot be tamed. Businesses in square 4 should be "milked," or their market attractiveness reestablished through product improvements and marketing investments. Businesses in square 5 should be carefully managed and appropriate strategies for them selectively chosen. Finally, those in square 6 often combine the disadvantages of the corner positions, making them less attractive possibilities.

The Strategic Challenges of the 1990s

In the 1990s, three main strategic challenges have emerged. First, intensifying further competition has pushed firms toward major restructuring; second, increasing environmental uncertainty has demanded greater strategic flexibility; and third, the legitimacy of business firms has been openly questioned.

Intensified Competition

Globalization and deregulation, two market forces unleashed in the 1980s, will continue to intensify. Standardization of norms and increased economies of scale in R&D, marketing, and manufacturing will accentuate the pressure on multinational and European firms to further rationalize their operations, leading to further globalization. Likewise, deregulation will continue unabated, as sectors such as health care, transportation, banking, and insurance are being liberalized. Further concentration, and thus increasing competitive pressures, both domestic and international, will result.

As J. Welch, CEO of General Electric, stated, "The 1980s were a walk in the park compared to what we will face in the 1990s" (1988). Increased competitiveness will force firms to search for competitive advantage through restructuring their strategic priorities.

Restructuring

In the future, companies will concentrate on a few selected core activities, leading to significant divestitures in businesses considered outside their main domain. When top management is unwilling or unable to face such a task, the company will fall victim to corporate raiders. In post-integration Europe, we envision major restructuring similar to that which took place in the United States during the 1980s. Firms will be forced to study carefully their productivity and close down inefficient operations. Moreover, fixed expenses will have to be reduced through a flatter, less bureaucratic organization, while a leaner staff at headquarters will also be essential.

Mergers and Acquisitions. In those industries where optimal scale economies have not yet been reached, we will witness a continuation of mergers and acquisitions. In the tire industry, for instance, Sumitomo Tire acquired Dunlop in 1985, which led Continental Gummi, a German manufacturer, to acquire General Tire in 1987. This in turn led Bridgestone, threatened in its U.S. market, to take control of Firestone, the number-two American manufacturer, in 1989. As the U.S. market became increasingly dependent on a few worldwide competitors, few options were left for Europe's Michelin but to take over Uniroyal-

Goodrich, which it did in 1989. As the 1990s attest, further concentration is about to come. The next victim in the tire industry could be practically any company, such as medium-sized competitors Toyo Tire and Pirelli. Unfortunately, European companies cannot shelter themselves and therefore have little choice but to join in the global mergers and acquisitions game.

Deregulation in the financial sector will lead to major concentration, as well—both in the United States and in Europe, as we have witnessed in Denmark recently. The main strategic issue today for banks and other financial institutions in Europe is embodied in the following questions: Is one better off being the acquirer or the acquiree? When should one make a move? There is no doubt that in postintegration Europe, mergers among banks and other financial institutions will dramatically increase, both domestically and across borders.

Airlines represent another regulated industry where increased competition will lead to concentration through mergers and acquisitions. This has already occurred in the United States and would have begun in France had the commission in Brussels accepted the merger of Air France, U.T.A., and Air Inter. Concentration will spread throughout Europe, leading, in our view, to a few international carriers and a spate of small local airlines.

Thus, the single market movement can be seen as the belated reaction of European businesses (and governments) trying to establish a viable competitive posture on a world scale by eliminating excessive fragmentation. This statement is supported by the fact that five years ago only 15 percent of major European mergers took place across borders. In 1990, 55 percent of major mergers involved partners from different countries. Similarly, in 1985 European mergers accounted for 8 percent of all global mergers. In 1990 this percentage has exceeded 40 percent.

Competitive Innovation. The major competitive arena has traditionally been considered to be an "industry" protected by the various incumbent firms through "entry barriers." Deregulation and new technologies, however, have blurred the conventional boundaries of what constitutes a given industry. In the financial services industry, for instance, are the new capitalization products offered by insurance companies and the like any different from conventional banking ones? How should bankers react to reduced deposits as investors put their savings into insurance policies because of fiscal incentives? Strategic competitive innovation aims at breaking down traditional industry boundaries and subsequently changes the rules of the game. This provides huge opportunities for some, but added competition and enormous threats for others, challenging if not seriously threatening existing market leaders.

The insurance industry (which went without any form of internal competition for far too long) might well be threatened by the banking industry on several fronts. At present, banks enjoy a good public image and can leverage their existing distribution channels (a large number of local branches) to eat into the traditional insurance business (car, home, or other policies). At the same time, mass retailers or large department stores are likely to enter the banking and insurance business. Carrefour, the French hypermarket chain, has already done so. The lack of protective legislation is opening up possibilities for newcomers to enter any market they choose. The implications of such free entry will be far-reaching, changing boundaries, competitive profiles, and profit margins radically.

Environmental Uncertainty

Blurred industry boundaries and competitive innovation are encouraging the proliferation of new entrants and thereby increasing uncertainty and unpredictability in the environment. Other factors contributing to increasing uncertainty are outlined below.

Market Efficiency. Because of deregulation and more sophisticated technology, markets are becoming increasingly efficient. The more efficient a market, however, the less predictable it becomes. Thus, interest rates, foreign exchange rates, and commodities prices (such as oil or minerals) cannot be anticipated, as new information is instantaneously discounted and becomes incorporated into the current demand and/or price.

Increasingly Shorter Life Cycles. Rapid technological improvements are now numerous, making the average life cycle of new technologies shorter and shorter. This is true not only of DRAM (dynamic random access memory) chips, but also of telecommunication equipment, robotics, financial services, and so on. Moreover, competitors are trying to outperform each other by speeding up product innovation, thus creating even more uncertainty and contributing to further market unpredictability (Allaire and Firsiroty, 1989).

Political Uncertainty. Important political changes have significantly altered the geostrategic priorities of multinational firms. Among such changes are the following: continuation of the processes of liberalization in the Soviet Union; economic and perhaps political unification of Western Europe; reunification of East and West Germany; democratization of Eastern Europe and possible economic association with the European Community; rapid economic development of Asian countries (Indonesia, Malaysia, India); and liberalization and democratization in South America (Brazil, Argentina, Chile).

Irreversible Commitments and Strategic Obsolescence

As the technological and competitive environment changed during the 1980s, many firms became victims of their single-minded pursuit of a specific competitive advantage. General Motors lost close to 10 percent of its market share as the trend toward smaller cars caught on. Caterpillar lost over $1 billion as the dollar appreciated and Komatsu invaded its traditional markets. In France, Renault lost over 20 billion Fr, and in Italy, Zanussi failed to succeed in the consumer electronics industry despite valiant efforts and considerable investment. None of these firms was poorly managed and their executives knew (maybe too well) how to compete. But most of them approached competition in the 1980s as they had done ten years earlier. They implicitly assumed that the environment and the rules of the game had not changed. Accelerated change caught them unaware, making their highly specialized skills (once considered assets) their worst enemies and contributing to their overall inability to adapt (Makridakis and Héau, 1987). In the environment of the 1990s, overspecialization and the blind pursuit of competitive advantage may prove just as fatal.

One way of learning from the past and preparing for the future is by studying successful firms in those industries where uncertainty was predominant during the 1980s. In high-technology industries, for instance, firms like Airbus, Ariane, and Philips spread risk through diversification or strategic partnerships. In the fashion industry, firms like Benetton attempted to reduce risk by becoming increasingly flexible not only in the deployment of their resources but also in their response to the changing tastes and preferences of consumers.

Risk Spreading

Diversification is not a new strategic response to risk reduction. Past experience has shown, however, that, while diversification creates value by reducing risk, it does not lead to superior returns. This means that benefits from reduced risks are usually followed by lower returns, forcing a trade-off between the two. A more successful approach to spreading risk is through strategic alliances and partnerships. They became increasingly fashionable in the late 1980s to the extent that even firms such as IBM (which had refused to share ownership or technology in the past) have begun to pursue them frantically.

We believe that various forms of strategic alliances and joint venturing among European firms such as those between Volvo and Renault, or Rhône-Poulenc and Hoechst, will continue to proliferate. For one, technology has considerably improved the ability of partners to communicate speedily and with more ease, thereby reducing the transaction cost of such ventures. Furthermore, the opening of new markets in Eastern Europe is going to increase the incidence of such partnerships. Deregulation in public services and the standardization and connectability of telecommunications and energy networks will require increased cooperation among national producers within Europe. In a city like Prato, Italy, over ten thousand small enterprises collaborate with each other through various formal or informal agreements.

We envision two main categories of strategic partnerships: those such as Airbus or GEC-Alsthom, where partners pursue scale advantages that none can achieve individually; and those such as Volvo-Renault or Bull-NEC, where the partners share complementary skills. Strategists must understand the limitations and dangers involved in the second type of alliances and partnerships, however, as the strategic motives of the partners often diverge and the agreement dissolves. In this case, partnerships do not provide equal benefits for both parties. For instance, one partner may be interested in a new technology, which, once obtained, makes further cooperation unnecessary. Another partner may be looking for managerial know-how or marketing expertise, which cannot be easily transferred, thus making the pursuit futile. Moreover, strategic partnerships among existing or potential competitors are often problematic, particularly when the purpose is to learn from each other rather than to share joint resources. In such cases, cooperation among firms within the same industry is nothing more than a hidden form of competition (Hamel and Prahalad, 1989).

Multiple Competitive Advantages

As we have maintained throughout this chapter, every firm needs to be competitively superior in order to survive. Yet competitive advantages might disappear as market needs change (as happened when people stopped buying the Ford Model T) or new technology destroys the basis on which such advantages were built (digital technology and the manufacturing of analog watches). A strategy based on a single advantage might also fail if a competitor offers a successful substitute (postal mail versus Federal Express or faxes).

Contrary to popular writers on strategy who have emphasized the dichotomy "low cost" versus "differentiation," we see successful companies in the 1990s as those that do not think in terms of either/or trade-offs. Rather, they move over time from one competitive advantage to the next, building a whole array of competitive strengths in the process (Gilbert and Strebel, 1989). Japanese and Korean companies are good examples of this: they traditionally enter a market at the low end, establishing volume and cost supremacy. They then improve their quality and service and build a powerful image. Finally, they innovate and conquer all segments of the market. European firms must therefore follow similar strategies if they want to avoid the fate of Jaguar, which, with 80 percent of its sales in the United States, could do nothing to the competitive attack of Honda, Nissan, and Toyota, and had to sell to one of the industry leaders, Ford Motor Company.

Competitive advantage is based on a never-ending pursuit of further strengths. By relying on a whole array of competitive advantages, firms in the 1990s will therefore be much less vulnerable to an unexpected shift in the competitive scene. How to move from one competitive strength to the next is partly a function of market opportunities and trends, and partly a result of leveraging a firm's core competences.

Strategic Flexibility

In the face of an unpredictable environment, the ideal strategy would consist in not investing at all—by so doing, a firm would constantly keep all its options open. But noninvestment is impossible, since new technologies must be exploited, changing market demands met, unit costs cut, quality improved, brand image strengthened, and so on, all of which require investment. Thus, firms will have to invest—sometimes heavily—harness the advantages from such investments, and at the same time avoid the risks associated with the uncertain environment. As we see it, this could be achieved by either minimizing commitments or increasing flexibility in order to respond to market or competitive changes.

Minimizing Commitments. Firms will increasingly use subcontracting. Japanese carmakers today are relying for 70 percent of the value of their components on such subcontractors. Markets for components and intermediary items will thus become increasingly specialized and therefore more efficient. European firms will have to limit self-manufacturing or operations to those tasks that are related to their core capabilities. A sophisticated system of brokers and other intermediaries will have to be developed to satisfy the subcontracting needs of European firms.

Firms will reconsider their pursuit of ever-increasing scale economies (Piore and Sable, 1984). New technologies will make smaller plant sizes possible, which will correspond to increasingly differentiated needs. For instance, scrap usage already allows minimills in Northern Italy to be more cost-efficient than large integrated steel mills; optimal scale in car production has also been reduced through flexible manufacturing systems, while economical production batches are being reduced to double digits (see Chapter Five).

Firms will also try to postpone their irreversible commitments to as late as possible during the manufacturing process. Benetton is an illustration of late differentiation of products. Benetton sweaters are knitted using undyed yarn and stored until consumer demand indicates that season's color choice. Customers are constantly monitored, as the sales of forty-five strategically located stores are electronically linked to the company's final dying facilities. Benetton can therefore offer the exact shade demanded by the market and in so doing it has turned its flexibility into a competitive advantage that allows it to increase the number of yearly collections.

Increasing Flexibility. Insofar as a firm can be thought of as a bundle of resources, the 1990s will witness an increasing quest for flexibility in terms of increased modulation of product design (in order to combine scale advantages and customization), increased use of computerized manufacturing systems, new financial instruments, and a broader range of skills in the labor force through education and training.

Another dimension of strategic flexibility may be gained by speeding up the time before goods reach the market. As the demand for new products or services can change unpredictably, the difference between a "threat" and an "opportunity" will lie in the firm's ability to react the moment a change in demand is confirmed. In that respect, small entrepreneurial firms might have a competitive advantage, as they can often adapt more rapidly than their large competitors. Speeding up the time to the market could be improved by: creating multidisciplinary teams, where R&D scientists, production engineers, and marketing people work closely together and are isolated from central bureaucratic control in order to operate as efficiently as possible; letting competing teams work on the same product development (in such cases the spirit of competition and cross-learning offset redundancy and higher costs); introducing a sense of urgency by setting up specific challenges or deadlines that exploit group pride and collective commitment; or fostering entrepreneurship through the relentless pursuit of opportunities.

Corporate Legitimacy

The pursuit of economic growth and the accumulation of wealth have, historically, been the legitimate goals of business enterprises in Western Europe. Yet the very success of businesses as agents of resource allocation and economic progress has also increased their social responsibility. Having successfully obtained deregulation and, in general, less interference from both trade unions and the state, firms today are more directly responsible to public opinion and society itself than was the case years ago. Corporate decisions have major social implications and in this respect they need to be as much concerned with ecological and ethical trends as with profit making. Public opinion can censure firms directly (by not buying their products or services) or indirectly (through public outcry, which eventually reintroduces government controls). Firms will become increasingly accountable to society, a role they have not been used to playing.

The traditional view is that management is ultimately responsible to the stockholders, who have the final claim over the firm. But many writers and lay people have questioned such an established view. On may expect the following types of questions to be increasingly raised:

- Who will govern business firms? Who will be represented in such governing bodies? What should their role be and to whom is management ultimately responsible? In Scandinavian countries as well as in Germany and Holland, workers' representatives are seated on the supervisory boards of companies and some key decisions require their approval. Should customers or other interest groups also be represented on supervisory boards in addition to workers?
- What protects stockholders if the board of directors is inefficient or overly lenient? How can managers be forced to best utilize the assets at their disposal? Do corporate raiders, megamergers, and leveraged buy-outs always have the negative impact attributed to them? Or do they play a useful role by forcing underperforming companies to restructure?

Sensitivity to environmental issues has been on the rise. Many critics have complained about the excessive depletion of resources; others have raised outcries over increasing pollution, acid rain, and global warming. The perceived importance of ecological issues is likely to increase, and strategists must be prepared to deal with these issues.

Another aspect of corporate responsibility is the whole area of ethics. How far can management go in its single-minded pursuit of profit? For proponents of economic liberalism, management's only concern must be to maximize profits. It is then up to society and legislation to tax firms in order to take account of externalities and achieve socially desired goals. Such arguments, however, are not easily accepted by most people, who expect business to be ethical whether or not they are legally bound to do so. Recent scandals have demonstrated how sensitive public opinion has become on such issues as bribery, product safety, and insider trading. Swiss banks always benefited from their policy of secrecy, yet they have abandoned it in the case of Ferdinand Marcos and Manuel Noriega. Similarly, drugs have become such a social evil that international money laundering is no longer tolerated.

Ethics extends to internal rules and behavior. Can employees refuse to do something illegal or work on projects they consider immoral? Should firms be forced to hire minorities or handicapped people? Should sexual harassment (open or covert) lead to dismissal?

Ethical issues are difficult to deal with because they depend upon social groups or given cultures. For instance, bribery, which is forbidden in Northern Europe, is often tolerated in Mediterranean countries. In such a case, what should the policy of a Northern-based company be toward its affiliate branches operating in Southern Europe?

It is our experience that corporate management is poorly prepared to deal with the ethical issues to be confronted. Most executives have never learned how to deal with such issues. This is one reason that ethics is among the most cited new courses in business schools. The time of the robber barons is gone.

Strategy Revisited

Strategists will have to accept that the present is different from the past and adapt the strategies of their companies accordingly. Below we discuss the importance of opportunism and luck, learning, and core competences as essential elements of the new strategic realities.

Opportunism and Luck Instead of Detailed Planning. Analytical strategic planning increasingly will be neither feasible nor useful owing to the unpredictability of key technological and market factors. Successful firms will be opportunists: in fact, there will be little difference between an opportunity and a threat as long as the company can identify a forthcoming change before its competitors. Being an opportunist does not exclude the need for a long-term vision that provides consistency and commitment toward the achievement of specific objectives. European firms such as L'Oréal in France, SAS in Sweden, and Daimler-Benz in Germany all include this kind of vision as an integral part of their corporate strategy, holding the firm together and creating a strong sense of shared values. We believe that opportunism coupled with a long-term vision and the commitment to realizing it will become indispensable.

We might think of strategic management as consistent luck in seizing opportunities. Such luck comes not only from identifying forthcoming opportunities and threats but also from superb execution and minute attention to details. Thus, we can summarize strategic management as: a shared commitment to a long-term collective ambition, an opportunistic attitude in the medium term, and superior execution in day-to-day operations.

Learning. Most of the popular strategic concepts of the past (the experience curve, industry analysis, and competitive assessment) are becoming not only useless but even dangerous, as they provide a false sense of security and encourage firms to specialize when they should be learning and adapting. But learning and adapting can only be achieved through experimentation.

Encouraging experimentation means encouraging dissent and accepting mistakes and failure. In many companies, top management is committed to experimentation as a vehicle for successfully dealing with change and innovation, and so are many younger executives, who are willing to experiment with new approaches. The main obstacle to learning and adaptation comes from the upper middle managers who see their positions threatened by a changing environment that diminishes the value of their expertise and therefore their importance in the organization.

A chief executive in charge of a six-billion-dollar firm told the author that he had reserved twenty-five days in 1990 to teach first-line supervisors "how to disobey their boss." Similarly, Chairman Jan Carlzon of SAS stated, "I want them [his managers] to make mistakes. . . . You give people a framework and within the framework you let people act. . . . The dangerous thing is to not make decisions." While experimenting, however, one learns little from success, as victory always has many parents; learning comes mostly from failure. As one executive put it, "Failure is the tuition for learning the business." Thus, not only must dissent be encouraged, but proper rewards and incentives must be provided for trying and even failing. In too many European firms, risk taking is still threatened by the emphasis given to short-term results and the stigma attached to failure, both of which discourage learning and innovation.

Learning and innovation often require "unlearning" of some of the principles that were considered the cornerstones of yesterday's strategies. For instance, the challenge is not to choose between one strategic imperative or another, but to manage more than one simultaneously. A firm will need to be at the same time both local and global, to be a low-cost producer while its products are of a high quality and differentiated. This, of course, requires the ability to understand multiple viewpoints and to realize that creative and innovative ways can be found to avoid trade-offs and achieve several objectives at once.

Core Competences. So far, we have stressed the importance of guided opportunism and the need for adaptive learning. Learning must also be cumulative, however, allowing firms to develop core competences in critical areas. Core competences correspond to superior capabilities of creative people who must work effectively together as a team. Core competences must be built throughout the organization and cut across traditional business functions and hierarchical levels. In our view, the ability to maintain existing core competences and add new ones in critical areas will become the essence of strategic management.

As products, technologies, and markets are becoming increasingly unpredictable, strategic management will have little choice but to shift its emphasis from a product/market orientation (that is, where do we compete) to building core competences (that is, with which resources from those that we have at our disposal do we fight). To give an example, Philips's strengths do not reside so much in its various businesses (color televisions, compact disc players, semiconductors, computers, lighting) as in the web of its managerial, technological, and marketing competences.

As a matter of fact, a company can minimize its risks by diversifying its portfolio of core competences. Since such competences are based mostly on people, they can easily be redirected when the firm is faced with environmental change. All it takes to adapt to market changes is to redirect the portfolio of core competences (and therefore competitive strengths) to new market demands. For instance, Philips's scientists can use their training and experience with compact disc players to quickly develop and manufacture optical read/write computer floppy disks once it is determined that the demand for such disks exists. Thus, successful strategic flexibility comes from the organizational capability to redirect core competences away from situations where the danger of failure looms high and leverage them toward new opportunities as they emerge. Thus, the ability to unbundle and rebundle core competences will become the basis of corporate renewal and the essence of business strategy.

Conclusion

In conclusion we see four strategic challenges. First, barriers in terms of geography, regulation, scale, and technology are breaking down. This leads to a blurring of the boundaries of what constitutes a certain given industry (or business) and to changes in the rules of competition.

Second, markets are becoming increasingly efficient. As a consequence, it will be difficult, if not impossible, to predict future changes in the vast majority of industries and markets. Furthermore, increased efficiency will lead to lower transaction costs and more efficient communication, which will transform firms into networks of relationships — some strong and continuous (fully owned facilities) and others weak and temporary (strategic partnerships or alliances).

Third, as markets become increasingly efficient and information is equally accessible, there will be similar access to capital, technology, production methods, marketing, and other skills. Such equal access will shift competition from tangibles (money, technology, machines) to intangibles (creativity, innovation).

Fourth, what will make the difference between success and failure will be a firm's ability to unleash and exploit the creative power of its people. With routine-type assignments being increasingly taken over by computers, the tasks of strategists will be to find practical ways of increasing operational efficiency as well as to formulate and implement creative strategic alternatives. Their efforts will have to be centered upon their ability to develop and exploit the core competences existing within their organizations. Nurturing and preserving these core competences will therefore become the most crucial part of a strategist's job.

References

Allaire, Y., and Firsiroty, M. "Coping with Strategic Uncertainty." *Strategic Management Review*, 1989.

Cool, K., and Diericks, I. "Asset Stock Accumulation and Sustainability of Competitive Advantage." *Management Science*, 1989, *35* (12), 1504–1510.

Doz, Y., and Prahalad, C. K. *The Multinational Mission: Balancing Local Demands and Global Vision*. New York: Free Press, 1987.

Dyas, G., and Thanheiser, H. *The Emerging European Enterprise: Strategy and Structure in French and German Industry*. London: Macmillan, 1974.

Gilbert, X., and Strebel, P. "From Innovation to Outpacing Strategies." *Business Quarterly*, 1989, *54* (1), 19–22.

Hamel, G., and Prahalad, C. K. "Do You Really Have a Global Strategy?" *Harvard Business Review*, 1985, *63* (4), 139–148.

Hamel, G., Doz, Y. L., and Prahalad, C. K. "Cooperate with Your Competitors and Win." *Harvard Business Review*, 1989, *67* (1), 133–139.

Haspeslagh, P. "Portfolio Planning: Uses and Limits." *Harvard Business Review*, 1982, *60* (1), 58–73.

Lorange, P., Scott, M., and Ghoshal, S. *Strategic Control*. St. Paul, Minn.: West, 1986.

Makridakis, S., and Héau, D. "The Evolution of Strategic Planning and Management." In W. King and D. I. Cleland (eds.),

Strategic Planning and Management Handbook. New York: Van Nostrand Reinhold, 1987.

Piore, M., and Sable, C. *The Second Industrial Divide*. New York: Basic Books, 1984.

Porter, M. "How Competitive Forces Shape Strategy." *Harvard Business Review*, 1979, 57 (2), 137–145.

Porter, M. *Competitive Advantage*. New York: Free Press, 1985.

Welch, J. F., Jr. *Managing for the Nineties*. General Electric Annual Meeting of Share Owners, Apr. 27, 1988.

PART THREE

Critical Cultural and Managerial Issues

CHAPTER 8

Managing Across Cultures and National Borders

André Laurent

For the social scientist, the move toward a single market Europe represents a superb example of socially constructed reality. It is fascinating to observe that the strategic significance of integration is currently recognized possibly even more in Japan and the United States than within Europe itself. A new social reality is created in the minds of individuals and groups when their attention is actively invested in considering the implications of such a reality on their own affairs. When the newly conceived situation challenges some of the existing equilibrium between global partners, the emerging social reality takes even more preeminence through a variety of mechanisms ranging from implicit denial to active rejection, proactive involvement, idealization, or even withdrawal. From this point of view, integration has already occurred, as Japanese and Americans have begun talking about a "Fortress Europe" whose aim is to put them in a position of competitive disadvantage. Single market Europe also provides a vivid illustration of the symbolic nature of social realities and an interesting example of symbolic management and visionary leadership.

1992 as Past History

The European Community started more than thirty years ago with the progressive signing of several treaties that established the embryonic economic foundations and ties that were necessary to allow for the achievement of more ambitious goals. As concrete economic policies were being endlessly and painfully debated in Brussels by technocrats, Eurocrats, and politicians, utopian thinkers and visionary leaders were running the real show by inventing important symbols: a European flag, European passports, the ECU, and even 1992 itself, the date set for "official" integration. Progressively, a utopian dream was slowly but solidly transformed into a tangible reality of a powerful nature through the use of artifacts. For years airline passengers have been reminded on every trip that there are two types of Europeans, those who need to complete a disembarkation card, and those nationals of one of the EC countries, who do not.

The ground had been carefully cultivated and the mental images readied for more important changes to come once 1992 passed into 1993—distant enough to be looked upon as a dream, a utopian idea, a faraway cloud, or, at best, a long-term prospect. Nineteen ninety-two did not seem a real danger to anyone although it was promising many sweeping changes for almost all countries, and the great majority of organizations and people at the same time. Airbus Industries, Eureka, Esprit, and a host of cross-boundary business partnerships were giving substance to the project. The Anglo-French agreement to finally dig the Chunnel convinced even the most pessimistic observer that if the French and the British can put their act together, "going to bed under the sea," then there can be no limit to European cooperation. Europessimism was progressively being replaced by the imperatives of survival. With its magic number of 325 million consumers, the target integration date of 1992 was providing Europe with a glimmer of hope. Perhaps the twelve member countries could, after all, become a single "giant," ready to face the Japanese and North American competition head on. United they could stand, divided they would surely fall: a united Europe could not be pushed around as each individual country could.

All these powerful images have created a new reality celebrated by numerous conferences, workshops, and books like this one. Even Margaret Thatcher agrees that there is no way to turn back. Unlike the challenges and dangers it will bring, however, integration is a past event.

Integration as a Tough Challenge for the Future

A British and an Italian firm have brought their interests together in the creation of an ambitious joint venture. The headquarters of the new company could not be better located than in Brussels. The top management team is composed of three Italian executives and three British executives, all transferred from their mother companies to work for the joint venture. The joint venture has been running for three years. Today, whenever the top management team gets together for a meeting, the challenge of working side by side remains as big as or bigger than it ever was. The most significant element of this challenge has little to do with the economic aspects of the business, which are going very well, but more to do with subtle issues of a cultural or cross-cultural nature. For instance, British and Italian managers simply do not share a similar conception of what an effective meeting is all about. The British executives assume that only one person should talk at a time. The Italians hold quite the reverse assumption. For them a meeting would be a complete waste of time and a useless ceremony under such norms of smooth and controlled interaction. For the Italians, critical problems that are likely to generate heated, interpersonal conflict should be dealt with, up front, during such meetings. The British know how to seem untouched in the middle of such storms and behave as if no conflict exists. Their preference is for handling such issues outside the official meeting room, bringing up only those issues that are for official approval during meetings. Moreover, the British prefer to do one thing at a time, such as first participating in a meeting, then taking phone calls, then reading the newspapers. Italians can merge these different activities in the same setting without any apparent problem.

Needless to say, these seemingly unimportant differences in approach raise significant challenges for the parties involved. Yet these differences represent only the tip of the iceberg. Italian and British managers differ on much deeper grounds. For instance, as they hold different ideas as to how and to what extent they should trust each other, the long-term success of the joint venture becomes a delicate issue. Their differing perceptions of trust exert significant influence on the long-term decisions they take, which, consequently, determines the extent of success of their joint venture.

Although we indicated earlier that integration is already a phenomenon of the past, we can argue equally well that it has not happened as yet. In fact it may take a very long time to see a Europe free of cultural and/or national barriers. Precisely in those settings where one could expect that progress in cross-national understanding and cooperation would be the most advanced, we actually find huge problems for effective collaboration among different European nationals in spite of a binding common interest. The challenge of integration is, therefore, to develop an ability to build on Europe's rich cultural diversity. Unfortunately, if not properly handled, such diversity can turn out to be as much a danger as a source of opportunities. This chapter aims to provide guidelines for better exploitation of European cultural diversities and for improving the achievement of organizational objectives.

Universality in Management Theory and Practice: Illusions and Reality

Managers involved in international business seem to welcome, appreciate, and enjoy the wealth of cultural differences that they encounter around the world. They cherish the cultural diversity of styles in music, literature, dance, and cuisine. Curiously enough, the same people — who applaud diversity in these artistic spheres of life—often dream of uniformity and universality when it comes to management. One may wonder why.

An important reason could be that most managers do not recognize their own peculiar ways of managing and organizing as being influenced, if not determined, by their own cultural habits. Individualism, for example, is of such sacred value in Western cultures that most of us tend to reject the notion that our own thinking, values, and behaviors may reflect collective cultural patterns. Yet we may be prompt to notice such patterns in others. Our own cultural traits are so much part of ourselves that we cannot see them anymore. As we become blind to our own cultural norms, we often assume others to be similar to ourselves and we become greatly surprised (and most often upset) when others, coming from different cultures, do not behave or act as we do.

Awareness of one's own culture is as much a prerequisite to understanding other cultures as self-awareness may be to understanding other individuals. Cultural myopia—the inability to see one's cultural makeup—leads to implicit ethnocentrism in management, a tendency to hold one's way as being the best and to expect it from, or to impose it on, others. Basically other cultures are implicitly perceived as unfortunate deviations from the norm—the norm being obviously that of our own culture.

This parochial view of the world may also occasionally breed a naive attraction for what is perceived as exoticism in management practices, leading to two polarized postures: other cultures are seen either as "primitive" in their own interesting ways, but having nothing to offer to the art of managing; or as universally better, particularly if they happen to have enjoyed economic success in the last few decades.

In the latter case, managers fall into the trap of being fascinated by "exotic" management dances without realizing that they are artistic expressions of other societies, and thereby reducing them to the level of mere tricks or gimmicks. This fascination leads to an inability to learn from alternative ways of managing and to a failure in transferring management know-how across cultures. Effective transfer of management know-how and successful cross-cultural interaction require a coupling of our ability to learn about ourselves and others with an educated awareness of cultural differences in management approaches, together with a positive evaluation of such differences.

The lack of appreciation of the cultural nature of management conceptions, style, and practices carries huge opportunity costs for multinational business. Most executives continue to view cultural differences as a handicap to global operations, while only a handful of multinational corporations have started to realize that cultural diversity may represent one of their most valuable assets.

Learning from cultural differences and exploiting them to gain advantages require a deep recognition of the fact that there is no universality in the art of managing, nor is there a single universal theory of organization. If the idea is accepted that the world of management is a puzzle of different truths— even within Europe—and that every society has some unique insight into effective management, then each culture has a contribution to offer every other society for the overall improvement of management theories and practices.

This new perspective may then allow us to build on our own cultural strengths, watch for our cultural weaknesses, learn from those of other societies, and properly adjust new learnings to the unique characteristics of specific cultural environments, including our own.

Management approaches are like maps that we can use to identify the territory of organizations. Different social territories obviously require different maps. In spite of this evidence, some managers are still hoping that their own cultural map will work anywhere, thus confusing the map with the territory; or they believe that there exists some privileged cultural map— Japanese or American—that would work universally better whatever the territory. This is obviously false and suggests that Europeans must devise their own maps adapted to exploit their rich cultural diversities.

Cultural Differences in Management Assumptions: A Research Inquiry

In recent years, leadership has frequently been defined as a symbolic activity. Effective leaders influence organizations and nations by shaping visions that inspire people by imparting meanings to situations or events. As the attribution of meaning is that part of reality that is most culturally defined, a proper understanding of leadership—particularly in international settings—cannot be restricted solely to the consideration of behavior. The different styles exhibited by British and Italian managers should only be seen as cultural artifacts.

Behind the superficiality of behavior such as that described in the British-Italian joint venture above lie deep meanings that need to be decoded. The challenge for international management is that the same behavior may mean very different things in two different cultures, and that, conversely, two very different behaviors may also mean exactly the same thing.

Should managers know more than their subordinates about their work? Should they have at hand precise answers to most of their subordinates' questions? Could it be that managers are more motivated by obtaining power than by achieving objectives? Is arbitration by a single person desirable when problems get more complicated? Should multiple reporting relationships be avoided at all costs? How about the bypassing of hierarchical lines—should that be encouraged? What does it take to be successful in your own company? If you could do only five things as a manager, what would they be? Such questions and many others were included in a systematic survey of upper-middle managers attending INSEAD's executive programs as an attempt to better understand their assumptions about the management of organizations (Laurent, 1983).

As expected, a wealth of individual differences emerged in response to such questions. When the patterns of differences were analyzed, variations in responses could be partly explained by characteristics such as age, education, job, professional experience, hierarchical level, and company type. Less expected, however—particularly in an institution that places great emphasis on an international ethos—was the fact that the nationality of the respondents emerged as an explanation for far more variations in the data than any of the respondents' other characteristics. Overall, the nationality of the manager had three times more influence on his managerial assumptions than any other factor. As a result of this finding, a series of further research studies were conducted in order to assess and identify the impact of national cultures on executives' conceptions of management and their explicit or implicit assumptions about business organizations.

An example of a typical pattern of national differences appeared in reaction to the following statement: "It is important for a manager to have at hand precise answers to most of the questions that his subordinates may raise about their work." Respondents had to express their view on a five-point scale from "strongly agree" to "strongly disagree." Although only a minority (13 percent) of both Swedish and American managers agreed with the above statement, a majority (59 percent) of both French and Italian managers did (see Figure 8-1). Whereas most French and Italian managers expect the boss to have the answers, Americans and Swedes apparently do not.

In this particular instance, Swedish and American versus French and Italian patterns of responses seem to reflect fairly different underlying models of an organization.

Implicit Models of Organization:
U.S. Instrumental View Versus French Social View

American managers hold more of an instrumental and functional view of organizations than do most of their European counterparts (Inzerilli and Laurent, 1983). An organization is perceived primarily as a set of tasks to be achieved through a problem-solving hierarchy where positions are defined in terms of tasks and functions. Authority is functionally based, too. Under this model, a manager's superior knowledge about the subordinates' work is not necessarily needed and could even be detrimental to the proper functioning of a decentralized problem-solving hierarchy.

French managers hold more of a social and personal view. They conceive the organization more as a collectivity of people to be managed through a formal hierarchy where positions are clearly defined in terms of level of authority and status. Moreover, authority is attached more to individuals than it is to their

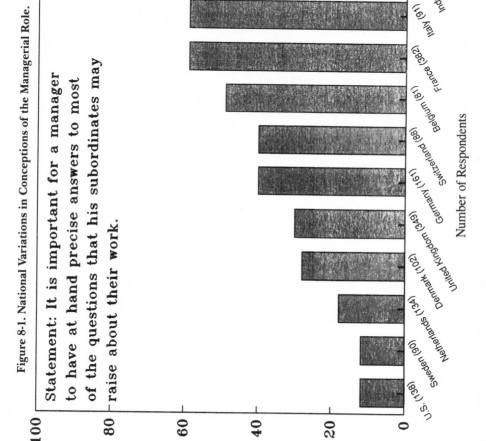

Figure 8-1. National Variations in Conceptions of the Managerial Role.

Statement: It is important for a manager to have at hand precise answers to most of the questions that his subordinates may raise about their work.

Source: Laurent, 1986.

offices or functions. As a result, the authority of managers is enhanced by their superior knowledge. If they are found to know less than their subordinates about the task, their authority base could suffer. Thus, managers must pretend to know more than their subordinates even if they do not.

One can imagine the astonishment of the newly appointed American manager in a French company who gets so many unexpected questions from his French subordinates, or the frustration of the French subordinates whenever the American boss replies, "I don't know" or "Ask Bill—he might know." Alternatively, one can well imagine the disappointment of the new French manager in the U.S. company who keeps waiting for his American subordinates to ask questions but whose telephone never rings or whose schedule is half empty.

If the parties involved lack an understanding of cultural differences in managerial assumptions and values, a mutual loss of esteem and credibility may deteriorate such relationships and make international operations a nightmare with disastrous results.

When managers are exposed to the description of such different models as the U.S.-instrumental and the French-social models of organization, they tend to nod as these descriptions elicit concrete behavioral examples from their international experience. One such example is the way in which business cards differ in typically American and French organizations. Consistent with the instrumental model, American business cards will tend to provide titles that may give a fair indication of the activity of the cardholder. This is not the case for the French manager's title, which may express a great deal about his or her power and status within the firm but very little about his or her actual area of responsibility.

As another instance, a French manager working for a U.S.-based company reported his experience when meeting his new American boss for the first time. The French manager's expectations about the meeting were that he would receive a few directions from his new boss. He actually found himself very unprepared when his American boss initiated the meeting by asking, "What are your objectives?" For once the French manager did not have any precise answer at hand because in his previous experience he had always been told what his objectives ought to be.

Such differences in expectations for the same situation may create significant misunderstandings between individuals that are culturally bound. Obviously, a better awareness and education about the cultural components of such situations may help to manage them better.

Interestingly, when the survey responses were analyzed across ten national samples of managers from Western countries, a North-South continuum appeared quite clearly from the results. While most managers from Northern Europe (Sweden, Netherlands, Denmark) and the United States felt it unimportant and even undesirable for managers to have at hand precise answers to their subordinates' questions, most managers from Southern Europe (France and Italy) felt the other way around. Managers from Great Britain, Germany, Switzerland, and Belgium fell into the middle of that continuum.

United States Versus Japan: Autonomy of the Individual Versus Welfare of the Family

The extension of the survey to samples of managers from Eastern cultures helped to avoid the trap of too simple an interpretation, when it was found that a strong majority of the Indonesians (67 percent) and the Japanese managers (77 percent) saw it as very important for a manager to have at hand precise answers.

When this management assumption came under discussion with the top-management group of a U.S.-based multinational—a group comprised of seventeen Americans, one German, one British, and one Japanese—it appeared that among the twenty participants of the seminar, only one had agreed with this questionnaire item. Thus the curiosity arose as to "who could possibly have agreed with such a stupid statement," as one of the American managers put it. His argument—supported by his fellow countrymen—was that not only is it unimportant for managers to have at hand precise answers to most of their subordinates' questions, but it is simply impossible. He then went on to say that were it possible, it would be highly undesirable, as this would discourage subordinates' initiative and create unhealthy dependency.

The argument was solid. Who could be the "villain" within the group who would endorse a different position? Not by accident, the said "villain" was from across the Pacific. The Japanese manager stated first that he had no hesitation whatever in strongly agreeing with the statement. Then he simply said, "If one of my employees comes to me with a question about his personal and family welfare, it is so obvious that as a manager I should have at hand precise answers."

This argument puzzled the rest of the group even more. One participant made the point that the statement under discussion did not have anything to do with employees' welfare but was only addressing the issue of work.

It then became evident that the Western reading of the situation was essentially technical, instrumental, and task-related (a subordinate comes to the boss with a question about the work), whereas the Japanese reading of the same situation was a different one. The Japanese concept of work is more diffuse and more embedded in the social texture of an organization extended to include the families of its employees. In such a concept, a different meaning was immediately inferred that was welfare-related.

An alternative interpretation of the very strong Japanese support for the omniscient manager may help to better assess the complexity of the interaction between cultural values and management beliefs. In the Japanese culture, the respect for hierarchy and the importance of saving face are such that most subordinates would avoid embarrassing the boss with a question that he could not possibly answer. Indeed, under those circumstances, bosses can easily be expected to have the answer to all questions they are being asked. The above brief consideration of alternative cultural models may help executives to better realize that none of them is intrinsically better or more effective than the rest, and this certainly applies to Europe in its effort to improve cross-border interactions.

German, British, and French Management Styles:
The European Mosaic

For Western executives, cultural differences in manage-ment may be easier to perceive when looking East; however, important differences abound within Europe that have been largely ignored or overlooked. Such differences have clearly emerged from the comparative research conducted at INSEAD (Laurent, 1986).

By and large, and more than others, German managers emphasize professional competence and coordination skills as key ingredients of organizational success. British managers favor interpersonal skills and the ability to influence others and negotiate effectively. French managers view the ability to orga-nize and control as particularly critical. Italian managers, more than the rest, know how to maintain flexibility in bureaucratic structures. Who is more right is obviously the wrong question. They are all right, or wrong, in their own way. Doses of coordina-tion, influence, control, and flexibility are important ingre-dients for any organization to succeed. For historical reasons, people and organizations in different cultures have developed more sensitivity to certain requirements as they are particularly relevant for succeeding in the place where their organization functions.

German managers, more than others, believe that creativ-ity is essential for career success. In their mind, the successful manager is the one who has the right individual characteristics. Their outlook is rational: they view the organization as a coordi-nated network of individuals who make appropriate decisions based on their professional competence and knowledge.

British managers entertain a more interpersonal and sub-jective view of the organizational world. According to them, the ability to create the right image and to get noticed for what they do is essential for career success. They view the organization as a network of relationships among individuals who get things done by influencing each other through communicating and negotiating.

French managers look at the organization as an authority

network where the power to organize and control the actors stems from their positioning in the hierarchy. They view the organization as a pyramid of differentiated levels of power to be acquired or dealt with. French managers perceive the ability to manage power relationships effectively and to "work the system" as particularly critical to their success.

Cross-Cultural Management:
A Learning and Development Opportunity

Without any doubt, managers feel more comfortable with models that translate their own cultural values and they are likely to be more effective within the boundaries of such models. For the same reason, however, these very same models may look strange and may be less effective when working outside their own cultural boundaries. International and expatriate managers have some difficulty in realizing that the "foreigners" are themselves, not the local people.

In a survey of a large U.S.-based chemical corporation that puts great emphasis on a worldwide multiple assessment system for the identification of high-potential managers, the following results were quite illustrative. The question was "What does it take to be successful in your company?" Managers were given a list of sixty different criteria from which they were asked to pick the most important ones. The top criterion in the American affiliate was "ambition and drive." The top one for the French affiliate was "being labeled as having high potential." The pragmatic American achiever looks instrumentally at how he or she should behave in order to be successful. The political French player looks socially at which group he or she should belong to in order to ensure career success. Both of them are right in their own cultural assessment of the same human resource management system. This result was later replicated in a survey of another U.S.-based corporation, in spite of the absence of a similarly formalized system of managing human resources (Derr and Laurent, 1989).

As management and organizational practices reflect cultural values and assumptions, one should obviously expect that a particular approach that may work very effectively at home could turn into a disaster abroad—just like expatriate managers—or at least could require limited or substantial adjustment. Management by objectives may look very different when staged by Italian actors. In an Indonesian organization, the inclusion of negative feedback in performance appraisal interviews may be systematically delegated to a go-between so as to avoid the unhealthy pollution of harmonious hierarchical relationships. Quality control circles may operate in a squared fashion in a French unionized plant. A matrix-type organization that involves multiple reporting relationships may have a hard time in Latin cultures, where subordination also means loyalty to the person of the superior and where multiple reporting will be experienced as a case of divided loyalty (Laurent, 1981).

Obviously some approaches are likely to work better in some places than in others. The "instrumental" approach may fit the U.S. environment better and the "social" approach may fit the French environment better. The simple recognition that management methods are contingent upon cultures is not enough, however. The conclusion that managers and organizations should in some way adapt some of their practices to different cultural environments represents only a first step for international business.

More important, a systematic probing into alternative cultural models of organization can bring the most precious awareness and understanding that no model is universally better or worse. Managers of international firms must understand that every one of these models—including their own—contains some unique and specific insight into the art of managing as well as some significant drawbacks, some distinctive competences, and some appalling handicaps. When blindly pushed to their extreme forms, all of these models may become pathological.

By confronting their own assumptions with those of other cultural groups, members of every society can learn a great deal about themselves and develop higher organizational effectiveness by building on their own identified strengths and minimizing the impact of their discovered limitations. This process may have occurred in Japan a few decades ago. It has clearly happened in recent years in the United States, where managers are developing more insight into the pros and cons of American management by looking at it in the Japanese mirror. It is not clear whether a critical assessment of management practices has happened in Europe yet.

National Versus Multinational Cultures

Multinational organizations, by the very nature of their identity and operations, are constantly facing both the challenges and the opportunities of national differences in management styles and they may, from that angle, offer interesting insight to the builders of a single market Europe. In spite of this reality, the amount of explicit attention given to this dimension has been limited in the past.

Cultural differences are more often talked about in corridors and at cocktail parties than seriously discussed in international work settings. If ignored or not explicitly recognized as legitimate for discussion, they can hardly be used to develop synergy between and across headquarters and subsidiaries—a high opportunity cost. As the differences are there, they are then likely to reappear insidiously in negative ways—a direct cost.

A frequently held assumption in the world of international business is that national differences in management conceptions can be washed away, or at least significantly reduced, by the unifying corporate culture of large multinational corporations or by the unifying effects of, say, integration. Research evidence shows otherwise. Although some degree of behavioral adjustment takes place at a superficial level, deep-seated cultural assumptions and values with regard to power, authority, structure, hierarchy, control, or coordination do not seem to change as a result of the corporate mold. Systematic studies of matched national groups of managers working in the affiliated companies of large U.S. multinational firms in Europe indicate that managers clearly keep their national identities when it comes to deep-seated managerial assumptions. Across fifty-six different items of inquiry into such assumptions, the overall research results gave no indication of convergence between national groups within multinational firms. If anything, the opposite tendency was observed. That is, the Germans were becoming slightly more German, the Dutch more Dutch, and so on—in spite of, or because of, their living and working together in the same corporation (Laurent, 1983).

Within the European affiliates of another U.S. multinational, for instance, only 25 percent of the German managers agreed that "the main reason for having a hierarchical structure is so that everyone knows who has authority over whom," while 50 percent of the Italian managers did. On the other hand, only 25 percent of the Italians believed that "in order to have efficient work relationships, it is often necessary to bypass the hierarchical line," while 70 percent of the British agreed to this statement. Conversely, when only 30 percent of the British managers recognized that "most managers seem to be more motivated by obtaining power than by achieving objectives," 87 percent of the Italians did. Finally, while only 15 percent of the Swedes thought it was important to have ready answers to most of their subordinates' questions, 65 percent of the Italians answered in agreement with this statement (see Figure 8-2).

Similar findings were obtained from groups of M.B.A. students coming from most European countries after a year of studies in the multicultural environment of the INSEAD campus. British and French students (the two largest national groups) showed consistently unchanged national attitudes as well as differences in their assumptions and values in spite of their intensive cross-cultural interaction during their year of studies at INSEAD. So did Eurocrats of various nationalities after eighteen years of collaborative international work based in the same Brussels office facilities. Attitudes and values acquired in a certain culture do not seem to be significantly altered by cross-cultural interaction with individuals of different nationalities.

The current emphasis on corporate culture may lead multinational organizations to strive even more than in the past for worldwide consistency in their management practices as a way of strengthening their corporate culture. While the need for

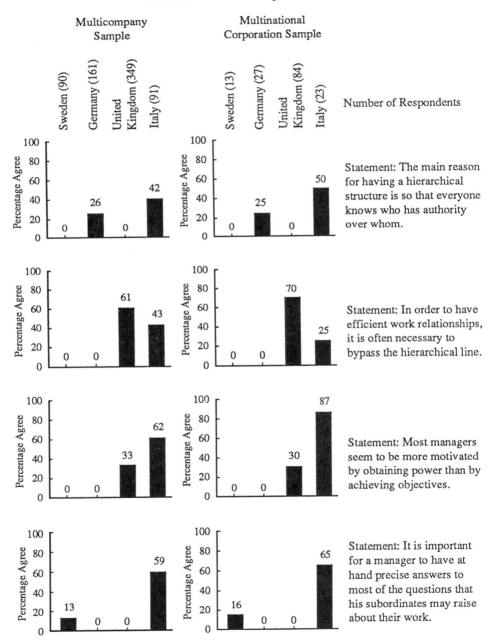

Figure 8-2. National Differences in Management Conceptions Across and Within Corporations.

consistency is there, worldwide effectiveness also calls for corporate values of a higher order that recognize, respect, appreciate, and build on the cultural diversity in management conceptions and styles around the world. For their own success and evolution, corporate cultures of multinational corporations may have a lot to learn from the unique insight of different societies.

Single Market Europe: Merging Identity and Diversity

Managers in postintegration Europe face a unique situation and challenges that, in essence, are not so different from those challenges already faced by multinational corporations around the world. How can we deal effectively with cultural diversity in a meaningful, operative, and successful framework? How can we develop synergies between different cultural traditions? How can we learn from such differences? How can we build on differences in order to develop a sum that is bigger than the mere addition of its constituting parts? How can we foster cooperation across national boundaries?

As compared with multinational corporations, single market Europe has four major advantages. First, its social fabric is a lot richer than any industrial or commercial corporation now in existence. It is populated by individuals and groups from highly diverse backgrounds and with long traditions of intellectual accomplishment. Second, European visions and ambitions extend far beyond narrow industrial and commercial interests. Third, it is less likely that European cooperation will be hampered by pathologies usually associated with the existence of central power. Finally, Europeans will realize that they must succeed with their integration objectives or become second-class citizens, unable to compete in the emerging high-tech and value-added industries.

On this ground, the illusory melting pot where all national traits and characteristics mix to become a single bland culture does not appear too much of a danger. The United States of Europe might not happen tomorrow, but there is no way to reverse into the position of twelve individual nations each fighting its own battle for survival.

The richness and potential of Europe lie in its diverse cultures, an asset that should be preserved. The major challenge—which is immense—will be our capacity to merge the value of identity with the value of diversity. In this we still have a long way to go.

References

Derr, C. B., and Laurent, A. "The Internal and External Career: A Theoretical and Cross-Cultural Perspective." In M. B. Arthur, D. T. Hall, and B. S. Lawrence (eds.), *Handbook of Career Theory.* Cambridge, England: University Press, 1989.

Inzerilli, G., and Laurent, A. "Managerial Views of Organization Structure in France and the USA." *International Studies of Management and Organization,* 1983, *13* (1/2), 97–118.

Laurent, A. "Matrix Organizations and Latin Cultures: A Note on the Use of Comparative Data in Management Education." *International Studies of Management and Organization,* 1981, *10* (4), 101–114.

Laurent, A. "The Cultural Diversity of Western Conceptions of Management." *International Studies of Management and Organization,* 1983, *13* (1/2), 75–96.

Laurent, A. "The Cross-Cultural Puzzle of International Human Resource Management." *Human Resource Management,* 1986, *25* (1), 91–102.

CHAPTER 9

Identifying Management Talent for a Pan-European Environment

Manfred Kets de Vries, Christine Mead

The globalization of business is proceeding at a fast pace, accelerated by such events as the movement toward a single market Europe, the opening up of Eastern Europe, and the Canada-U.S. trade agreements. As companies seek to internationalize their operations they run into a number of blockages, many of which have their roots in cultural differences. It is not surprising that the more international a company becomes, the more it must be aware of prevailing cultural differences. These differences appear at every level of the organization, from attitudes toward work, authority, responsibility, and decision making to such mundane matters as office layout, perks, and even ways of greeting colleagues. Obviously, it can be argued that executives who can better understand cultural issues and more successfully adapt to various cultural settings will be of greater value to international organizations than executives who are less able to do so. This raises the question of whether a new kind of manager, a "global" one, will be needed: a person who will play the role of catalyst while at the same time being sensitive to cultural diversity and functioning effectively in different cultural environments.

What should executives be prepared for when operating in different cultures? What aspects of culture make their task more difficult? And what can be done to facilitate adaptation to other cultures?

One of the earliest and probably most famous definitions of culture was proposed by the anthropologist Edward Tylor in the opening lines of his book *Primitive Culture* (1871). He suggested that "culture... is that complex whole which includes knowledge, belief, art, morals, law, custom, and any other capabilities and habits acquired by man as a member of society." Although Tylor was specific in listing the various behavioral forms culture can take, culture has remained very elusive as a concept. Many facets of culture are imperceptible and intangible, escaping even those individuals who are part of that culture itself. This is largely because many aspects of culture are taken for granted, an attitude that becomes understandable if we define culture as the totality of learned ways of believing and behaving. As such, it becomes an ever-present force that will unconsciously affect any situation of leadership and any organization.

In studying international business, we touch upon the problematic area of the interaction of corporate and national cultures and, inevitably, the issue of cultural adaptiveness. A number of companies have experimented along these lines, one of which is Schlumberger, a successful international organization in the oilfield-service industry operating in ninety-two countries. What first stands out in studying Schlumberger is the importance placed on research and technology. This aspect is an integral part of the corporate culture, and candidates hoping to work for the quiet giant are expected to subscribe to its strong orientation toward superior research and technology. But although the company is very technology-driven, there are other values that have to be taken into consideration. The late Jean Riboud, former CEO of Schlumberger, touched upon them when describing the company's "spirit" during his reign (Auletta, 1984):

1. We are an exceptional crucible of many nations, of many cultures, of many visions.
2. We are a totally decentralized organization.
3. We are a service company, at the service of our customers, having a faster response than anybody else.
4. We believe in the profit process as a challenge, as a game, as a sport.
5. We believe in a certain arrogance; the certainty that we are going to win because we are the best — arrogance only tolerable because it is coupled with a great sense of intellectual humility, the fear of being wrong, the fear of not working hard enough.

Although Jean Riboud did not explicitly talk about what makes a manager capable of leading Schlumberger to success, certain subtle mechanisms are at work in the firm to make its operations so successful. It is not only that Schlumberger people fit a certain profile, but there are other factors that also play an important role. Headquarters at Schlumberger is very small. Although strategic direction is largely determined at headquarters, the company has a strong regional structure. A great deal of operational autonomy is given to the people in the field. Space is created for each national culture. Career progression does not depend on time spent at the head office. At each location the management team is made up of five or six different nationalities so that there is not one dominant national culture, but rather a group of executives from different cultures who share a set of common values. And this corporate culture becomes a major lever in assuring coordination among the many different units of the organization and making its people, coming from more than one hundred different cultures, work so effectively together.

It is the objective of this chapter to take a closer look at the question of what factors foster European leadership and to what extent culture plays a role in successfully managing across borders.

It goes beyond our present scope to review the various qualities needed for effective leadership and the question has been dealt with elsewhere (see Bass, 1981, 1985; Bennis and Nanus, 1985; Devannah and Tichy, 1986; Kets de Vries and Miller, 1984). Of course, that does not mean that these qualities should not be taken into consideration when drawing conclusions about effective European executives. In this chapter, however, four questions will be addressed: How do pan-European companies (like international ones) choose people to be their future leaders, and how can they be sure that those chosen will be culturally adaptable and operate competently across borders? What kind of management development and training enhances understanding and adaptability? In what organizational context does pan-European leadership thrive? And, finally, what can be said about career path management and repatriation? Answering such questions may be useful in assisting European corporations to plan for their future executives.

The Selection Process

Personal Characteristics. For many companies, technical competence is the primary criterion for choosing someone to work abroad (Harvey, 1985; Zeira and Banai, 1984; Mendenhall and Oddou, 1985, 1986; Tung, 1981, 1982). If an executive has done a good job in the home country, the assumption is that he or she will automatically be able to repeat his or her successful performance in another country. This happens particularly in cases where people are being sent to other countries to set up a new plant, establish an oil rig, or expand an existing factory. In such cases, there is little or no preparation for cultural variations, since the work is perceived as mainly technical. After all, the assumption is being made that an executive is someone who has the confidence to sort out any problems deviating from normal working procedures. If something goes wrong, he or she should be able to "fix" it.

Researchers interested in the question of what personal qualities are likely to be found in someone who is culturally adaptable propose such characteristics as open-mindedness, self-confidence, ability to deal with ambiguity, ability to relate to people, and curiosity. In looking at people with top manage-

ment potential, Shell, a European company operating internationally, narrowed twenty-eight qualities down to the four most
important abilities: helicopter view, imagination, power of analysis, and sense of reality (Muller, 1970). Gunnar Hedlund (1986),
taking the Jesuit order as an ideal model for an international
organization, is more specific. He suggests six essential qualities
for effective functioning in an international context: (1) an
aptitude for searching and for combining things in new ways;
(2) the ability to communicate ideas and turn them into action;
(3) the command of several languages, as well as knowledge of
and sympathy for several cultures, in order to provide "a stereo
quality to perception and interpretation"; (4) honesty and integrity; (5) the willingness to take risks and experiment; and (6) faith
in the organization and its activities.

In addition, there are a number of values or assumptions
that indicate cultural understanding and adaptability. The most
obvious, perhaps, is the belief that every culture has developed
its own way of managing and that one country's way is not
necessarily superior. Another is the feeling that home is where
one is located rather than where one "comes from." Moreover,
the perception of where one's roots are — whether in oneself, the
family, or the country of birth — can also affect how easily people
move from culture to culture.

Selection Criteria. Expanding on the personal qualities
needed for cultural adaptability, researchers have developed
lists of criteria considered to be important for the selection of
international managers. Among them, Michael Harvey (1985)
has suggested thirty characteristics, including mental flexibility,
social and cross-cultural exposure, and physical and emotional
stamina, which can be weighted according to country and type
of job. The search for appropriate selection criteria requires
careful attention. For instance, a number of surveys have concluded that the greater the consideration paid during the selection process to adaptability and ability to communicate, the
higher the success rate in the assignment (Tung, 1981). We can
wonder if these selection criteria are applicable to executives on
international assignments only, as factors such as interpersonal

skills will improve effectiveness in noninternational assignments, too.

Zeira and Banai (1984) argue that the criteria for selection must be augmented to include the host country's nationals.
At present, the people who are to work with the expatriate
executive and the cultural aspects of the country itself are rarely
taken into consideration at the selection stage. Zeira and Banai
suggest that the better the fit between the stakeholders' expectations and the expatriate manager's ability to deal with them, the
fewer the chances for potential conflict.

Early Socialization. With respect to the availability of managers with a potential for successfully working in international
environments, there are a growing number of individuals
rooted in more than one culture. It can be argued that children
of parents of different nationalities who have changed countries
several times when young probably have a different sense of
belonging in any given culture than those who grew up in the
same place. If the former grow up bilingual, their ways of
looking at things are likely to be much wider than those of
children who grow up speaking one language only. Growing up
with different languages provides the kind of stereo-quality
perception mentioned above, which enhances adaptability
when managing outside one's own home country.

Of course, it is not necessary to live in more than one
country to develop these abilities. A child living in Switzerland
speaking Italian at home, learning French and English at school,
and observing the different life-styles of people from different
cultural backgrounds (French, German, Italian) has already had
an intensive course in cultural adaptability. Or a child who
grows up in Brussels, where the local high school has children
with ten different mother tongues, has direct experience of a
multicultural world. Thus, children growing up in Europe with
all its different television and radio channels and easy crossing
of borders are being exposed to many different cultures from
early on. Given the impact of early socialization on adult development, we can argue that early exposure to different languages
or nationalities is a determining factor in how successful the

individual will be in dealing with cultural adaptability later in life. Moreover, it can also be stated that the chances of finding successful managers capable of operating throughout Europe will be greater than when young people were exposed to only a single national culture.

It is rare for a company to have access to the ideal candidate at the time an international position becomes available. The question of management training for better cultural understanding therefore becomes critical. Of course, for management training to be effective, it helps if the individual has acquired in early life a certain amount of responsiveness to cultural differences.

The Question of Management Development

Surprisingly little is done in the form of management development to prepare people for international assignments. The exception is the kind of training that can be found at the very few truly international business schools such as INSEAD or Institute for Management Development (IMD). As far as company training is concerned, according to Tung (1981, 1982) only 32 percent of U.S. multinational enterprises provide training for international assignments. The European and Japanese companies surveyed along the same lines reported higher rates of training: 69 percent among the European companies and 57 percent among the Japanese.

In Europe, great progress is being made to provide an M.B.A. education of which the objective is to enhance the students' ability to become effective managers of firms operating in many countries. INSEAD, for instance, has a strictly enforced policy: no nationality can dominate the student body (this is achieved by limiting the percentage of students of any single nationality to less than 25 percent of the total number). Given the number of nationalities present, being at INSEAD is like working at the United Nations. There are some students who speak five or six languages, while the majority speak more than two. Thus, cultural learning is not taught in a formal course; it is practiced throughout a student's stay at INSEAD. Socialization therefore becomes the most effective way of learning about the French, the English, the Germans, the Italians, and other European and non-European cultures. INSEAD provides a practical and effective approach to training executives for pan-European companies. Moreover, it is no longer unique, as other business schools are imitating its approach throughout Europe. In our view, this is the best way of training M.B.A.s to become the executives of the pan-European firms of tomorrow.

Experiential Training. Research is being conducted to determine the best approach to training aimed at enhancing cultural understanding. In a study on training parent country professionals in host country organizations, Zeira and Pazy (1983) suggest a combintion of both on-the-job and off-the-job training. Using Lewin's theory of effective change processes, they argue that learning, in essence a process of change, requires a period of "unfreezing": the loosening of habitual structures of thought and behavior and the opening up of new ones. Off-the-job training, particularly in another country, provides an occasion for the loosening up. At the end of the learning process, the opposite procedure is required—the refreezing or building of the new structure and linking it to behavior already in place, which best occurs in on-the-job training. What this suggests in terms of how international executives are groomed is that the training be done during the assignment in another country. Whatever training is undertaken prior to departure is most effective when it is geared toward making an individual ready to be open to change and to learn in the new environment he or she is going to face. Of course, certain cultures (given the person's background) are going to be more compatible than others.

Many European companies follow a policy of stationing their executives abroad for several years followed by a number of years at headquarters (for example, Philips, Shell, Rhône-Poulenc). This pattern serves the purpose of creating a more consistent corporate culture than would be the case if managers remained in only one country or region. Moreover, it provides headquarters with international experience, as management staff is composed of both people from most European (and non-European) nationalities and executives who have worked in several European countries and are well aware of their differences, cultures, and specific problems or needs.

Zeira and Pazy (1983) report on an approach to managerial development that they found successful in providing a high level of professional development as well as cross-cultural exposure. Their study involved groups of engineers in the aircraft industry being sent by their parent organization to work for twelve to eighteen months for a host country organization. Zeira and Pazy believe training is more effective when it takes place within another culture, as well as within a practical work environment. The host organization also benefits from the cross-cultural experience, as its executives learn to work with people from other cultures.

The Reaction of the Family. A critical element in the success of expatriate executives is the experience of their spouses and children (Bartolomé and Evans, 1980). The most frequent reason for an executive failing to complete an assignment in another country is the negative reaction of his or her spouse. An executive from Rhône-Poulenc who had worked both inside and outside of Europe estimated that spouses were responsible for 80 percent of early returns. Research done by Harvey (1985), Tung (1981), and Mendenhall, Dunbar, and Oddou (1987) supports the contention that family circumstances account for expatriate executives' failure in the majority of cases. Despite this, only half the companies interview spouses during the selection procedure, and a far smaller percentage of spouses are included in the training programs to help them better cope with the new environment they will be forced to live in. Although we realize that the role of the spouse is only one factor among many others, ignoring it can be a costly omission for both the company and the family.

A supportive spouse and family, particularly in a situation where the executive may find himself or herself cut off from other relationships, may be the essential factor in enabling an effective cultural adjustment to be made. Furthermore, marrying into another culture provides a person with intensive long-term experiential training in cultural understanding and adaptability.

Forms of International Organizations

Management training leads to the question of what kind of international organization best promotes cultural understanding and adaptability. Obviously, it would be foolish to suggest that there is an ideal type of structure suitable for all organizations and cultures. There are numerous kinds of multinational enterprises, Europe-wide joint ventures, parent-subsidiary relationships across national borders, and other forms of alliances. However, there are certain structural factors that can help organizations best exploit their international operations.

Referring to human resource management, André Laurent (1986) suggests that certain factors can promote a truly international organization. These factors include:

- Explicit recognition by headquarters that its own ways of managing human resources reflect assumptions and values based on its own culture
- Understanding that these ways are neither universally better nor worse than others — they are different, and they are likely to exhibit strengths and weaknesses when applied abroad
- Explicit recognition by headquarters that its foreign subsidiaries may have other, preferred ways of managing people that are intrinsically neither better nor worse, but could possibly be more effective locally
- A willingness on the part of headquarters to acknowledge cultural differences and take active steps to make them open to discussion and therefore usable
- The building of a genuine belief by all parties that more creative and effective ways of managing people can be developed as a result of cross-cultural learning

Types of Multinationals. With the purpose of designing a conducive corporate environment, Howard Perlmutter (1969) goes beyond basic beliefs and attitudes and introduces a number of conceptualizations useful for understanding the multinational corporation. Using ideal-type configurations, he proposes four orientations for multinationals: ethnocentric, polycentric, regiocentric, and geocentric. In the case of an ethnocentric orientation, key positions are occupied by the home country nationals, and foreign subsidiaries take on a subservient position. In polycentric companies, the foreign subsidiaries are run by local nationals and have a great deal of autonomy as long as there are results. The head office takes a more hands-off position.

The regiocentric orientation differs in that the action takes place in various regional headquarters. The connotation of country is replaced by that of geographical region—Scandinavia, Iberia, Central Europe, and so on. Management development in regiocentric firms is for regional positions. Finally, in the case of the geocentric orientation, a complex network of interdependencies exists between headquarters and subsidiaries. Organizational identity is determined both by local and more universal factors. Management development of persons showing high potential for leadership positions can take place anywhere in the world (Heenan and Perlmutter, 1979).

Gunnar Hedlund (1986) further develops the conceptual evolution from ethnocentrism via polycentrism to geocentrism. He mentions that one of the signs of geocentricity is the use of third-country nationals in top management positions. Other aspects are reliance on global profitability goals and increased rotation of personnel. A recentralization of authority at headquarters often accompanies the shift to geocentrism to allow for more centralized strategy making in response to global competition. Interdependence is reciprocal: products, know-how, money, and people flow in complex patterns, not from the core to the periphery, as in the ethnocentric firm.

Hedlund's view that "for commercial and practical purposes, the nations do not exist, and the relevant business arena becomes something like a big unified home market" (1986, p. 18) is not realistic for a number of reasons. He comments on the strong differences that continue to exist between nations and regions, and notes that the primary loyalty of many employees is still to their home country, which counterbalances the proclaimed increased homogenization of demand. He argues that cultural differences in management style mean that uniform, worldwide control systems are unlikely to be viable. Moreover, the size of the organization may prohibit effective and speedy global coordination. Most firms do not have enough executives able to create and carry out ambitious global strategies. The specialization of subsidiaries can become so extreme that it would be detrimental to assign narrow strategic roles to them and wasteful not to use the creativity and entrepreneurship of people at all nodes of the network. Finally, centrally guided global product strategies looking at the world as one market may lead to neglecting opportunities to exploit existing differences between nations.

These limits to the "mononational" version of geocentrism illustrate the danger of seeing geocentricity as the scaling up of the national corporation and the reestablishing of a central strategic management at the apex of one big, global hierarchy. A special case of geocentrism, distinguished by its heterarchical nature, is what Hedlund believes to be the way in which international companies should move. Concerning Europe, however, the limits to pan-European management and organizations are less restrictive, as there are some commonly shared goals. Cultural differences are less pronounced than those between industrialized and Third World countries.

The "New" Multinational Corporation (MNC). Fundamental to the idea of the MNC, whether European or global, is the interface between structure and strategy. Thus MNCs may first identify their structural properties and then look for strategic options to best exploit those properties. As a consequence of being made up of multiple organizational structures, it is not always possible for MNCs to promote people by giving them jobs higher up in the career path. Movement among companies located in different countries becomes more common, especially as it builds up in the "nervous system" of the complex organizational structure of the MNCs. The core of the firm consists of people with long careers and much experience in the enterprise. These managers constitute the communication network of the corporation, and as such they are a strategic resource. More all-encompassing and long-term contracts can be expected, as can participation in the ownership of the company. There is probably duality in the career system: a limited core of lifetime employees and a much larger number of people with briefer, loosely coupled associations with the firm. Such duality provides both stability and flexibility. In its ideal form, the core provides the memory, information, and experience, while the others help to prevent rigidity by establishing channels for new ideas.

A great deal of rotation of personnel and international travel are necessary in order for the internalization of norms to take place. In the new MNC, organizational culture becomes the new "control" device. Every organizational participant is aware of what the organization stands for—its missions, core values, and prohibitions. Recruitment to the core should include, as basic criteria, willingness to travel and to change functions within the company. Moreover, different reward and punishment systems are necessary to deal with negative feedback and to encourage the long-term investment of individuals in the company.

The implication of this new type of MNC is that organizations are becoming "flatter," with less emphasis on hierarchy, greater lateral communication, complex networking, and loosely coupled, interdependent organizational units with innovative human resource management practices. Finally, a broad range of people in the firm develop the capacity for strategic thinking and action. This can be done by decentralization of strategy formulation, active use of task forces to identify key problems and major strategic issues, and open communication of strategies and plans, as well as early opportunities for developing the management capabilities of the core group. Strategic thinking must be a permanent activity at all levels of the organization. A good illustration of this direction is Proctor & Gamble's Eurobrand teams, where different national subsidiaries are given the role of developing product-market strategies for the region based on the work of a cooperative team of managers across those subsidiaries (Bartlett and Ghoshal, 1986, 1987a, 1987b). Other organizations are establishing "centers of excellence" concerned with such functions as R&D and manufacturing.

Most international organizations use some form of periodic assignment to headquarters for international managers, as well as rotation of assignments within regions. In addition, most organizations seem to have three levels of managers: those who operate only within their own country, those who are assignable within their region, and those who are assignable globally. The more ethnocentric a company is, however, the more this last category tends to be made up of parent country nationals.

Some European companies are global in nature, others tend to concentrate on the EC markets, and still others are regional, national, or even local. As integration approaches, more of the regional, national, and local firms will have to change their strategic thinking to include all of Europe as their potential market. These are the companies that most need to develop managers who can operate within other European cultures as effectively as in their own. MNCs have already gained extensive experience in operating within many cultures. Thus they have an advantage over newcomers, who must adapt to the new cultural dimensions of management without making too many mistakes or any fatal ones.

The Issue of Career Path Management

In addition to the concerns of taking up a new assignment in another country, there are also the problems of reentry. Many executives dread a stay at headquarters after an assignment at a subsidiary. For example, an executive from Rhône-Poulenc felt that his job on return was boring and routine and that his decision-making power had been taken away from him. But he also realized that reentry was essential to keep his personal network at headquarters alive. The question of what kind of job someone returns to is problematic for the manager involved and for the organization. From the individual's perspective, he or she has probably grown used to a good deal of freedom not to be found in the more bureaucratic set-up at the head office. The life-style may not be as glamorous, the fringe benefits not as interesting, and the tax burden quite different. The returning manager may still be at the same level as colleagues who did not venture forth and thus feel that his or her initiative in spending several years abroad has not been duly rewarded. Moreover, he or she may find there are few possibilities to use what was learned abroad and also that headquarters staff is apparently uninterested in the way things really are out in the field.

The basic results of a number of investigations are not very conclusive (Mendenhall, Dunbar, and Oddou, 1987). There does not seem to be a clear relationship between expatriation and career advancement. In most cases, an international assignment is initially seen as a step up a career ladder. On return, however, expatriate executives may or may not find that they have been assigned a higher position in the company. For example, if the communications within the company are poor and they have remained isolated from a number of strategic decisions, they may have lost whatever position and influence they had in the company prior to their international assignments.

Similarly, unless expatriate executives have made sure that headquarters knows of their successes while they were abroad, their work may go unrecognized and they may lose opportunities for promotion. Given advances in international communications, extreme degrees of isolation probably exist only in theory. However, the *feeling* of isolation is a very real one for executives returning to headquarters after a gap of some years. With increasing executive mobility, they may no longer know the top level of management personally. The environment at headquarters will probably not be the same. They as individuals have been changed by their experiences in another culture (Adler, 1986). The "fit" may not be quite as good as before they left for the assignment abroad.

Facilitating Return. Suggestions for improving the reintegration of returning executives include a succession plan developed with the manager prior to departure, which would include length of stay, projected responsibilities while abroad, systematic management reviews, and subsequent job position on repatriation. Another mechanism is to set up a corporate human resource center whose director reports directly to the CEO. Such a center becomes an indication of the importance top management places on assignments abroad. Its purpose would be to inform executives abroad about corporate policies, strategies, and actions, as well as to let the CEO know about the performance and potential of executives abroad.

The firm could also organize a support network involving communication through travel and company newsletters. Six months prior to return, internal job searches could be initiated on behalf of the returning executive. Some companies (for example, Japanese firms) have also institutionalized a mentoring relationship, which becomes a source of additional support while executives are abroad or when they first return to headquarters.

The training and development needs of returning executives should not be ignored. Some firms rotate the location where training takes place so that local executives, who may never have worked at headquarters, get a chance to develop personal contacts with international and headquarters executives.

Part of the difficulty with managing career path in international assignments is the barrier between host country executives and parent country executives. In many cases, top management positions are always held by parent country people, and career advancement above a certain level is blocked for the host country executives. Moreover, the ability to speak the language of the parent country often seems to be one of the key hurdles. Opening top executive ranks to nationals other than those of the parent country is frequently the last step to be taken, perhaps because there is still too large a cultural gap between nationals of different countries (Zeira and Pazy, 1983). They may believe, perhaps only unconsciously, that executives from their own countries are the only ones capable of holding the top jobs in the corporation. If the practice of reserving top executive positions for one nationality is given up, it is usually done by assigning managers to a third country, neither their own nor the parent country.

Conclusion

In this chapter, we have described the various factors that contribute to making executives successful in international careers (see summary Figure 9-1). Most of these factors apply not only to managers of Europe-wide firms but also to those of global firms. As shown in Figure 9-2, we conclude that there are three spheres of influence for the development of executives capable of successfully operating in varying cultural settings. The strongest influences on both leadership qualities and the ability to adapt culturally stem from early personality characteristics. Leadership and adaptability can be further enhanced by early responsibilities, international work, and educational experiences. Finally, the organizational structure and the depth and extent of the prevailing corporate culture provide a framework for cultivating and encouraging further development of the leadership qualities necessary to manage successfully across various countries or cultures. To summarize:

- Cultural understanding and adaptability will be key factors for effective functioning in different foreign environments.
- Cultural understanding and adaptability are strongly influenced by the degree of cultural diversity within the family and the cultural exposure of the individual executives.
- The existence of leadership qualities is highly dependent upon upbringing and early career challenges.
- Developing successful international management qualities necessitates challenging foreign assignments from the early career stages onward.
- A favorable organizational environment — that is, the existence of a corporate culture conducive to foreign assignments and the inclusion of certain human resource management practices (career path management, mentoring, reentry management) — usually enhances the successful

Figure 9-1. Factors Contributing to the Development of the Global Leader.

PERSONALITY DEVELOPMENT		PROFFESIONAL DEVELOPMENT		ORGANIZATIONAL DEVELOPMENT
ADAPTABILITY FACTORS		TRAINING AND EDUCATION:		ORGANIZATIONAL STRUCTURE
* Cultural diversity in family * Early international experience * Bilingualism * multiple roots	P E R S	* Analytical skills * Professional skills * Study in other cultures * Interpersonal skills * Languages	O R G A	* Geocentric/ regiocentric * Use of 3rd country nationals * Flat/lateral relationships * Multicultural
LEADERSHIP FACTORS	O N A L I T Y	MANAGEMENT DEVELOPMENT	N I Z A T I O	INTERNATIONAL HUMAN RESOURCE MANAGEMENT
* Self-confidence * Responsibility * Curiosity * Imagination * Communication skills * "Core values" * Career goals and expectations	S C R E E N	* Early responsibility * Variety of tasks * Early international experience	N A L S C R E E N	* Career path responsibility * Re-entry management * Selection criteria * Communication * Mentoring * Culture complexity factor
		PERSONAL DEVELOPMENT		
		* Supportive spouse * Adaptable spouse * "Moveable" children * Variety of interests		

Figure 9-2. Model for Analyzing the Spheres of Influence on the Making of a Global Leader.

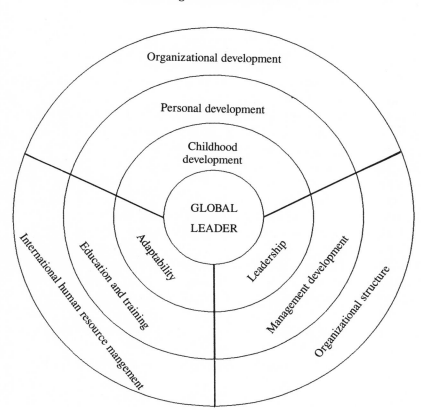

development of executives capable of operating in cultures different from their own.

- An organization that is multicultural, both because it is different in each country and because in each location (particularly headquarters) there are executives of different nationalities and from different cultures, provides a conducive learning environment for global executives.
- The ability of spouse and children to accept living in a different culture while being supportive of the manager is essential for the success of international executives, who will

be unable to last (to say nothing of being effective) if their family is unhappy outside their own country.

References

Adler, N. *International Dimensions of Organizational Behavior*. Boston: Kent, 1986.

Auletta, K. *The Art of Corporate Success*. New York: Putnam, 1984.

Bartlett, C., and Ghoshal, S. "Tap Your Subsidiaries for Global Reach." *Harvard Business Review*, 1986, *64* (6), 87–94.

Bartlett, C., and Ghoshal, S. "Managing Across Borders: New Strategic Requirements." *Sloan Management Review*, 1987a, *28* (4), 7–17.

Bartlett, C., and Ghoshal, S. "Managing Across Borders: New Organizational Responses." *Sloan Management Review*, 1987b, *29* (1), 43–53.

Bartolomé, F., and Evans, P. *Must Success Cost So Much?* New York: Grant McIntyre, 1980.

Bass, B. *Stogdill's Handbook of Leadership*. New York: Free Press, 1981.

Bass, B. *Leadership and Performance Beyond Expectations*. New York: Free Press, 1985.

Bennis, W., and Nanus, B. *Leaders*. New York: Harper & Row, 1985.

Devannah, M., and Tichy, N. *The Transformational Leader*. New York: Wiley, 1986.

Harvey, M. "The Executive Family: An Overlooked Variable in International Assignments." *Columbia Journal of World Business*, 1985, *20* (1), 84–92.

Hedlund, G. "The Hypermodern MNC—A Heterarchy?" *Human Resources Management*, 1986, *25* (1), 9–35.

Heenan, D. A., and Perlmutter, H. V. *Multinational Organizational Development*. Reading, Mass.: Addison-Wesley, 1979.

Kets de Vries, M.F.R., and Miller, D. *The Neurotic Organization: Diagnosing and Changing Counterproductive Styles of Management*. San Francisco: Jossey-Bass, 1984.

Laurent, A. "The Cross-Cultural Puzzle of International Human

Resource Management." *Human Resource Management*, 1986, *25* (1), 91–102.

Mendenhall, M., Dunbar, E., and Oddou, G. "Expatriate Selection and Training and Career Pathing: A Review and Critique." *Human Resources Management*, 1987, *26* (3), 331–345.

Mendenhall, M., and Oddou, G. "The Dimensions of Expatriate Acculturation: A Review." *Academy of Management Review*, 1985, *10* (1), 39–47.

Mendenhall, M., and Oddou, G. "Acculturation Profiles of Expatriate Managers: Implications for Cross-Cultural Training Programs." *Columbia Journal of World Business*, 1986, *21* (4), 73–79.

Muller, H. *The Search for the Qualities Essential to Advancement in a Large Industrial Group*. The Hague: Shell Publication, 1970.

Perlmutter, H. "The Tortuous Evolution of the Multinational Corporation." *California Journal of World Business*, 1969, *4*, 9–18.

Tung, R. "Selection and Training of Personnel for Overseas Assignment." *Columbia Journal of World Business*, Spring 1981, pp. 68–78.

Tung, R. "Selection and Training Procedures for U.S., European, Japanese Multinationals." *California Management Review*, 1982, *25* (1), 57–71.

Tylor, E. *Primitive Culture*. New York: Putnam, 1871.

Zeira, Y., and Banai, M. "Present and Desired Methods of Selecting Expatriate Managers for International Assignments." *Personnel Review*, 1984, *13* (3), 29–35.

Zeira, Y., and Pazy, A. "Training Parent Country Professionals in Host Country Organizations." *Academy of Management Review*, 1983, *8* (2), 262–272.

CHAPTER 10

Understanding the European Consumer

Myths and Realities

Pierre Valette-Florence

The greatest strength of the entity called Europe lies in its ability to create a single European identity, yet Europe's greatest attraction rests in its diversity. As a single Europe looms closer, marketing managers must attempt to gain a better understanding of the European consumer. Can they assume that the European consumer possesses characteristics that transcend national boundaries and so formulate global marketing strategies? Or should they recognize that consumers are different in a way that depends upon their specific country of origin, and thus develop marketing strategies specifically geared toward the various EC nations and cultures? We believe that the biggest challenge facing marketing managers operating across Europe lies in their capacity to conceive and implement appropriate strategies and in their ability to accept and use to their advantage the subtle differences that exist from one country or culture to another.

The purpose of this chapter is to evaluate consumers in Europe—their commonalities and differences—and, where

possible, to identify the origin of such differences. The first part
of the chapter explores the question of whether a single European culture exists at present. In the second part we investigate
the methods currently available to study consumers and present
the conclusions of major studies that have been carried out on
the European consumer. The third part examines the marketing
implications of the information we have gleaned about European consumers and discusses some of the consequences for
marketing strategies. Finally, the concluding section summarizes the chapter and formulates a number of suggestions for
marketing executives.

European Culture or European Cultures?

Culture is a collective characteristic derived from common norms, values, and behavior, where the norms are prescriptions governing life in a society, values are expressed as ideals to
strive for (for example, democracy, justice, liberty, or equality),
and behavior is the most visible manifestation of culture (as
such, culture includes all means of communication, from language and clothing to buying habits and actual tastes). Given the
above description of culture, can we talk about a single European culture, or is it more accurate to talk about various European cultures?

The countries that consitute the EC share a range of
characteristics, suggesting the existence of a common identity.
This is most clearly perceptible in terms of institutions (democracy, justice, education, and so forth), which, although not identical, are nonetheless extremely similar. In addition, consumers
in Europe are used to comparable, although not identical, ways
of life: most shop in supermarkets, practically all watch television (in fact, preferring television news programs to the written
press), and so on.

Similarly, when faced with major events such as marriage,
childbirth, and death, the majority of Europeans share a set of
values that clearly differentiate them from other cultures. The
typical way in which people from European countries express
their emotions is different from that of, say, the Eastern societies.

In Eastern countries death is viewed as an everyday, common-place affair, whereas in Europe it is generally followed by anger, frustration, and extreme sadness all combined together. Orien-tal cultures place a great deal of importance on the harmony of the *group*, whereas Westerners value *individuality*. As Jean Stoezel (1983) remarks, sociological processes stay the same from one country to another within the EC. However, their development is established at different levels, which are specific to each of the countries.

In addition to starting from a similar base of life-style, religion, and so on, the people of the countries of the EC are faced with technological developments in the areas of informa-tion (such as satellite television) and purchasing (such as on-line networks using videotext terminals — called minitels in France) that will further contribute toward the standardization of the profile of the European consumer.

As far as behavior patterns are concerned, a number of authors (for example, Dubois, 1987) have emphasized the uni-versal nature of certain sociological phenomena, such as the generation gap or the way in which sex roles are changing. This leads to cultural subgroups that adopt similar behavior patterns across the European continent. In this context, teenagers exhibit common consumer behavior that can lead to Europe-wide stan-dardization of certain types of products, like records or jeans. In the same way, the ever-growing and generalized entry of women into the work force throughout Europe has led to food in the form of prepared dishes (frozen, precooked, vacuum-packed) becoming a widespread and permanent part of all supermarkets (or even smaller stores) from one end of Europe to another.

As can be seen by the standards of permissiveness shown in Table 10-1, even in abstract ideals there exist commonalities, showing that the opinions given throughout the countries of the EC are remarkably similar. Such similarity is, in itself, a guaran-tee of at least a common morality if not a common moral code.

Despite these numerous commonalities, a careful study also shows some remarkable differences among the various European countries. Climatic conditions, similarities in lan-guage, and ultimately religion have forged differences in life-

Table 10-1. Rate of Acceptability of Twenty-Two Types of Questionable Behavior.

	Europe	Belgium	Denmark	Spain	France	Great Britain	Holland	Ireland	Italy	West Germany
Murder in self-defense	535	510	539	624	579	533	527	460	554	444
Divorce	497	386	689	470	531	496	477	320	499	500
Abortion	407	350	640	283	489	401	435	170	429	388
Euthanasia	403	354	606	311	471	436	543	212	304	427
Homosexuality	326	304	517	282	316	342	564	272	252	351
Prostitution	293	286	412	250	302	296	468	213	207	345
Adultery	285	256	263	257	400	252	264	181	276	263
Lie benefiting the liar	285	337	200	321	332	272	333	255	195	315
Theft by retention	285	302	198	390	298	242	265	239	276	278
Underage sexual relationships	273	318	146	242	378	177	470	142	273	263
Suicide	265	217	338	221	348	273	325	183	183	281
Tax evasion	264	330	239	280	322	269	314	335	185	251
Fare-dodging	214	211	161	241	247	205	241	249	166	221
Failure to report an accident	208	165	142	216	244	233	208	196	195	178
Rebellion against the police	203	203	159	214	251	173	224	168	181	207
Social security fraud	202	209	129	232	325	267	145	183	142	194
Corruption	191	227	117	156	249	161	201	150	195	188
Receiving stolen goods	175	174	121	213	209	186	157	154	145	153
Constraint on freedom to work	170	164	166	168	174	169	179	157	166	171
Drug taking (marijuana)	166	152	187	208	176	173	205	162	144	139
Political assassination	153	164	133	151	181	175	158	144	126	137
Temporary car theft	135	136	109	172	148	123	132	117	135	121
Average rate of acceptability	270	261	282	268	317	262	311	212	238	264

Source: Stoezel, 1983, p. 41.

Note: The larger the figure, the greater the level of acceptability.

Figure 10-1. Cultural Groups in Western Europe.

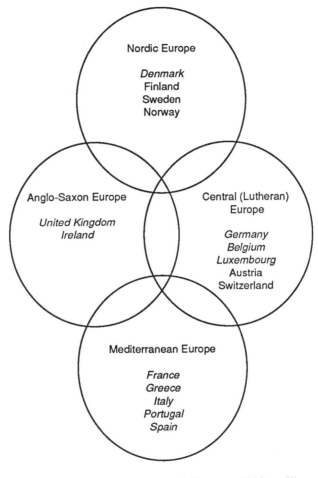

Nordic Europe

Denmark
Finland
Sweden
Norway

Anglo-Saxon Europe

United Kingdom
Ireland

Central (Lutheran) Europe

Germany
Belgium
Luxembourg
Austria
Switzerland

Mediterranean Europe

France
Greece
Italy
Portugal
Spain

Source: Adapted from Usunier and Sissman, 1986, p. 85.

Note: Italicized countries are members of the EC.

styles, of which the Nordic and Latin are probably at opposite ends (see Figure 10-1). However, cultural differences also exist within single countries. No one would argue that individuals as different as Sicilian farmers and Milanese office workers share the same life-style or consumer habits.

Jean Stoezel (1983) clearly shows in his European survey that socio-demographic factors (place of residence, educational background, family structure, and religious beliefs and practices) determine cultural values and influence life-styles. In some countries these socio-demographic factors are influential in determining certain cultural subgroups that share an identity closer to that of a subgroup in a neighboring country than to that of another group within the given country itself. For example, German factory workers may have more in common (and share more similar buying habits) with factory workers in Italy than they do with doctors or school teachers within Germany (even in the same town). Other crucial factors that determine culture might create groups of consumers that differ because of language, for example, rather than nationality (the Flemish-speaking Belgians may be more like the Dutch than their own countrymen, the French-speaking Belgians), or because of occupation (a Greek fisherman may have more in common with a Spanish fisherman than with an Athenian banker).

Marketing managers require an operational way of investigating the behavior of European consumers. They must, therefore, be provided with analytical tools that can be used to better understand European consumers and their similarities and differences.

Methods for Investigating the European Consumer

The investigation into the European consumer distinguishes between global approaches centered around identification of social and cultural values, which can be termed "macro," and more specific approaches directly related to product use, which can be termed "micro."

The choice between macro and micro approaches should be guided by the product being marketed. If the target audience is clear-cut, pan-European approaches (macro) can be employed. Music is a typical product that transcends frontiers. Thus, a general survey of the extent of receptivity of the main target group purchasing records (the younger generation) to a different medium will, doubtless, be enough to set up an appro-

Figure 10-2. Consumer Evaluation Approaches.

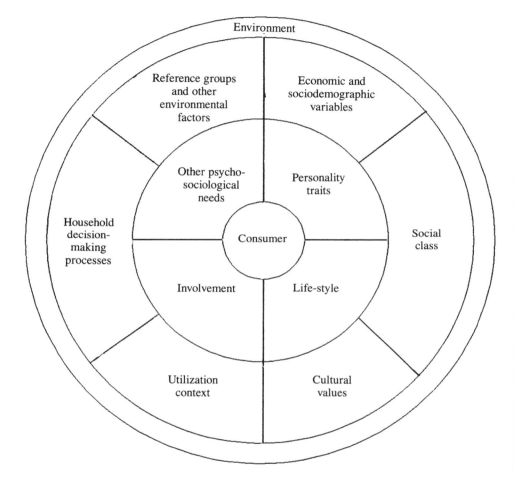

priate advertising campaign. On the other hand, the marketing of furniture would require a far more detailed analysis of individual tastes and the "art of living," which is different in each European country. In such a case a micro approach is required, as the target audience does not possess universal characteristics that are similar throughout the various EC countries.

Figure 10-2 sets out the different approaches that provide

the means for evaluating the European consumer. Such approaches differentiate between environmental (macro) factors and individual (micro) factors. The environmental factors include: cultural values, social class, reference groups, economic and socio-demographic factors, utilization contexts, and the decision-making process within the family.

Since the time of Stoezel's European report it is now possible to make use of some biannual studies of European consumers, their cultural values, and their aspirations, which are known as the Eurobarometers (1984). Although of an undeniable interest in sociological terms, these studies are perhaps too general to be used directly by marketing practitioners, who require more concrete information about consumers if such information is to be used for product positioning and advertising purposes.

Several studies of the sociocultural factors are available. The best known are those of Rokeach (1973) and Kahle (1983). Such studies provide useful explanations of domestic activity for the United States (Beatty and others, 1985) and France (Valette-Florence and Jolibert, 1990) and the differences between them. An additional study, by Munson and McQuarrie (1988), is geared more toward the individual consumer. These studies can provide valuable information to marketing managers although such information might at times be too general, as is often the case with macro approaches.

The individual (micro) factors are related to: life-style, personality traits, facets of involvement, and needs of a psychosociological nature.

Personality Traits. Among the numerous approaches to personality, two principal ones (psychoanalytic and behavioristic) have emerged. The psychoanalytic approach attempts to bring out the deep motivation of individuals through in-depth interviews, while the behavioristic one equates personality with a set of factors that manifest themselves as human behavior and can be revealed by the use of specific lists. These two approaches can be extremely useful in helping us better understand purchasing motivation (Plummer, 1985). Although it seems inadvisable to use such methods to the exclusion of all others, they can be valuable tools in conjunction with other approaches. For instance, it would be interesting to know whether on a Europe-wide level the segments identified in, say, a French study remain the same. Moreover, it would be extremely valuable to know if the weighting methods used by French women would be equally applied by all women across Europe or if they would change according to the nationality of the women considered.

Life-Styles. Lately, life-style studies have become very fashionable. Such studies initially originated in the United States, but have also become widespread in Europe. From a marketing point of view, the life-style of an individual can be measured according to three different levels related to personal value system, attitudes, activities, and consumption patterns (Valette-Florence, 1986). Values are well rooted in the consumer and are easy to measure. Thus, they constitute one of the most promising directions for consumer research. It is our belief that the use of value-system studies will increase across Europe and will thus allow us to improve our comprehension of the European consumer. Another way of investigating life-styles relates to AIO (activities, interests, and opinions) surveys. Such surveys seek to better understand the attitudes and behavior of individuals in relation to one or more products. Their purpose is to help marketing executives develop insights for more successful segmentation. Their value is greatest when they are carried out at regular intervals. The only AIO study undertaken on a Europe-wide scale is the one made in 1980 on behalf of the EC Commission (*European Consumers*, 1980). We expect studies of this type covering the whole of Europe to become a regular tool for better understanding the activities, interests, and opinions of European consumers.

An alternative approach to AIO consists of identifying consumption patterns based on the actual purchases of goods and services made by consumers. To the best of our knowledge, no such study is conducted on a European scale, although in France the Research Center for the Study of Observations on

Life Conditions (CREDOC) carries out such a study, as do institutes in other European countries. We expect that as companies begin the process of formulating pan-European marketing strategies such studies will increasingly be conducted on a Europe-wide scale.

On a practical level, and leaving aside cost considerations, marketing managers need to better understand specific consumption patterns so as to position new products more successfully. Moreover, it would be highly beneficial to uncover possible complementarities and become aware of changes in consumer tastes and buying habits on a year-by-year basis. As catalog sales and videotext purchasing (by minitel in France, for example) become widespread in Europe, the scope and interest of such Europe-wide studies will naturally become of increasing importance. Recent studies on the purchases of cosmetic products have shown a clear association between socio-demographic profiles and purposes on the one hand, and such profiles and the type of communication media used on the other.

Facets of Individual Involvement. The nature and intensity of the involvement of an individual consumer with a given product are best understood through the following five facets presented by Laurent and Kapferer (1985): (1) personal interest in a category of products and its meaning and importance for the consumer; (2) the hedonic value of the product (its capacity to provide pleasure) and its emotional meaning for the consumer; (3) the symbolic nature attributed by the consumer to the product itself, its purchase, and its consumption; (4) the perceived importance of the negative consequences of a bad choice; and (5) the chance of making such a bad choice again.

For any given product it is possible to measure the importance attached to each of the above facets. Thus, there is minimum involvement in the case of batteries and maximum involvement with dresses and perfumes. Such an approach can be used to improve positioning and advertising strategies. Europe-wide comparisons would permit us to determine whether or not the different facets of involvement are of a similar intensity and

importance across countries, and thus help us determine segmentation and advertising strategies.

In a recent study, Kapferer and Laurent (1986) demonstrated ten types of consumption patterns by measuring these
facets of consumer involvement for twenty products. The major
conclusions to be drawn from their study can be summarized
below:

1. The often evoked strong/weak dichotomy concerning in-
    volvement is not true. The minimum and maximum in-
    volvement groups represent only 16 percent and 9 percent
    respectively of the respondents. This means that the major-
    ity of consumers interviewed were in between and there-
    fore amenable to influence in buying the product or ser-
    vice presented to them.
2. Each of the facets of involvement varied distinctly accord-
    ing to the group in question. It is this differentiation that is
    of greatest interest, as it can allow us to attribute specific
    buying behavior to each group.
3. Various groups showed contrasting consumption patterns.
    For example, the "conformist purchasers" were charac-
    terized by an overevaluation of the symbolic value of the
    product. In the champagne category, such groups ac-
    counted for almost half of all champagne purchases (48
    percent).

When extended to the whole of Europe, the findings of
such studies can be used to help marketing executives make
better decisions about the desirability of global versus differentiated strategies for various European countries and/or products.

Criteria for Selecting Specific Methods of Investigation

Three types of studies are possible: at the levels of culture,
concerning the individual consumer, and dealing with a specific
product. At the same time, certain methods can be applied to
more than one level of investigation. For example, the consumer
involvement aspects refer to both the individual and the prod-

uct levels. Similarly, brand sensitivity studies are not only related to the products being studied, but also to the individual buyer and his or her evaluation. The means-end chain analysis deals with all three levels at the same time. It is based on in-depth interviews of individuals and attempts to establish links between their personalities and values and their buying habits (Gutman, 1986). Methodology elaborated by Valette-Florence and Rapacchi (1991) for this purpose suggests the choice of either a macro or a micro approach. Finally, it is a good idea to distinguish between specific market studies and those that are more general. In such a case the former are carried out on behalf of the corporations that commission them, whereas the latter are usually performed by Europe-wide organizations, like that of the Eurobarometers mentioned earlier and sponsored by the commission in Brussels.

In the future, more studies will be carried out in an attempt to cover all three levels of interest (cultural, individual consumer, and specific product) and as many factors that could influence them as possible. For instance, recent work done by Kapferer and Laurent (1989) in France clearly shows the multitude of factors influencing consumer buying decisions. Furthermore, their conclusions substantiate the importance of several specific evaluation criteria (for example, brand loyalty and awareness do no necessarily vary equally). Finally, their studies also confirm how valuable their approach can be in a Europe-wide context, where the degree of involvement and brand awareness varies considerably from country to country (Laurent and Kapferer, 1986). Another approach with high future potential consists of modeling the behavior of the consumer and then producing a typology derived from such a model (Roehrich, Valette-Florence, and Rapacchi, 1989). It seems that the results of such modeling are superior to those provided by traditional typological analyses (Valette-Florence and Rapacchi, 1990).

Cultural Similarities and Differences:
Marketing Implications

The major concern of marketing managers operating across Europe focuses on the use of global or differentiated strategies. The similarity of social norms across Europe, the standardization of communications, the frequent interactions among people of different nationalities—be it in the course of business, studies, or vacationing—cross-imitation effects, and so forth point to future growth in global or pan-European marketing. Similarly, transcultural products such as rock music, fashion, and certain food items (prepared meals or low-calorie products) also suggest an increase in the tendency toward global marketing.

On the other hand, Theodore Levitt's (1983) well-known assertion that "different cultural preferences, national tastes and standards, and business institutions are vestiges of the past" may be an oversimplification as far as the European consumer is concerned. Even homogeneous markets such as that for motorbikes may require differentiated marketing in certain cases. For example, Honda created the "Transalp" model specifically for the French motorbike market, which is known to be different from most of the other European markets. With a highly developed market for trial bikes, Honda had to adapt its products to meet the specific French tastes.

A counter-trend to global strategies consists of addressing the marketing of products or services to specific cultural targets and audiences. The most striking example of such a counter-trend can be found in the United States, where specificity has been carried to the extreme, affecting the food or hygiene product mix depending on whether the target audience is Black, Hispanic, or non-Hispanic white (Sexton, 1972; Sondhein and others, 1979). In Europe, the same situation might eventually emerge for the North African immigrants living within the EC. As Dubois (1987) perceptively noted, the relative intensity of cultural disparities within a country (as opposed to those that exist between countries) determines the strategic choices of the corporation just as much as the marketing manager's willingness or ability to adapt his or her firm to changes in such cultural disparities.

Given the extent to which their products are recognized universally, corporations such as Coca-Cola, Levi-Strauss, Bic, and Gillette have used undifferentiated marketing for a long time, thus achieving substantial economies of scale. The same is true for small-scale luxury products such as those of Louis Vuitton and Chanel and certain alcoholic beverages. In such cases, the extremely high symbolic value of the product being sold counterbalances cultural disparities through product image and imitation effects.

At the same time, major multinationals such as Nestlé, Unilever, Proctor & Gamble, and General Foods are quick to define marketing strategies that are specifically adapted to local cultures. For example, Nestlé uses its advanced freeze-dried technology to market a different type of coffee in each country that is specially adapted to the local palate of each culture or country (Kapferer, 1989). This type of strategy seems to be the prerogative of giant corporations, the only ones in a position to sacrifice the advantages of standardization in order to maintain their world leadership. However, as newer, more flexible manufacturing technologies (see Chapter Five) become commonplace, the vast majority of corporations will be capable of producing custom-built products targeted to specific cultures or even smaller groups of consumers, thus increasing the possibilities of differentiated marketing.

Finally, an intermediate solution exists, consisting of global marketing of a product while varying some elements of the marketing mix (often with great subtlety). Since the McDonald's clientele outside North America is made up principally of teenagers, unlike its counterpart in the United States, where it consists predominantly of families, the company was obliged to modify the localization as well as the conception of its fast food establishments. Similarly, it had to adapt its beverages to local cultural tastes and hence to sell beer in France and guarana in Brazil, while only marketing traditional soft drinks in North America. Similarly, food giants such as Gervais Danone maintain the same quality standards worldwide, but adapt their yogurt (making it more or less tart) to satisfy different European tastes.

Repercussions on the Elements of the Marketing Mix

Variations on the three alternative strategies outlined above are infinite, as are their repercussions on the marketing mix. The extent of such variations depends on the cultural and behavioral differences of the consumers involved. In addition, sales and advertising practices must also be examined. Although rarely taken into account, sales techniques are very influential for the purchaser of high-involvement products (for example, perfume), technical products (cameras), or durables (cars and refrigerators). In such cases, the interface of consumer and salesperson acting in an advisory capacity may prove dominant. The analysis of European disparities in terms of the sales process has been found to be extremely useful, especially concerning the key arguments provided to the customer by the salesperson, which vary considerably from one country to another. Such disparities must be taken into account when formulating marketing strategies. Advertising is no doubt the area in which cultural variations appear in both their most marked and their subtlest forms. It is here above all that the marketing manager must be able to adapt in an imaginative way to all of the many European cultural variations. For instance, a Peugeot 205 advertising campaign used in several European countries incorporated nearly identical visuals. The only difference is in the translation of the French word *garce*. Even though much stronger and more derogatory, the English word *bitch*, the Dutch word *biest*, and the German word *Bärnst* were used after having been tested and found acceptable. In Italian, however, the subtler and perhaps more Latin *ti odio* ("I hate you") was chosen, as it was found that the stronger translation of *bitch* was not compatible with the Italian conception of capricious women. These linguistic and cultural subtleties clearly denote the need to adapt advertising messages when they are being used across various countries.

Furthermore, even transnational products such as cars and pantyhose need advertisements adapted to the specificities of different European cultures. This is perhaps the single most important message that marketing executives must accept, as in the final analysis, there is no such thing as universal or global advertising and marketing. However, it is also true within individual countries, such as the United States and Canada, as segmentation and positioning are always critical factors determining product success.

Conclusion

Like a precious stone that is better displayed from different angles, the European consumer is best perceived from different viewpoints. The myth, should the reader still be in any doubt, is that the European consumer is a single entity. The consumers of the various EC countries no doubt share a set of common values; however, discrepancies exist and will continue to do so in the future. To uphold the myth of global marketing—except for certain products such as Coca-Cola or jeans—and marketing transnational targets is counterproductive. Products must undergo some degree of adaptation to cultural differences. The same holds true for advertising. As a matter of fact, most of the errors in international marketing are, in our view, due to faulty assessment of local cultures.

The reality of the European consumer is quite different from the myth. We envision an increasingly cosmopolitan European consumer who will demand differentiated products and the use of differentiated marketing strategies. A wide array of approaches are now in existence that will permit marketing executives to better identify such a consumer and his or her changing needs and tastes. The future implies the slow emergence of a common approach and methodology that can be applied throughout Europe so that the findings of one study can be compared with those of another. Moreover, new methods of investigation, new statistical developments, and new tools of analysis will doubtless appear. New sociocultural trends will also arise and they will need to be identified as soon as possible, often using new technologies.

Getting to know the consumer better will be the key to marketing success in the integrated market. Marketing executives will have to make sure that they are equipped to achieve such a task. This chapter was written to provide them with a description of the main issues and approaches related to

Europe-wide marketing. To paraphrase the eighteenth-century German writer Novalis, the marketing manager of tomorrow should not stumble on cultural barriers and differences — on the contrary, such barriers and differences should stimulate him or her even more.

References

Beatty, S., and others. "Alternative Measurement Approaches to Consumer Values: The List of Values and the Rokeach Value Survey." *Psychology and Marketing*, 1985, *2*, 181–200.

Dubois, B. "Culture and Marketing." *Research and Applications in Marketing*, 1987, *2* (1), 43–63.

Eurobarometers. Brussels: Commission of the European Communities, 1984.

European Consumers. Brussels: Commission of the European Communities, 1980.

Gutman, J. "Analyzing Consumer Orientations Toward Beverages Through Mean-End Chain Analysis." *Psychology and Marketing*, 1986, *3*, 28–42.

Kahle, L. *Social Values and Change: Adaptation to Life in America.* New York: Praeger, 1983.

Kapferer, J.-N. "The Face Value of Brand." In J.-N. Kapferer and J.-C. Thoening (eds.), *The Brand.* Paris: McGraw-Hill, 1989.

Kapferer, J.-N., and Laurent, G. "Consumer Involvement Profiles: A New Practical Approach to Consumer Involvement." *Journal of Advertising Research*, 1986, *25*, 48–56.

Kapferer, J.-N., and Laurent, G. "The Sensitivity of the Mark." In J.-N. Kapferer and J.-C. Thoening (eds.), *The Mark.* Paris: McGraw-Hill, 1989.

Laurent, G., and Kapferer, J.-N. "Measuring Consumer Involvement Profiles." *Journal of Marketing Research*, 1985, *22*, 41–53.

Laurent, G., and Kapferer, J.-N. "Conflict in the Channel: The Case of European Store Brands." Annual conference of the European Institute for Advanced Studies in Management, Brussels, Oct. 28, 1986.

Levitt, T. "The Globalization of Markets." *Harvard Business Review*, May–June 1983, 92–102.

Munson, J., and McQuarrie, E. "Shortening the Rokeach Values Survey for Use in Consumer Research." *Advances in Consumer Research*, 1988, *15*, 65–70.

Plummer, J. T. "How Personality Makes a Difference." *Journal of Advertising Research*, 1985, *24* (6), 27–31.

Roehrich, G., Valette-Florence, P., and Rapacchi, B. "Combined Incidence of Personal Values, Involvement and Innovativeness on Innovative Consumer Behavior: An Application on Perfume Purchase." Proceedings of the 129th Esomar Seminar, Vienna, Nov. 6–8, 1989.

Rokeach, M. *The Nature of Human Values.* New York: Free Press, 1973.

Sexton, D. "Black Buyer Behavior." *Journal of Marketing*, 1972, pp. 36–39.

Sondhein, J., and others. "Hispanic Marketing: The Invisible Giant." *Advertising Age*, 1979, pp. 5–20.

Stoezel, J. *Values of the Present Times: One European's Inquiry.* Paris: PUF, 1983.

Usunier, J. C., and Sissman, P. "The Intercultural in the Service of Marketing." *Harvard-L'Expansion*, 1986.

Valette-Florence, P. "Life-Style Studies: Concepts, Field Investigation and Actual Problems." *Research and Applications in Marketing*, 1986, *1*, 94–109; *2*, 42–58.

Valette-Florence, P., and Jolibert, A. "Social Values, AIO, and Consumption Patterns: Exploratory Findings." *Journal of Business Research*, Special Issue on Social Values, 1990, *20* (2), 109–122.

Valette-Florence, P., and Rapacchi, B. "Structural Analysis and Cluster Analysis: A Complementary Approach." *Research and Applications in Marketing*, 1990, *5* (1), 73–91.

Valette-Florence, P., and Rapacchi, B. "Improvements in Means-Ends Chain Analysis Using Graph Theory and Correspondence Analysis." *Journal of Advertising Research*, Feb./Mar. 1991.

CHAPTER 11

Appreciating the Diversity of the Single Market Community

Michelle Bainbridge, Spyros G. Makridakis

Heaven is where the police are British, the cooks French, the mechanics German, the lovers Italian, and it is all organized by the Swiss. Hell is where the cooks are British, the mechanics French, the lovers Swiss, the police German, and it is all organized by the Italians.

Anonymous

The above story has been told innumerable times when addressing audiences composed of various European nationalities. It brings out the common European stereotypes, emphasizing how these stereotypes could put into question the extent of pan-European success, depending on whether this rich cultural diversity is used as a source of potential competitive advantage or, if it is left unexploited, allowed to become a factor leading to failure.

There is no doubt that Europe does not have a unicultural environment. Western Europe is made up of seventeen countries whose inhabitants speak more than ten major languages and a host of minor ones. Within the European Economic Community alone, there are nine official languages. Moreover, the customs, attitudes, values, and spending patterns of the various nationalities differ widely from one country to another and there are even huge differences to be found between regions within the same country. A recent study on "European lifestyles" conducted by Market Intelligence (MINTEL) among eight thousand European nationals confirmed such differences and highlighted the potential opportunities and/or problems that a single market may create.

The finding, for instance, that British households are more than twice as likely to possess a microwave oven than the average household in the EC presents as much a threat as an opportunity for manufacturers, as they seek ways to increase the number of microwaves sold in countries whose consumption lags way behind that of the British. While, on the other hand, French cheese exporters may well have a difficult time persuading British housewives that Camembert beats Cheddar in light of the fact that, in the same survey, 64 percent of those Britons questioned professed to preferring their own traditional dishes to "foreign muck." Will the French cheese producers be able to persuade other European nationals that unseemly, malodorous cheeses are excellent in taste and help digestion? If they can, the opportunities presented to them are huge, as their potential market will expand more than sixfold. But, as psychologists well know, changing well-established customs and tastes is not a trivial matter, nor can it be done overnight.

In addition to wide cultural diversity, the countries of Europe also differ in demographic and socioeconomic terms. Of the twelve EC member countries, four (France, Italy, the United Kingdom, and West Germany) are considerably larger than the rest — accounting for more than 70 percent of the total EC population and 80 percent of the total GNP. The remaining eight countries are much smaller, ranging from a mere 370,000 inhabitants in Luxembourg to 39 million inhabitants in Spain. Similarly, there are wide economic disparities between the rich Northern countries (excluding Ireland) and the poorer Southern countries. The disparity in per capita GNP between Denmark and Portugal is over $12,000 (Denmark's GNP is more than six times higher than that of Portugal). Huge differences in income exist within single countries between industrialized or urban regions and rural ones. In Italy, for instance, the per capita GNP of the north is twice as high as that of the south, and unemployment in the south is more than two and a half times the rate in the north.

Demographics: The Graying of the EC Population

Population growth in all twelve EC countries has slowed down to the point that in most countries there is practically no growth and in certain countries, such as West Germany, the population is actually declining. Moreover, it is only the smaller countries (Greece, Ireland, and Portugal) that exhibit annual growth rates in excess of 0.5 percent. The overall population growth rate of the twelve stands at less than 0.1 percent, and even this small net increase may disappear before the end of this century, raising concern of a declining population and the prospect of a huge army of retired people.

Birth Rates. Since the middle of the 1960s, birth rates have slumped in all of the twelve EC countries. The growing prosperity of the 1950s and 1960s was reflected in an almost universal baby boom, with birth rates rising as much as 20 percent during some parts of this period. During the late sixties and early seventies, however, the baby boom stopped almost as abruptly as it had started.

Figure 11-1 shows the average number of children per woman in 1985 for the twelve countries of the EC. The country exhibiting the highest figure, Ireland, stands at only moderately more than the zero growth threshold (2.4 children per woman), while Spain, with the second highest figure, achieves only the 2.1 children per woman necessary to maintain the population at its present level. All the other countries fall below this level, meaning that the new generation of Europeans will be smaller than that of their parents. West Germany faces a particularly worrying future. If the present level of 1.3 births per woman continues, future generations will number less than two-thirds that of their parents. Indeed, if present trends continue, the EC market of 325 million prople will peak around the year 2000 and drop to less than 300 million by the year 2040. Moreover, the EC's share of the world population will drop from 6 percent in 1990 to less than 3 percent by the year 2040.

In addition to the rise in acceptance and availability of contraceptive techniques and abortion, the explanation for this

Figure 11-1. Average Number of Children per Woman, 1985.

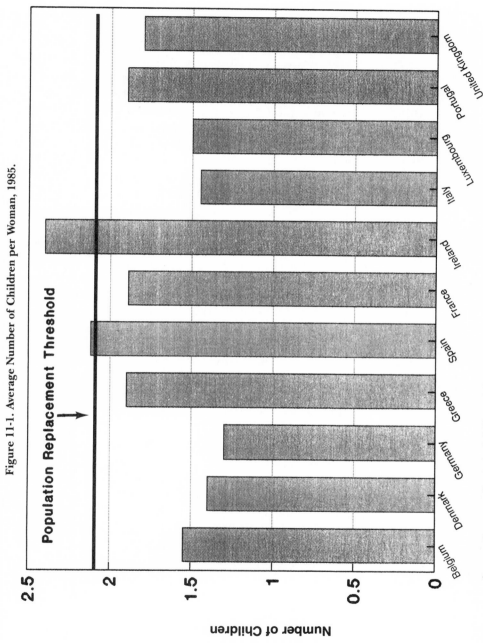

Source: Eurostat, Statistical Office of the European Communities, Luxembourg, 1988.

surprising drop in the birth rate seems to lie more in the attitude of women in modern European society. Even in Ireland, where contraception and abortion are still illegal, the average annual growth rate of the population fell from 1.5 percent between 1971 and 1981 to 0.6 percent between 1981 and 1987. Although it can be argued that such a decline is a direct result of the resumption of emigration, fertility has also dropped. The number of births dwindled from 74,000 in 1980 to around 60,000 today. Overall, the decline in the rate of population increase is dramatic, as can be seen from Figure 11-2, which shows the rate for the twelve in 1960 and 1984.

Attitudes in society, although varying considerably among the different EC countries, have resulted in a rise in the number of working women, which has definitely contributed to a fall in fertility rates. Table 11-1 shows the number of working women as a percentage of the total female population for the twelve countries in 1977 and 1986. This table demonstrates that, without exception, the ratio of working to nonworking women has increased considerably over the ten-year period. As the trend of increasing numbers of working women continues, we foresee a continuation of declining birth rates, and thus population growth rates, in the EC.

Another important factor that depresses the birth rate is the age at which women marry and produce their first child. Here a definite split between the Northern countries and the Mediterranean countries exists. In all the Northern countries (with the exception of Ireland), women are marrying and consequently producing their first children at a later age. In France, for example, the mother's average age at the birth of her first child has risen by almost five years since 1960. In the Mediterranean countries, however, the opposite has occurred: women (and men, for that matter) are marrying and starting families at an earlier age. The explanation for this divide in societal attitudes seems to lie in the fact that economic prosperity has been but a relatively recent phenomenon in the poorer countries of Spain, Italy, Greece, and Portugal. Thus, the economic restrictions to marriage that existed in the pre-1960s era have now disappeared and young couples can afford to set up house

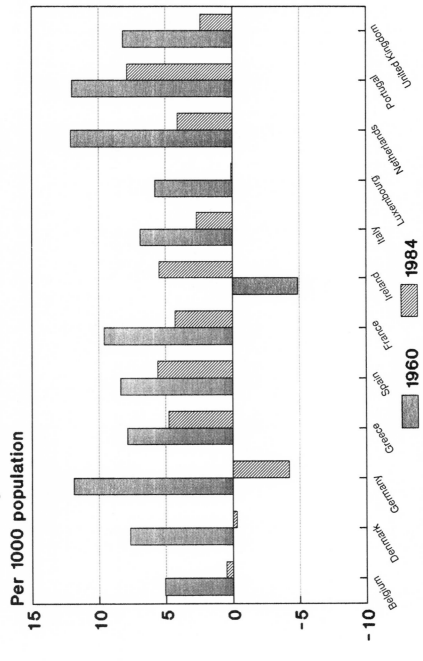

Figure 11-2. Rate of Population Increase (Natural Increase – Net Emigration).

Source: Eurostat, Statistical Office of the European Communities, Luxembourg, 1988.

and have children at an earlier age. As economic prosperity increases, however, we expect the poorer Southern countries to become more like their Northern counterparts, with increasing numbers of more highly educated women choosing to work, at least for a period of time, before marrying and starting a family.

Marriage and Divorce Rates. Another phenomenon that has changed indiscriminately across the countries of the EC is the rates of marriage and divorce (see Table 11-2). In all cases the number of marriages per 1,000 population has decreased over the last twenty-five years and the number of divorces per 1,000 married couples has increased. It is England that exhibits the highest marriage rate today, with 7 weddings per 1,000 population; but the incidence of divorce in England is the second highest in the community, with 12 divorces per 1,000 married couples. Of the other countries that make up the EC, marriage is the least popular in Spain and France with Ireland and Italy close behind (in Ireland there is no second chance, as divorce is still not recognized in this predominantly Catholic country).

**Table 11-1. Working Women as a Percentage of
Total Female Population in the EC.**

	1977	1986
Belgium	28.8	33.1
Denmark	42.3	50.9
West Germany	31.1	34.3
Greece	21.3	27.3
Spain	20.5	21.9
France	32.5	35.6
Ireland	19.7	21.9
Italy	24.5	28.8
Luxembourg	25.8	30.2
Netherlands	20.9	27.6
Portugal	31.5	35.1
United Kingdom	34.6	39.0
Average for EC	28.8	32.5

Source: Eurostat, Statistical Office of the European Communities, Luxembourg.

Table 11-2. Marriage and Divorce Rates in the EEC.

	Marriage Rate		Divorce Rate	
	1960	*1984*	*1960*	*1984*
Italy	7.7	5.2	1.3	1.0
France	7.0	5.1	2.9	7.7
West Germany	9.4	5.9	3.6	8.7
Spain	7.7	4.8	—	0.5
Portugal	7.8	6.9	0.4	—
Greece	7.0	5.6	1.5	2.5
Denmark	7.8	5.6	5.9	12.6
Ireland	5.5	5.2	(not recognized)	
Luxembourg	7.1	5.4	2.0	6.4
Belgium	7.2	6.0	2.0	6.8
Netherlands	7.8	5.7	2.2	9.9
United Kingdom	7.5	7.0	2.0	12.0

Source: Eurostat, Statistical Office of the European Communities, Luxembourg.

The lowest incidence of divorce appears, as one would expect, in the traditionally Catholic countries of Southern Europe—Italy, Spain, and Portugal. (We exclude Ireland from these statistics, as there is no way of ascertaining the number of couples no longer living communally but without officially recognized divorces.)

Life Expectancy. Perhaps even more striking is the cumulative effect of falling birth rates *and* the lengthening life span. The last thirty years have witnessed lofty increases in life expectancy in all twelve countries of the EC. During the thirty-year period from 1950 to 1980, average life expectancy at birth rose in all countries of the community—in some countries by as much as fifteen years for women and thirteen years for men. Today, the longest life expectancy at birth for both men and women is to be found in the Netherlands (seventy-three and eighty years, respectively), while the shortest is to be found for men in Portugal (sixty-nine years) and for women in Ireland (seventy-six years). Interestingly enough, Greece possesses the third longest life expectancy at birth for men and the second shortest life expectancy at birth for women.

The result of falling birth rates combined with longer life expectancy produces an overall aging or graying of the population, which will undoubtedly have far-reaching social and economic consequences for the European Community.

The Senior Segment. The most important aspect of the changing age distribution of the population is the declining ratio of the potentially productive age group (those who are of working age — fifteen to sixty-five years old) to the nonproductive age groups (those that are either of pre- or postworking age). The obvious reason for such concern lies in the fact that production comes mainly from the working-age group and thus this group must bear the burden of the other two. Hence, any change in the age distribution of the population has significant repercussions for the reallocation of resources, as a shrinking work force will have to pay for the rapidly expanding numbers of retirees (who, it seems, will be living longer after they retire).

As pensions are paid in Europe on a current basis (workers' payments are redirected immediately toward the payment of pensions), and the birth rates have been slowing down for a number of years, there is considerable concern about the ability of decreasing numbers of workers to provide pensions for increasing numbers of retirees. Furthermore, the overall costs of social security benefits and health care for these elderly people are on the rise, an increase that will have to be borne by the smaller group of workers. Finally, as the number of years of schooling required to adapt to the higher levels of competence needed is increasing, new entrants will come into the work force at a later age, further shrinking the actual number of workers in Europe.

Table 11-3 is an estimate of the percentage of total population that the over-sixty-five age group will represent by the year 2010.

If present trends continue, by the year 2030 countries such as Germany will have more people drawing from pension schemes than contributing to them. The same is true to varying degrees throughout Europe. Even the stereotypical Italian mother surrounded by smiling bambini is on the way out. Today

Table 11-3. The Estimated Percentage of the Over-Sixty-Five Age Group in the Year 2010.

Country	Percentage of People over Sixty-Five Years of Age
West Germany	20.4
Luxembourg	18.1
Italy	17.3
Greece	16.8
Denmark	16.7
France	16.3
Belgium	15.9
Spain	15.5
Netherlands	14.6
United Kingdom	14.6
Portugal	14.1
Ireland	11.1

Source: Authors' estimates drawn from information contained in Eurostat publications, Statistical Office of the European Communities, 1989.

in Italy only thirteen children are born for every ten women, while old-age pensioners are expected to represent 17.3 percent of the population in 2010. Greece, Denmark, and France can expect somewhat more stable futures, with smaller changes in the percentage of the total population represented by the over-sixty-five age group, and Spain and Portugal seem reasonably fortunate in that they have maintained smooth birth rates over the last thirty years. Ireland, while exhibiting the strongest population growth at present, may not be so fortunate, as exceptionally high unemployment rates have induced young people (particularly the skilled) to emigrate, thus leaving behind a large proportion of less-educated, less-productive older workers.

Notwithstanding the direct costs involved in financing hefty pension schemes, the effects of such fluctuations on the economy are multiple. Patterns of demand will change if large fluctuations in the age distribution of the population continue to occur. This will mean a sharp decline in industries that are geared toward the baby market, while industries directed more toward the needs of an aging population (for example, medical care, pharmaceuticals, and housing for retirees) will witness a large increase.

Today, old-age pensioners are by no means the old folk set in their ways and their buying habits that their predecessors were. They are increasingly active and, more important, they are increasingly affluent. Their demands, although quite different from those of the younger members of society, could become areas providing huge growth. Companies are starting to recognize the huge potential demand represented by this segment of the population. Elizabeth Arden recently introduced the Millennium line of cosmetics especially for the over-thirty-five age group, while other cosmetic companies, targeting the mature rather than the youth markets, have launched a variety of antiaging facial creams.

The financial service area is another industry that could reap considerable benefits from evolving demographic changes (as it already has, to some extent). The widespread fear concerning the inability of governments to pay tomorrow's pensions has led to an increase in retirement schemes run by private enterprise (government fiscal policies encourage saving for retirement by exempting certain sums from income taxes). In 1987 insurance companies in France collected over six billion dollars from people saving for potentially lengthy retirements. In Britain two-thirds of the country's savings are held by people over the age of fifty-five, making the elderly the prime target group for financial services. Meanwhile, in Germany, the baby boomers are expected to inherit the previous generation's wealth, which, for the first time this century, has not been devalued by costly wars and hyperinflation. Thus, the need for sound, high-return opportunities will increase considerably in Germany and elsewhere.

The Density and Distribution of the EC Population

The density and distribution of the EC population vary widely among the twelve countries and the various regions of the EC conglomerate. Moreover, there are striking differences between rural and urban areas.

Population Density. Population density within Europe is relatively high. The 2.2-million-square-kilometer combined area of the twelve is roughly four times smaller than that of the United States and ten times smaller than that of the Soviet Union. Thus, even the least populated of the EC countries, Ireland, has almost twice as many inhabitants per square kilometer as the United States.

Even though the overall population density is relatively high, the population of Europe is not at all homogeneously distributed across the community. Ireland, paradoxically possessing the highest birth rate in the EC, is the least populated, with a mere 51 inhabitants per square kilometer. The Netherlands and Belgium, with 352 and 323 people per square kilometer, respectively, practically tie for first place as the most densely populated countries of the twelve, and are three times more densely populated per square kilometer than France. West Germany and the United Kingdom are next with comparable population densities of 245 and 232 people per square kilometer, while the majority of countries fall in the 100 to 200 people per square kilometer range (Italy, 190; Luxembourg, 141; Denmark, 119; Portugal, 110; and France, 101). Spain at 76, Greece with 75, and Ireland are the countries with the lowest population densities.

Marked as the differences in terms of size and density of the population between countries, even more dramatic are the differences that exist between regions *within* single countries. Highly populated, generally industrial or administrative centers, and sparsely populated, frequently rural regions are to be found within most of the community countries.

The most striking feature of the population map of the EC is the unevenness of the distribution of the people across Europe (see Figure 11-3). We can see quite clearly that the most densely populated regions of the community stretch along a diagonal line from northwest England, to the industrial regions of northern Italy, passing through southern Holland, northern Belgium, and the Rhine/Ruhr conurbation in Germany. The Paris–Ile-de-France area, the most populous in France, lies slightly away from this diagonal line of concentration, owing its

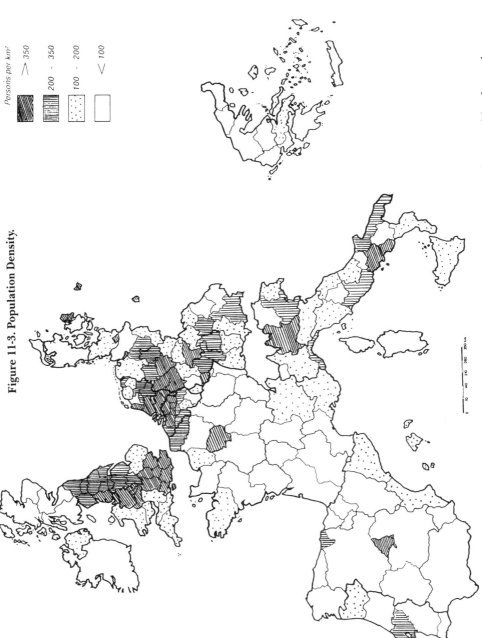

Figure 11-3. Population Density.

Persons per km²

> 350

200 - 350

100 - 200

< 100

0   70   140   210   280   350 km

Source: Authors' adaptation from *Europe in Figures.* Statistical Office of the European Communities, Luxembourg.

highly populated condition to a long history of centralization that reaches back as far as Napoleon.

Despite the fact that the concentration of the population in a limited number of towns and cities has invariably led to the depopulation of the surrounding rural regions, it cannot be automatically concluded that the low-density regions are necessarily poorer, depressed areas. On the contrary, they are often regions of highly mechanized, efficient agriculture with significant per capita income. Champagne, to the east of the Ile-de-France region, is such a case, with vast, extremely efficient agriculture ensuring an income that is slightly higher, per head of population, than that of the Côte d'Azur — an area renowned for being the home of the rich and famous.

Rural Areas Versus Urban Centers. The exodus of the population from the rural areas to the big cities is a phenomenon that has been felt throughout the countries of the EC, starting as early as the seventeenth century in the United Kingdom, West Germany, and France, and continuing later on in countries such as Italy and Spain. In a recent issue of *World Health* magazine, it was estimated that by the year 2000, 75 percent of Europeans will be living in cities. Already, 60 percent of all West Germans live in towns or cities of more than 20,000 inhabitants, with 15 percent of the population concentrated in the Rhine-Ruhr district alone. The Paris conurbation, encompassing a mere 2 percent of the land area of France, is home to a staggering 19 percent of the population. In Holland at the end of 1987, 51 percent of the population was living in urban municipalities, with practically half the population concentrated within the Amsterdam-Rotterdam-Utrecht triangle (which makes up the Randstad region). Even in countries such as Spain and Greece, the proportion of the total population living in large towns is very high: two-fifths of all Spaniards live in towns of over 10,000 inhabitants, and the urban population of Athens and Salonika in Greece accounts for more than 40 percent of the total population. Only Portugal has a high proportion of rural inhabitants: in 1980 more than half the Portuguese were living in settlements of less than 2,000 inhabitants.

It is interesting to note that in many countries the trend toward internal migration to cities has been halted or even reversed in the last few years. In France, for example, the 1982 census showed that only towns with under 200,000 inhabitants were still growing and that the biggest migratory influx between 1975 and 1982 was into the Languedoc-Roussilon region in the south. Similarly, in England the most rapid population decline has actually taken place in inner-city areas, with most urban centers having stabilized if not declined in terms of population.

An aspect that has certainly played an important role in the decision-making process concerning population location is that of urban congestion. With the relative general rise in prosperity and the acquisition of cars, the choice of locating away from the center of large conurbations, where land costs are high and pollution and overcrowding a problem, is open to those so wishing. It has been estimated that in the high-rise neighborhoods of European cities population density can be as high as 15,000 people per hectare. There is also some evidence to suggest that such high population densities may have important psychological and behavioral impacts on human beings. The problems associated with urban congestion are present to some degree or another in all of the central urban zones of Europe. Thus, it seems reasonable to expect that in the postintegration environment, lesser-developed areas will witness strong rates of expansion as cheap and effective telecommunications provide the potential to locate away from large consumer centers.

European Community: Economic Facts and Figures

At present, the combined GNP of the twelve totals around three and a half billion dollars, while that of the United States stands at four and a half billion dollars. Since the EC population is about 30 percent greater than that of the United States, however, its per capita GNP is considerably lower ($11,000 versus $18,500). Japan's per capita GNP is also higher than that of the EC, by almost $5,000.

There are huge income discrepancies among the various EC countries. As mentioned in the introduction to this chapter,

Germany, France, Italy, and the United Kingdom make up 80 percent of the total community wealth. Per capita income also varies a great deal, topped by a group of wealthy countries (Denmark, Germany, and Luxembourg) whose per capita GNP stands at around $15,000 (about the same as that of Japan, but roughly $3,500 lower than that of the United States). The second group of countries, with a per capita GNP of between $10,000 and $12,000, includes France, the Netherlands, Belgium, the United Kingdom, and Italy. The third group includes Spain, Ireland, and Greece, with a per capita GNP between $6,000 (Spain and Ireland) and $4,400 (Greece). Finally, Portugal's per capita GNP is the lowest of the community countries, standing at only $2,900. Figure 11-4 shows the 1987 per capita GNP of the twelve EC nations together with those of the United States and Japan.

The Structure of the EC Economies. The economies of the twelve EC countries experienced a period of slow growth following the 1973 energy crisis. This left them lagging behind the United States and gave Japan a chance to catch up and then overtake even the largest and most developed of the EC economies.

Figure 11-5 shows the per capita GNP of Germany, France, the United Kingdom, and Italy together with those of the United States and Japan for the years 1970, 1975, 1980, 1985, and 1988. The numbers speak for themselves. The relative growth of even the strongest of EC nations failed to adapt to the new realities of the middle and late 1970s, let alone those of the 1980s. Part of the reason for this must be attributed to Europe's old institutions, the protection expected and provided by governments, and the existence of many unwritten agreements that seriously constrained competition (see Chapter Two for additional details).

From the late 1970s and early 1980s on, firms ceased to face strong competition either from abroad (because of protectionist measures) or from within their own countries (because of gentlemen's agreements or outright monopolistic or oligopolistic barriers). Moreover, they failed to invest, as they did not

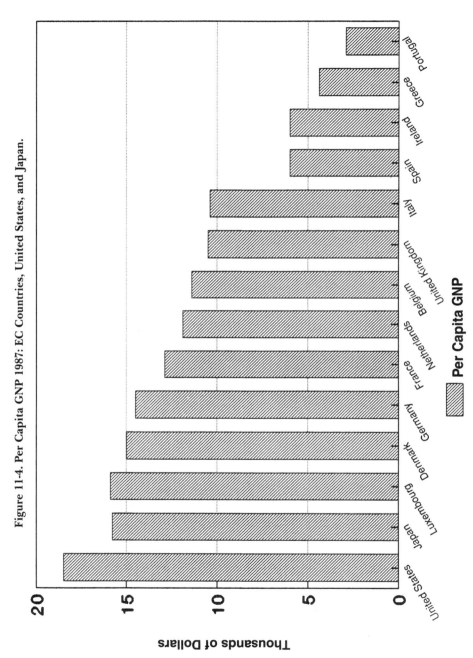

Figure 11-4. Per Capita GNP 1987: EC Countries, United States, and Japan.

Per Capita GNP

Source: Eurostat, Statistical Office of the European Communities, Luxembourg, 1989.

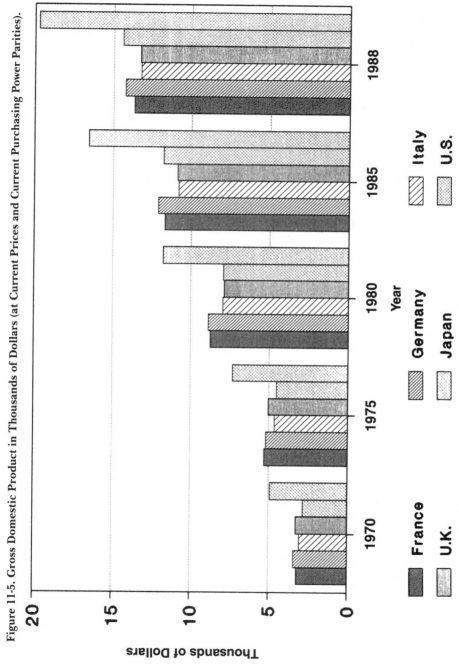

Figure 11-5. Gross Domestic Product in Thousands of Dollars (at Current Prices and Current Purchasing Power Parities).

Legend: France, U.K., Germany, Japan, Italy, U.S.

Source: Eurostat, Statistical Office of the European Communities, Luxembourg, 1989.

believe that the returns on their investments could compensate for the risks involved.

As integration approches, the present inefficiencies of the national economies will have to be ironed out with a view to their eventual disappearance. The prospect of a single market where goods, services, capital, and people will be free to move within the community has increased competition and intensified the drive for higher efficiency and lower costs. Thus, the fragmented and protected economies are already becoming more interdependent. Intracommunity trade has steadily increased and cross-border mergers, acquisitions, and alliances are becoming more common. If the commission achieves its objective of a truly integrated single market there is no reason the GNP of the twelve should trail behind that of the United States or Japan. As some studies have pointed out (see Chapter Two), if the medium- and long-term benefits of the single market are considered, EC growth rates and economic gains may exceed even those envisioned by the Cecchini report, bringing the EC economies to a parity with the United States and Japan.

Structural Funds. A major problem at present is the large discrepancies between the more and less affluent EC countries (see Figure 11-5) and the more and less affluent regions within single countries. To smooth out these discrepancies and to "help redress the principal regional imbalances in the Community" (article 130 of the Treaty of Rome), the commission has set up ambitious structural funds to facilitate and accelerate the economic development of poorer countries and regions, and those areas that have been witness to high unemployment caused by either agricultural or industrial decline. The means employed by such funds vary from direct grants or aid to encourage development of regional infrastructure (for example, transportation or communication links) to financial aid for retraining the long-term unemployed. They also include interest-reduced loans from the European Investment Bank (which was specifically set up for this purpose). Even though the size of the various structural funds is relatively large (in the 1988–1992 period, their total will amount to 50 billion ECU, or $55 billion), questions have been raised as to whether these funds are sufficient to accomplish the tasks involved (especially because the disparities between "rich" and "poor" countries have become even greater since Portugal and Spain joined the EC). For this reason various instruments have been proposed, tailored to the particular needs of the different countries, regions, and areas. Some are aimed at improving the infrastructure, others at raising the standards of living, while some are targeted more specifically at long-term structural unemployment or particularly high rates of unemployment found in the under-twenty-five age group.

Trade Within the EC. One of the reasons for which the European Community was created was to encourage trade among the member states. In this respect, the community has achieved notable success. Today around half of all EC trade is conducted among the twelve. The share and structure of trade differ greatly, however. West Germany and the Netherlands show considerable surpluses, for example, while Italy, the United Kingdom, and France run substantial deficits. The smaller EC countries that also run substantial commercial deficits with their EC partners feel somewhat threatened by the pressure to be fully integrated. Moreover, the free movement of goods, people, capital, and services associated with the integration directives presents additional threats for these countries, which may see even larger deficits following integration. Figure 11-6a and b shows the intercommunity trade among the major partners involved.

EC and EFTA. The main trading partners of the twelve EC countries as a whole are the United States and the six countries that make up the EFTA. The EFTA countries represent the largest single market for EC goods, accounting for 24.5 percent of all EC trade. At the same time, the twelve accounted for 61 percent of EFTA's imports — at a value of more than $1 billion — while providing an outlet for 55 percent of EFTA's exports. In April 1984 the ministers of the EC and EFTA agreed to intensify efforts toward the fullest possible realization of the free movement of goods, services, capital, and persons with the aim of

Figure 11-6. Intercommunity Trade.

a. Percentage of EC Exports
(1977 and 1987)

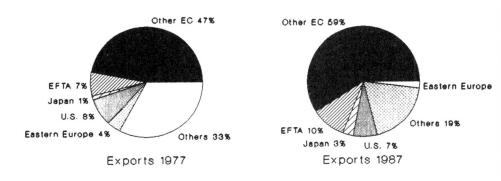

b. Percentage of EC Imports
(1977 and 1987)

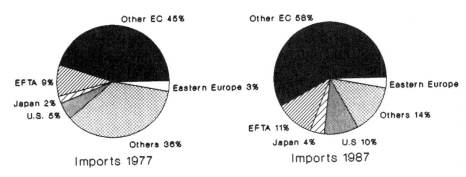

Source: Adapted from *Europe in Figures*, Statistical Office of the
European Communities, Luxembourg, 1988.

creating a dynamic and homogeneous European space; Austria, a member of EFTA, officially applied for membership to the EC in 1989. Although the application has not yet been considered, it is extremely likely that Austria will be accepted soon after full integration (since the EC governments decided that no further countries could be considered for membership after 1992).

The Cultural Environment

As mentioned in the introduction to this chapter, the European Community is by no means unicultural. It is also fair to say, however, that culturally speaking the peoples of the twelve countries of the EC are, in fact, more alike than they are different. Europeans have, historically, been in constant contact with each other over the centuries (through either trade, travel, or war). They thus share similar values and religious beliefs (practically all the peoples of the countries of the EC are Christians) and have very similar systems of government. In the Declaration on European Identity, published in 1973 by the EC, the diversity of cultures in Europe was seen "within the framework of a common European civilization."

Although it is extremely difficult to define culture (see Chapters Eight and Nine), there are several factors that can be used to distinguish cultural differences. Prominent among a host of considerations are language; socioeconomic variables; religion; and attitudes toward work, leisure, and saving (or spending). The twelve EC countries can be separated into two major cultural groups and four smaller ones. Thus, even though the Germanic cultures distinguishable in Northern Europe, for example, are quite different from those of the Mediterranean cultures of Italy and Greece, the Italians and Greeks have still managed to achieve notable success when working in Germany, just as the Germans have when setting up business in Italy and Greece. Moreover, even though the stereotypes mentioned at the beginning of this chapter do indeed exist for each and every country of the EC, the cultural differences among the Italians, Germans, Spanish, English, Danish, Greeks, and so on are not so intrinsically incompatible as to make the problems insurmountable. The actual divergence among the cultures is seen, in fact, to be reasonably small when different nationalities work toward a common goal. Therefore, we do not see cultural differences as a major obstacle to European integration — on the contrary, if properly channeled we believe that cultural differences can become a source of numerous competitive advantages.

One aspect of culture that often sets Europeans apart is language. In Europe, there are nine official languages (plus a host of unofficial ones). Given this linguistic diversity, the findings of the Eurobarometer Poll (a triannual EC publication that tracks communication and culture within the EC) are not really surprising. The poll reported only 8 percent of the total population of Europe to be trilingual and a staggering 66 percent of all Europeans speaking only their native language. The greatest deficiencies were reported in Ireland, Britain, and Portugal, where between 75 and 80 percent of the population spoke only their native language. When moving in from these peripheries of Europe, the number of bilinguists and trilinguists increased dramatically. In Luxembourg, 99 percent of the population was bilingual, and in Denmark and the Netherlands, 60 and 28 percent of the population, respectively, spoke at least two languages fluently.

In 1988 the commission attempted to introduce measures to combat these deficiencies by making fluency in two languages mandatory in all secondary school curricula. Despite virtually unanimous support for the LINGUA program, England, West Germany, and Denmark opposed the legislation, claiming the sovereign right to decide at the national level (or in the case of Germany, the *länder* level) the content of secondary schooling (even though the study of a second language at school is standard practice in all three of these countries).

While European governments appear reluctant to introduce a mandatory second language into the curriculum, Europeans themselves seem to have no such qualms. Language-training companies have seen a doubling of their clientele. Most of this demand is for English, which is emerging as the most popular second language in the EC. Although the emergence of English as the de facto second language might well prove to be a thorn in the side of the Francophones, it would appear that too much progress has already taken place for anything else to happen. An EC official for the LINGUA program recently reported that trying to stop the progress of English was like "trying to stop the tide coming in." As increasing numbers of professional schools and businesses make fluency in two languages a minimum requirement for applicants, the bilingual and trilingual incidence rates should increase dramatically.

Critics maintain that language differences will create significant problems for pan-European operations and that such difficulties will eventually block the road to true European integration. These language obstacles are not, in our opinion, insurmountable. Last year, for example, British Telecommunications introduced the LINTEXT translation system to the police force at the British end of the Eurotunnel. This system permits English phrases typed into a computer to be translated into French and displayed immediately on another terminal. Although there remains a great deal of work to be done on computerized translation systems, which are prone to making mistakes when idioms or words with multiple meanings are used, they could offer considerable help in reducing the importance of linguistic hurdles.

Even though in day-do-day business existing linguistic differences may cause some superficial problems, it is simply too easy to contend that such differences are a major obstacle to pan-European integration or success. Japanese and Korean businessmen do not seem to have been unduly hindered by their native languages when exporting to countries worldwide—especially given the fact that the different European languages are less divergent than are those of the Japanese or Koreans. Moreover, some countries have a number of official languages and have still managed to succeed. Switzerland has three official languages, yet this reality has not prevented it from achieving outstanding economic success, as can be measured by a per capita GNP of $21,000—one of the highest in the world. The Indian constitution recognizes sixteen different regional languages (there are hundreds of unrecognized ones) and only 30 percent of the total Indian population have a language in common—Hindi. Yet they still profess a common nationality, as do the peoples of the Soviet Union, who speak 112 different languages and write using five different alphabets.

Language, then, is not an irresolvable problem for European integration. Indeed, since exposure to different languages increases cultural adaptability, as we mentioned in Chapter Nine, the language differences in Europe can actually be a source of great advantage for Europe's battle to global expansion. Different languages do not necessarily set peoples apart any more than sharing a single language automatically assures shared values, principles, or culture (and a safeguard against cultural shock), as any American who has ever visited England or any any Briton who has ever gone to Australia well knows.

In order for companies to be able to conduct day-to-day business across the EC, however, they must establish a common language in which to carry on negotiations. Considerable progress has already been achieved in this direction. For example, a spokesperson for Olivetti recently reported that "every Olivetti manager must get by in English" and that at headquarters internal memos from one Italian director to another were written in English. The same is true for many other pan-European corporations. Indeed, with the numerous cooperative programs launched by the commission and exchanges of students and teachers among the different countries, Europeans from all over the community are forced to communicate across different languages. "The official language is broken English," said the director of administration at the European Space Agency. Even at the EC headquarters in Brussels, a great deal of the work is accomplished during breaks, lunches, or dinners, when everybody reverts to English in the informal atmosphere of the dining room. Ministers and EC officials are willing to exchange ideas in the language that is common to all (English), something that is not the case during the formal meetings. There, each participant is expected to use the language of the country he represents, and insists upon doing so with everything laboriously translated by a team of interpreters.

As European integration advances, we expect to see the importance of languages diminish. The younger generations will become more fluent in languages other than their native tongue. Broken English (or French for that matter) will not be considered a handicap, but an indispensable advantage in communicating throughout Europe. Thus, the English language might play the same role tomorrow in Europe as it does today in India (where it is used as the common language not because of the Indian love of English, but because the babel of regional languages and dialects presents too much of a communication problem).

Another aspect of culture that often sets peoples apart is religion. In this respect, the EC shows much more homogeneity. Practically all the people of the EC profess to Christianity, with an approximate 65/35 Catholic and Protestant split (with the exception of Greece, whose national church is the Greek Orthodox). Although the influence of the church has declined throughout the countries of the EC, religion remains more dominant in the traditionally Catholic Southern countries and — although to a lesser degree — in Greece than in the Northern countries. Ireland is the Northern exception — where a very strong Catholic church still influences legislation and behavior a great deal.

Conclusion

Although the twelve EC countries are dissimilar demographically, economically, and linguistically, their people share similar values, have essentially the same religious beliefs, and are all governed democratically. They are bound by a common civilization. Within Europe, there are none of the examples of profound national hostility that are exhibited between Israel and its neighbors, Iran and Iraq, or India and Pakistan. The people of Europe will be more easily integrated to form a single economic and even political entity than, say, the people of Azerbaijan and Armenia, two Soviet republics.

True integration among the twelve EC countries cannot be successful until the extreme economic differences that exist today are reduced. The structural funds aim at diminishing the differences between the affluent North and the less prosperous South and between industrial regions and those that were predominantly agricultural historically or where industrial decline has caused high numbers of structurally unemployed. The objective of these funds is thus to help the unemployed and the less fortunate segments of society located in these countries or areas. By so doing, it is hoped that Europe will be socially just and that every European will be able to benefit from the creation of a common market.

In our view, geographical imbalances of the population are less significant than the economic ones, because the free movement of people will permit a more uniform redistribution of the population (at least in theory). With regard to the "graying" of the population, the substantial motives presently in existence do not seem to have had an effect on the birth rates. Indeed, birth rates have remained remarkably stubborn despite the variety of incentives introduced by national governments. The problem of falling birth rates is not a uniquely European (or EC) one, but appears to be linked to economic prosperity: it is present, to varying degrees, in practically all industrialized or developed countries—including the United States and Japan.

Linguistic differences are a fact of European life that will not be eliminated by integration directives. Nevertheless, the countries of the European Community are not fighting for predominance of their own languages (unlike the Belgians, whose linguistic wars have brought down more than one government), nor do they feel threatened by English becoming the common European language. Although it is recognized that a single language spoken across all the countries of the EC would be preferable to nine official languages, the disadvantages and extra costs involved are not going to put Europe at a competitive disadvantage vis-à-vis the United States, Japan, and other competitors.

Finally, in all EC countries the government and business leaders accept the cultural differences of the twelve, and they view them as a source of strength rather than weakness. Europe's advantages come from its long historical heritage and its rich cultural diversity. Such history and culture are the binding forces that make Europeans feel part of a larger community, one that extends beyond the boundaries of their own countries.

PART FOUR

Finance, Banking, and the Monetary System

CHAPTER 12

Forging a Financial and Monetary Union

Charles Wyplosz

On October 5, 1989, the German Bundesbank (Central Bank) hiked its discount rate of interest by a full percentage point, to 6 percent. The bank's goal was to check the drop in the value of the dollar, not to fight inflation. Seven other European countries had to follow Bundesbank's example in order to avoid a capital flight from their own currencies. England was obliged to increase its own interest rates to a record 15 percent, raising cries of protest from both the business community and mortgage-paying customers.

There is no secret among EC countries that interest rates are determined by Germany's Bundesbank; however, the Bundesbank's conservative policies are not always compatible with those of other countries more interested in increasing growth rates than in keeping inflation in check, the main objective of the Bundesbank. These countries feel even more concerned when interest rate hikes are not so much intended to keep inflation down as to fight a drop in the value of the dollar, an objective that has not been achieved by increasing interest rates in the past.

In order to balance the German dominance in monetary policy, EC government officials, central bankers, and leading economists are calling for more cooperation at the community level so that they can have a greater say about interest rates and other monetary matters. Thus, talks about monetary integration, a single central bank as in the United States, are initiated even by conservative members of the British government. For most EC states, monetary integration (or at least serious coordination at the community level) has become a necessity to be implemented as fast as possible.

Economic Aspects of the EC

The central objective of the Single European Act (allowing free movement of goods, capital, and people within the EC) is to permit competitive forces to operate to their fullest extent throughout Europe. According to economics textbooks, competitive forces act to provide the best of goods (and services) at the lowest possible price. The ultimate beneficiary of increased competition is the consumer, since he or she maximizes the amount of goods and services that can be purchased with a given disposable income. Those producers who survive the competition also benefit in the long run, as they achieve cost effectiveness and acquire competitive advantages in both home and foreign markets. Indeed, one often hears the explanation that the competitive advantages enjoyed by U.S. and Japanese firms have been accumulated because they have had to operate in highly competitive home markets. These home markets have become testing grounds, providing them with huge opportunities to repeat domestic success by expanding abroad, further increasing their competitive lead. The real world is obviously one where perfect competition is not the norm. In reality, most industries are of the so-called monopolistically competitive kind—that is, they are dominated by a small number of large firms that compete against each other. Industries closer to the pure competition model typically deal with activities that are not widely tradable (mainly services).

Competition and Firm Size. An important question is what is going to happen in industries where monopolistic competition currently occurs. Increased economies of scale might well prove to be the source of the largest benefits, as European firms will reach the size of their U.S. and Japanese competitors. This will enhance productivity gains, allow for greater product variation, and probably result in lower production costs. Through mergers and acquisitions, competition might be strengthened to the point where some companies become close to achieving monopolistic powers, raising the possibility that antitrust regulations might be required to avoid EC-wide monopolies. Thus, policymakers will have to maneuver on the razor's edge, as large, powerful firms are needed to harness economies of scale and compete successfully on a worldwide basis while at the same time firms with monopolistic powers must be avoided.

Competition and Labor Markets. European labor markets are notorious for their lack of flexibility. The major concern of labor leaders is as high and as well-protected levels of employment as possible, along with the highest possible wage. A way of looking at the labor markets and the firms they serve is as a bilateral monopoly: large firms and powerful trade unions share the prices that are being extracted from the ultimate consumers. Enhanced competition is designed precisely to cut these prices. If the Single European Act succeeds in increasing competition, it will reduce prices, forcing both capital and labor to accept a smaller share unless they manage to increase productivity like the Japanese. If the Single European Act leads to EC-wide multinational companies (MNCs), national unions may be in a disadvantageous position, having to bear a disproportionate share of the lower prices consumers will be paying. This explains trade unions' reluctance about integration and the maneuvers around the idea of a "social Europe" (a way of maintaining union power when confronted with large MNCs operating on a Europe-wide scale). The alternative could be Europe-wide unions capable

of balancing the increased bargaining power of Europe-wide
MNCs.

Financial Integration. The financial markets have enjoyed
the highest degree of protection from their individual European governments; moreover, liberalization is likely to have the
most sweeping effects in such markets (see Chapter Thirteen).
Explicit restrictions to capital movements and a host of banking
and other restrictions have sheltered financial markets and resulted in firms that are not fully competitive on a worldwide
basis. Protectionism, or the lack of it, will change the scene quite
radically, bringing huge opportunities and equal dangers for
financial institutions and European firms alike.

Changes in the financial sector will affect the conduct of
national monetary policies as well as the ability of individuals
and/or firms to choose countries with minimal taxation rates
(Neven, 1990). Limited capital mobility has led to widespread
differences in the fiscal treatment of capital income (see Table
12-1). As a result, it is fairly easy to envisage highly lucrative
borrowing/lending strategies based solely on the exploitation of
tax loopholes in various European countries. Given existing
regulations, these strategies have been available only to well-
organized and fairly large corporations. In a single market
situation, virtually everyone in the EC, including individuals,
will be allowed the same opportunities. Moreover, financial
intermediaries located in tax haven countries will be permitted
to advertise their services publicly in all EC countries. The
consequences involved are critical, as they concern most of the
EC's financial wealth.

Given such huge stakes, it is understandable why national
governments feel so strongly about EC legislation concerning
financial markets. The countries where taxation of capital income is low (Luxembourg, the United Kingdom, and the EC
neighbor Switzerland) want to see "free competition among tax
systems." Naturally, the countries where capital income taxation
is higher (France, Italy, the Netherlands) are keen not to lose an
important source of revenue. Other countries that have not
made up their minds will become the eventual power brokers,

Table 12-1. Withholding Taxes on Dividend Income.

Paying Country	Recipient Country											
	Belgium	Denmark	France	Germany	Greece	Ireland	Italy	Luxem-bourg	Nether-lands	Portugal	Spain	United Kingdom
Belgium	–	15	10–15	15	15	15	15	10–15	5–15	15	15	15
Denmark	15	–	0	15	30	0	15	15	15	10	10	15
France	15	0	–	0	25	10–15	15	15–25	15	15	10	15
Germany	10–25	10–25	10–25	–	25	10–20	25	10–25	10–25	15	15	10–25
Greece	25	42–53	42–53	25	–	42–53	25	42–53	35	42–53	42–53	42–53
Ireland	0	0	0	0	0	–	0	0	0	0	0	0
Italy	15	15	15	30	25	15	–	15	0–30	15	15	5–15
Luxembourg	10–15	5–15	5–15	10–15	15	5–15	15	–	2.5–15	15	15	5–15
Netherlands	5–15	0–15	5–15	10–15	5–15	0–15	0	2.5–15	–	25	5	5–15
Portugal	12	10–12	12	12	12	12	12	12	12	–	10–12	10–12
Spain	15	10	10	10	18	18	15	18	10	10	–	10
United Kingdom	*	*	*	*	*	*	*	*	*	*	*	*

Source: Giovannini, 1989.

*For the UK, tax treaties have been renegotiated. No withholding taxes are normally levied on dividends. The exact treatment can vary depending on the type of treaty.

determining what direction the tax system(s) will follow (although the recent changing of Germany's position toward that of France, Italy, and the Netherlands might aid the latters' cause).

Three broad possibilities are conceivable. The first consists of a withholding tax of equal amounts uniformly applied in each country. This would immediately eliminate the problem of searching for tax havens, but it would simultaneously put EC financial markets in a position of competitive disadvantage vis-à-vis tax havens in non-EC countries. The tax treatment of capital income is an *international* rather than a European issue, which means that the EC countries are under external pressure to opt for minimal tax levels if their financial markets are to become competitive with those of world markets. The British experience following the abandonment of all capital controls in 1979 illustrates what may be in store for the rest of the EC.

The second solution would be to impose exhaustive reporting of capital income by every depositor to the fiscal agents in the country of residence. This would permit each country to apply whatever income taxes it wishes to its citizens' capital, avoiding any loss of revenue. In addition to the bureaucratic difficulties that would have to be overcome to ensure compliance, this solution also puts the EC countries at a competitive disadvantage vis-à-vis those countries that are not EC members and therefore would not be obliged to adhere to such a stringent reporting system.

The third solution is to abandon the taxation of capital income. Although this is the logical and perhaps predictable outcome if competition among tax systems is allowed, it would unfortunately make the postintegration community look like a capitalist's paradise. Such a prospect would undoubtedly lead to the political question of whether the efficiency gains from capital liberalization are worth the inequity between labor and capital income thus introduced. Obviously, the EC countries leaning toward socialism will resist the social implications of exempting capital income from taxation. On the other hand, competitive realities necessitate more liberal policies, posing a serious dilemma for European policymakers.

Monetary Integration

There is widespread agreement that the European monetary system (EMS) owes at least part of its success during its first
ten years to the existence of capital controls in countries whose
currencies have had a tendency to be devalued: France, Italy,
Belgium, and Denmark (Giovannini, 1989).The issue now is
whether capital controls are a necessary condition for continued success, if not the very survival of the EMS.

Threats to the EMS. Figure 12-1 shows interest rates on one-
month interbank deposits in French francs and Italian lire. For
each currency, two rates are shown: the local market rate and the
London rate. What is interesting is the divergence between the
two. If we accept that such a divergence cannot occur if operators are allowed to engage in arbitrage between local and
international markets, then the one appearing in Figure 12-1
can only be attributed to the work of controls. The fact that this
divergence occurs only sporadically can be explained by the fact
that capital controls are only effective occasionally, and most of
the time they are unable to prevent sizable movement of capital
into or out of the country. It is known that, with time, economic
agents can circumvent controls, as countries with convertible
currencies that open to trade cannot implement perfect restrictions on capital movement. More important, the evidence
suggests that controls discourage the entry of capital as much as
they do the exit of capital, even when they are specifically designed to prevent exit only. Thus, countries that impose controls
may find themselves at a disadvantage (having unwittingly dis-
couraged outside capital from entering their markets).
    The fact that a divergence between the two interest rates is
only seen during the weeks or months preceding an EMS realignment goes some way in explaining the crucial importance
of controls, even if their effect is temporary and/or imperfect.
The speculative attacks preceding EMS realignments are made
by operators fearing a loss on their capital holdings in the
currency to be devalued as they move their capital to a currency

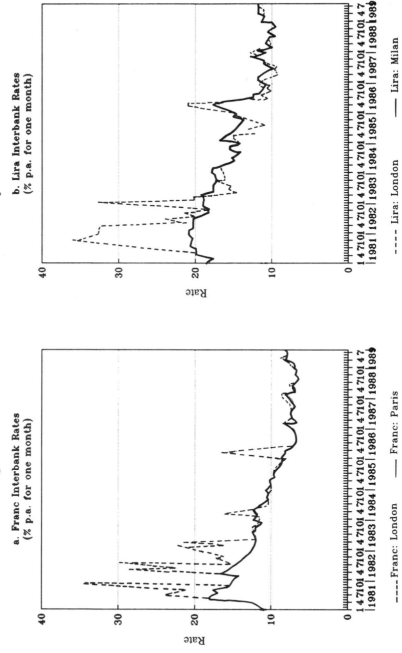

Figure 12-1. Interest Rates on One-Month Interbank Deposits.

Source: DRI-FACS data base.

to be appreciated. If there were no restrictions on capital motion, the size of such movements would be limitless and could theoretically lead to massive borrowing in, say, francs or lire in order to make short-term investments in, say, marks. Such borrowing would wipe out the foreign exchange reserves of the monetary authorities in France and Italy. As a result, any parity among the currencies would become indefensible and the EMS could, in fact, collapse.

Thus, restrictions to capital movements are aimed at protecting the very existence of the EMS during periods of realignment. The only other plausible scenario would be to let the local interest rates rise to the level of international rates. Indeed, as we see in Figure 12-1, London rates increase to the point where the yields fully offset the expected capital loss, which, on a per-annum basis and over a short period of time, amounts to spectacular rate increases. Monetary authorities in France and Italy are unwilling to let domestic rates rise to such levels for the sake of defending an exchange parity that is considered to be overvalued by the foreign exchange markets. The choice, then, is one of either relinquishing the parity or resorting to capital controls. The difficulty could be avoided altogether by eliminating realignments. However, in order for this to be a plausible solution, either a monetary union or a close, yet complex approximation in the form of complete harmonization of monetary policies across the countries of the EC would be essential.

If we accept that the liberalization of capital movements represents a serious threat for the EMS, a European monetary union becomes a logical and perhaps necessary option, even though it was in no way implied by the Single European Act. It is for this reason that the heads of the European states appointed the Delors Committee in 1988 to study the question of a European monetary union (EMU).

The EMU and the Delors Report. In discussions of a European monetary union, the question of national sovereignty is invariably raised. A monetary union exists de facto from the moment a number of countries undertake to establish irrevocably fixed parities for their respective currencies. In such a case, the question of whether the individual currencies retain different names makes no economic difference whatever. If a common currency is adopted, the important issue is the manner in which the union's monetary policies are determined and, even more important, the way in which the power to influence monetary policy is shared among the union's member countries. The sovereignty-based fear of "losing one's national currency" or the question of whether a central bank should be created are far less important. Interestingly enough, a recent Gallup Poll conducted among fifteen hundred top European executives for the Paris-based Association for the Monetary Union of Europe found that 83 percent were in favor of a common currency and a startling 76 percent believed that individual national currencies should eventually be phased out.

The key recommendation of the Delors Report is a three-stage strategy moving over time toward a full monetary union. A major aspiration of the report is for member countries to agree that a decision to accept stage 1 is a commitment to go all the way to stage 3.

Stage 1 requires, in addition to complete EC membership in the EMS (that is, the United Kingdom, Portugal, and Greece must join), the granting of outright independence for individual nations' central banks. Stage 2 is marked by the adoption of a new treaty permitting national transfer of monetary authority to a supranational body, the ESCB (European System of Central Banks), as well as the irrevocable locking of fixed parities among the currencies. The final stage moves to a position where the tasks normally performed by individual countries' central banks are taken over by the ESCB. (The Delors Committee was dominated by central bankers, which might explain the strong emphasis on independent monetary policies, first for national central banks and then for the ESCB.)

On the crucial point of when (or if) a monetary union will be achieved, the committee merely assumed that a monetary union was the ultimate goal (a view previously espoused in the Treaty of Rome and in just about every article written on 1992 since). Furthermore, the report remains surprisingly mute about how the ESCB would function. By rejecting the idea of a sole central bank, the report seems to advocate more of a U.S.-style federal banking system. Unfortunately, the committee's preoccupation with "cooperation" makes the report read more like an attempt to allay fear than a workable strategy aimed at creating a true European monetary union. The central problem of power sharing, by definition conflictual, is not really dealt with in the Delors Report.

In addition to being quite different in strategy from that used in the successful adoption of the Single European Act (in which vague political agreements came first, leaving the commission the delicate task of working out the details within the 1992 deadline), the decision to link stage 2 to the successful completion of a treaty and the transfer of power to the ESCB is one of the surest recipes for indefinite stalling. Thus, the committee's report successfully pushes the achievement of the ultimate goal (a monetary union) into the very distant future.

The full independence of central banks, crucial to stage 1, is a highly controversial political and economic issue. If central banks are to focus essentially on price stability in order to achieve lower rates of inflation, they must then ignore a wider range of concerns dealing with overall economic performance, including growth, public debt, unemployment, and productivity. Thus, several policymakers see European central banks independent of EC governments as absolutely inconceivable. By advocating a federal solution, the committee tries to evade the issue of how individual governments can influence monetary policies and in so doing achieve objectives other than simply lowering inflation (higher growth rates, lower unemployment, and so on). At the same time, it must be said that the federal banking system in the United States seems to succeed in achieving both strong growth and a low inflation rate.

The European Monetary System After Integration. With capital movements free since July 1, 1990, and supposing that the Delors Report is dutifully adhered to, the transition period before the institution of a monetary union is likely to be very lengthy. First, it cannot be taken for granted that the EMS will survive a period of great flux. Some steps will have to be taken to protect the existing system that has thus far proven to be a considerable success.

Despite early pessimism, the EMS has succeeded in stabilizing exchange rates among member countries at a time when those of countries not in the EMS became considerably more volatile (see Figure 12-2). The EMS must be credited with having had a strong disciplinary effect on member countries, some of which have a reputation for being less than prudent in their choice of monetary and fiscal policies. The unit of account, the ECU, has won public approval and even turned out to be a reasonable success with the banks. Moreover, the inflation rates of member countries have dropped well below those of the pre-EMS era.

The performance of the EMS has not been entirely flawless. First and foremost, the growth performance of EMS countries (see Table 12-2) has been rather disappointing. Even though one can always cite the second oil shock of the late 1970s in defense, the countries adhering to the EMS were not alone in facing this period of turbulence. One explanation for the low growth might have nothing to do with the EMS, but with the fact that the EMS member countries are characterized by particularly rigid labor markets. If we accept that labor market flexibility is a key factor in sustaining economic growth during periods

Table 12-2. Growth and Inflation (Percentage per Year).

	Bel-gium	Ger-many	Den-mark	France	Italy	Nether-lands	U.K.	Spain	United States	Japan
GDP growth: annual averages										
1970–1980	3.2	2.2	2.7	3.6	3.1	2.9	1.9	2.1	2.7	4.6
1981–1987	1.0	1.1	1.5	1.3	2.1	1.1	2.4	1.9	2.7	3.9
Inflation rates (GDP deflator)										
1980	3.8	8.2	4.8	12.2	20.6	5.7	19.7	9.5	9.0	3.8
1987	2.1	4.6	1.9	3.3	5.5	–1.0	4.0	4.5	3.3	0.7

Source: European Economy, Nov. 1987, 34; OECD, Economic Outlook.

Figure 12-2. Exchange Rate Variability
(Standard Deviation of Monthly Change).

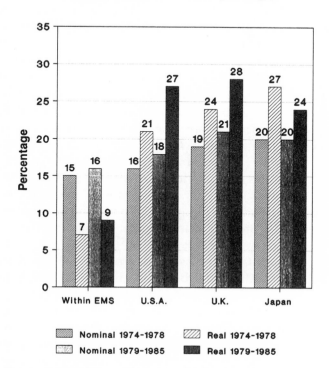

Source: Adapted from Ungerer and others, 1986.

of disinflation or external shocks like the oil crisis, then the above-mentioned rigid labor markets could explain the lackluster growth. This is not the case with non-EMS countries, which enjoy labor institutions providing important flexibility advantages (Giavazzi and Giovannini, 1989).

An alternative view postulates more than just bad luck as the critical factor for explaining low growth rates. Theoretically, all EMS currencies were supposed to have equal importance. In reality, it is clear that the German mark has enjoyed a degree of preeminence, raising claims that the EMS is merely a DM zone. The evidence in favor of this interpretation can be inferred from observing exchange market interventions, statistical stud-

ies of monetary policy instruments, and the behavior of interest
rates during realignment periods (Wyplosz, 1986). Two main
explanations have been offered. The first is that countries with a
track record of high inflation (such as France and Italy) have
willfully decided to follow the German stance in order to appear
to be uncompromising inflation fighters (Giavazzi and Giovannini, 1989). The second explanation is based on the idea that in
any fixed exchange rate system, inflation rates tend to converge
toward the lowest common denominator. Thus, countries facing
higher inflation occasionally need to depreciate their currencies; however, the speculative attacks that unfold in anticipation
of currency depreciations dry out exchange reserves and put
their central banks in a position of weakness. This reduces their
influence relative to the countries whose currencies are not
depreciated and has forced upon them the German preference
of systematically preferring low growth to high inflation.

The Options. One thing should be clear: the EMS may enter
a period of fragility and potential instability. Without the
cushioning protection of capital controls, realignments could
become sweeping events. Two main options are open: The first
one is to ban realignments altogether. The second one is to
reform the EMS. Failing to adopt one or the other of these
diametrically opposed solutions may require reinforcing capital controls through some alternative route.

Among EMS countries, banning realignments is only possible if inflation rates converge fully. This immediately raises the
question of what the reference inflation rate should be. Put
differently, whose inflation rate should be the one toward which
all other countries converge? Unless there is an explicit agreement, the chances are that there will be an automatic convergence toward the lowest inflation rate. All countries will end
up on a de facto DM standard, much as is already the case for the
Netherlands.

The alternative to the "Dutch solution" is an early move
toward a monetary union with a joint central bank of a federal
nature. The arguments are obvious. In a central bank setting, the
more inflationary countries (traditionally, France, Italy, and

Spain) would have a say on monetary policies, which could then be geared more toward growth objectives. Thus, Germany's power would be diluted. Clearly, there is little incentive for Germany to agree to such a power-sharing arrangement. The staunch opposition of Thatcher, whose country would have had the most benefit from a unified monetary system acting to lower the high inflation rates experienced in the United Kingdom, paradoxically prevented more monetary integration. Moreover, unless the British opposition changes, we may well see a "two-speed Europe" as far as monetary union is concerned.

The alternative solution is to amend the EMS to make realignments possible without capital controls. This could be done by allowing realignments to occur without discrete jumps in exchange rates. The idea is to arrange things in such a way that a realignment becomes a change in the central parity, leaving the actual exchange rate level virtually unchanged. This is possible when the newly established parity falls within the margins of fluctuations allowed by the previous parity. For ex-pample, the Italian lira could be at the low end of its margin before the realignment and then find itself at the top end of the new margin without actually moving at all. To make this system work, it would be necessary to have either more frequent and smaller realignments (a sort of crawling peg) or wider margins of fluctuation, or both. However, this "soft" EMS solution does not tackle the strong position of the DM. Sooner or later frustra-tions with weaker currencies can emerge on the part of member countries, which will demand more equality. (The Basle-Nyborg agreements of September 1987 have taken some initial steps in this direction, which could be further elaborated as part of the Delors plan—leading to monetary integration of EC countries.)

Fiscal Policies

From the preceding discussion, it should be clear that the independence of national monetary policy will be reduced once capital controls are removed. This will make the other stabiliza-tion instrument traditionally used by governments—fiscal pol-icy—more indispensable, meaning that governments may be forced to use fiscal policy more vigorously, for two reasons. First, they will have no alternative instrument once monetary policy is lost. Second, the enhanced credibility offered by the loss of monetary independence will eventually allow them to borrow more easily to finance their budget deficits. Alternatively, fiscal policy may tend to be more restrained because financial markets will impose discipline on reckless borrowers. When the public debt grows at present, the interest rate rises in the country involved. Once currencies become close substitutes for one another, the interest risk will spare private borrowers and become government-specific. In addition, treasuries will not be able to call upon their central banks for financing. The central bankers of the Delors Committee do not believe in the disciplinary effects of financial markets, as they suggest the establishment of deficit ceilings to balance the loss of ability of EC governments to determine their own monetary policy.

Fiscal Policy Implications of Monetary Integration. A main objection to monetary integration is that, should a country be subject to an adverse shock, such as increased production costs, the removal of exchange rates as a policy tool may be crippling. Given that such shocks do occur, a formulated process that will render them painless enough to avoid a breakup of the very ideas that integration means to foster is needed. The EC Commission proposes to combat this very problem through the implementation of "regional policies." Unfortunately, skeptics view these regional policies as resembling rather too much the ill-reputed Common Agricultural Policies. A better way to achieve administrative redistribution (which usually falls prey to organized interests) is an EC-wide insurance system targeted at individuals, not nations, much as the United States handles cases of regional distress (Calmfors and Driffil, 1988).

Ideas as to what to do and how to do so are not in short supply (Sachs and Sal-i-Martin, 1989). The problem is essentially political, however (and also highly symbolic). In order for regional policies to operate effectively, they must be sufficiently justified to quash complaints from other national governments that they give more than they get. The solution may lie in mixing redistribution policy with other budgetary functions. What is really involved here is nothing less than the early stages of a federal budget. Just as the liberalization of capital movement will create pressure for monetary integration, monetary integration will bring fiscal federalism to the forefront.

Capital flow liberalization also brings up the issue of tax harmonization. We have shown that the mobility of assets will make it impossible to retain widely different rates of taxation on capital income and that eventually these taxes will have to become harmonized. But changing certain taxes cannot be done in isolation. There will be a need to compensate with increases elsewhere—unless, of course, public spending is reduced at the same time, a desirable but unlikely prospect. Reducing public spending is so difficult, politically speaking, that even entertaining such an idea at all seriously is wishful thinking. Thus, what is most likely to happen is real pressure for fiscal reform coming from within each EC country. Moreover, there will also be pressure to harmonize tax rates on noncapital income in order to avoid movements of firms and individuals toward countries with lower tax rates.

Conclusion

In this chapter we have shown how the liberalization of capital movements might harm the EMS and slow down Europe's march toward full economic integration. More distant in time but probably more considerable in impact are the implications of a federal budget (making Brussels the real center of power) and the possibility of a harmonized tax system.

Because of their complexity and the potential they present for disagreement, the range of issues involved is dizzying. When the heads of state approved the Single European Act in 1985, they did not fully grasp the implications thereof, particularly those concerning the removal of all restrictions on capital movements. The irony is that there is still little indication that the member governments fully understand the implications even now. If insufficient progress is made in time, one distinct possibility is that European integration will gently slide into an early phase of euphoria where assets are painlessly redistributed among financial centers with no real economic benefits what-ever. Later on, as tension appears (for example, an increasing external surplus in Germany, matched by a deepening deficit in Italy, Spain, or France), certain countries will either adopt a de facto DM standard (the Dutch solution), reinstate capital con-trols, or, alternatively, break away from the EMS. Fortunately, there are less dramatic alternatives — for one, a reform of the EMS to make it both "softer" and more equitable to the various EC member states. In addition, all EC countries must be given a more equal voice in determining overall monetary policy, as such policy affects their own economic well-being.

References

Calmfors, L., and Driffil, J. "Bargaining Structure, Corporatism and Macroeconomic Performance." *Economic Policy*, Apr. 1988, *6*, 13–62.

Giavazzi, F., and Giovannini, A. *Limiting Exchange Rate Flexibility: The European Monetary System.* Cambridge, Mass.: MIT Press, 1989.

Giovannini, A. "National Tax Systems vs. the European Capital Market." *Economic Policy*, 1989, *9*, 345–386.

Neven, D. "Structural Adjustment in European Retail Banking Industry: Some Views from Industrial Organisation." In J. Dermine and I. Walter (eds.), *European Banking in the 90's.* Oxford, England: Basil Blackwell, 1990.

Sachs, J., and Sal-i-Martin, X. "Federal Fiscal Policy and Opti-mum Currency Areas." Unpublished manuscript, Economics Department, Harvard University, 1989.

Wyplosz, C. "Capital Controls and Balance of Payments Crises." *Journal of International Money and Finance*, 1986, *5*, 167–179.

CHAPTER 13

Integrating and Legislating Rapid Changes in the Financial Services Industry

Gabriel Hawawini, Eric J. Rajendra

A consensus has emerged among financial experts: first, we are witnessing a historically unparalleled transformation of the European financial services industry; second, the complete integration of Europe's fragmented financial markets will take longer to achieve than the morning of January 1, 1993. In other words, a long, complex, but irreversible process of change is unfolding across European financial markets.

This chapter examines the evolution and transformation of the financial sector in EC countries and evaluates the effects of various changes on European users and providers of financial products and services. The analysis focuses on the two most vital subsectors of activity for borrowers and investors: banking and securities markets.

Note: The key analyses and arguments presented in this chapter are given a more detailed treatment in a work entitled *The Transformation of the European Financial Services Industry: From Fragmentation to Integration*, coauthored by Gabriel Hawawini and Eric Rajendra, and published as a monograph (1989) by the Salomon Brothers Center for the Study of Financial Institutions of the Graduate School of Business Administration, New York University.

The Forces Driving European Financial Integration

A popular view holds that the integration of European financial markets was simply dictated into existence by various legislative measures of the European Commission in Brussels over the past three decades. Indeed, the 1957 Treaty of Rome clearly stated the desire to create a customs union among the signatories, which for the financial sector meant freedom of establishment, provision of services, and capital movements. This view presumes that the transformation of European financial markets has followed some neat timetable that has eliminated divergent financial regulations and structures in the various segmented national markets.

The historical realities of European financial integration show a rather different picture—one of fits and starts, and numerous obstacles based on national political interests and fear of ceding or sharing economic and financial control in individual EC markets. This is illustrated by the numerous chicken-and-egg arguments expounded: true financial integration cannot be realized unless monetary union is established first; monetary union is impossible without a convergence of national economic and monetary policies; national economic and monetary policies cannot be achieved without some form of political union. Each argument raised new debates and pushed further into the background the possibility of achieving any form of financial integration.

This rather bleak scenario changed dramatically in the last decade for the following reasons:

1. *Rising economic interdependence.* As European cross-border trade, investment, and capital flows increased, the need for greater harmonization of divergent national financial regulations became more evident. Europe increasingly came to view itself as an economic bloc whose state of economic and financial fragmentation was perceived to be a handicap resulting in lower productivity and lesser economic efficiency vis-à-vis the integrated markets of the United States and Japan.

2.   *Fallout from global financial deregulation.* The U.S. and Japanese deregulation in financial services that took place from the mid-1970s onward had a strong ripple effect on the major European financial centers, especially London. Fears of rising competition from American and Japanese institutions armed with skills gained in more liberal and competitive markets had the effect of promoting the calls for European deregulation. Although the United Kingdom led the process, other European countries quickly followed so as not to be left behind.

3.   *Increasing technological progress and applications.* Technology had a twofold effect on the European financial sector. First, it enabled nonregulated firms to provide financial services at a lower cost than established firms (for example, over-the-counter markets in securities and nonbank consumer credit firms). This phenomenon brought about competitive distortions that led, for all practical purposes, to effective deregulation. Similarly, the use of technology by securities firms in New York to service British investors was a major factor undermining the self-imposed regulation of the London Stock Exchange. Second, advancements in telecommunications and decision-support systems for trading, investing, and transaction data processing have had the tangible effect of integrating banking and securities markets across Europe.

4.   *Modification of the EC legislative processes.* The June 1985 publication of the White Paper on the creation of a unified European market greatly altered the consensus approach that existed among European commissioners in the legislative area of financial integration. Instead of waiting for thousands of national regulations and practices to be perfectly harmonized, they opted for a "dynamic disequilibria" approach whereby a certain level of healthy market "confusion" was to be permitted. This fundamental change in philosophy resulted in: harmonization of the most basic rules in the provision of financial services, mutual recognition of each member country's supervisory criteria, and

home-country supervision of the foreign activities of financial institutions.

As the process of transformation toward European financial integration accelerates, two questions are frequently raised: What are the potential benefits of financial integration? Can they be estimated in any tangible fashion?

Numerous academic and nonacademic studies (Hasse, 1988) have been undertaken to answer the first question. The perceived benefits can be summarized as follows: an improvement in the allocating efficiency of savings and investments; a pooling of national capital markets within the EC, lowering its dependence on extra-EC financial centers (and hence reducing its shock-sensitivity to external economic developments); a reduction in the risk of capital investments through increased diversification opportunities (true for both investors and financial intermediaries); the lowering of the cost of funding for borrowers as they diversify their sources of funds in an increasingly competitive financial environment; and the fostering of stronger (and potentially larger) financial institutions to compete with global giants from the United States and Japan.

The second question was answered in a study commissioned by the EC and executed by Price Waterhouse in 1988 to evaluate the opportunity cost of *not* having a financially integrated Europe. Although the study covered only eight countries and has been criticized for several key methodological shortcomings, it nevertheless serves a vital purpose as an illustrative example of the differences in prices for financial products and services (banking, securities, and insurance) across eight EC countries. The theoretical percentage price reductions of financial integration at the EC level are shown in Table 13-1.

Potential percentage price reductions are indicated for all eight countries and in three subsectors, with a range of 9 percent to 34 percent for the three subsectors taken together. Adjusted for the possibility that the European markets may not become perfectly competitive and integrated soon, more realistic percentage price reductions in the range of 4 percent to 21 percent were estimated (see Table 13-2).

Table 13-1. Theoretical Potential Price Reduction Resulting from Complete European Financial Integration.

	Belgium	Germany	Spain	France	Italy	Luxem- bourg	Nether- lands	United Kingdom
Banking	15%	33%	34%	25%	18%	16%	10%	18%
Insurance	31	10	32	24	51	37	1	4
Securities	52	11	44	23	33	9	18	12
Total	23	25	34	24	29	17	9	13

Source: Commission of the European Communities, 1988.

Across all subsectors, Spain and Italy show the greatest potential for price reduction, with the United Kingdom and the Netherlands proving to be already quite price-competitive. The remaining countries are in between these two extremes.

The most revealing nature of these estimations is not in the total figures for all financial services or even those of each subsector, but in specific product lines. For instance, Germany, relatively efficient in private equity transactions, seems to be leading Europe in inefficiency in consumer credit. Similarly, the United Kingdom, extremely efficient in institutional securities trading, is highly inefficient in private equity transactions, home insurance, and consumer credit.

Hence, from a retail or corporate consumer's standpoint, the benefits of an integrated Europe in financial services will be seen in different product categories, different subsectors, and different countries. The challenge for intermediaries will be to

Table 13-2. More Realistic Percentage Price Reduction in All Financial Services Resulting from Financial Integration.

	Belgium	Germany	Spain	France	Italy	Luxem- bourg	Nether- lands	United Kingdom
Spread	6–15%	5–15%	16–26%	7–17%	9–19%	3–13%	0–9%	2–12%
Center of spread	11	10	21	12	14	8	4	7

Source: Commission of the European Communities, 1988.

understand the existing inefficiencies, exploit the opportunities, formulate strategies that capitalize on micro-skills
(often at the product or functional level), and execute these
differentiated strategies on a Europe-wide basis.

Current Regulatory Barriers and EC Legislative Efforts

The obstacles to making truly pan-European banking or
securities strategies as discussed above lie in a differing mix of
direct and indirect barriers that exist in each EC country for
each of these financial sectors.

In the banking industry, for example, most EC countries
do not have visible barriers designed to favor domestic versus
foreign participants. Instead, one has to look to the various
practices that each country applies equitably to all participants
within its borders: capital controls, limits on equity participa-
tions in corporations, solvency and capital requirements, limits
on paying market interest rates on certain types of deposits,
restrictions on securities transactions, differences in tax treatment of interest and dividend income, and varying bank secrecy
laws.

On the other hand, in the securities industry, participants
are burdened not only with indirect barriers (in the form of
different practices and standards in each country), but also with
certain important direct barriers: regulations in certain national exchanges, which prevent foreigners from being licensed
as brokers; and limitations in some countries on the holding of
foreign securities by national pension funds and insurance
companies. In addition, of course, participants in some countries have had to contend with still lingering exchange controls
making multicountry portfolio investing extremely difficult. Or,
in the case of Germany and Belgium, participants wishing to
provide securities trading had first to obtain a full banking
license and offer a full range of services.

The EC is attempting to harmonize away these numerous
regulatory barriers and local practices, using the philosophy of
dynamic disequilibria discussed above. In practice, the situation

has spawned several key directives in both the banking and the securities sectors.

The Capital Movements Directive of 1988 (an extension of a 1986 directive) is common to both the above-mentioned sectors and can be viewed as a foundation directive. It enables free capital flows of all types and lays the groundwork for two other key directives, the Second Banking Directive and the Investment Services Directive, which, if achieved in entirety, will result in an integrated European financial market.

The latter two directives are supplemented by approximately twenty directives, which as a whole attempt to harmonize the most glaring differences among the EC countries. They push through the rather revolutionary notions that each country should recognize the other countries' supervisory criteria and that financial intermediaries properly registered in one country should be able to offer their services across the EC while being supervised by their designated home country.

Assessing the likelihood of success of these directives is at best a difficult task: numerous country-specific factors mix, both for and against financial integration. Nevertheless, certain guarded comments may be made and some outcomes anticipated.

First, despite historically based national dislikes for releasing full control of national money supplies, strong pressure from investors (private, corporate, and institutional) and financial intermediaries will probably result in the realization of the directive on capital movements. In fact, as integration progresses, countries that resist full liberalization of capital movements may in reality find themselves faced with hidden outflows.

Second, most of the directives on harmonizing banking and securities markets' rules, definitions, and standards will probably be realized and enforced within the next three to ten years (given the present situation in some of the newer member countries). In the case of the banking industry, these efforts are often part of a larger framework of international harmonization of standards (such as the Bank for International Settlement, bilateral central bank agreements, and the Organization for Economic and Cooperative Development [OECD]). In the securities industry, the growing use of standard technology applications frequently serves as an automatic harmonizer of disparate standards.

In both industries, there is no intrinsic national resistance to the creation, at least in theory, of a level European playing ground via these harmonizations. Yet some harmonization directives could prove to be difficult to enforce.

In the securities field, for instance, in order to realize the directive stipulating disclosure of large shareholdings, a certain level of honesty on the part of the shareholder will need to be relied upon, especially in those countries where bearer securities are cleared electronically. And the directive controlling insider trading, despite efforts to define the term, will in all probability result in monitoring nightmares unless the EC creates a strong-arm agency (like the Securities and Exchange Commission in the United States) with a mandate to monitor compliance across European equity markets.

In the banking arena, the Second Banking Directive may prove to be quite controversial. Numerous issues could cause conflict during negotiation or enforcement—for example, limits on bank equity participation in nonfinancial businesses, the practical split of supervision by home and host authorities, and the level of freedom to be given to non-EC institutions.

In a nutshell, we can be fairly confident in saying that, while the major directives under proposal in the financial sector will be approved in some form or another, the true test of their success (that is, their enforcement in each EC country) will take place in a checkered fashion for at least five to ten years after integration.

Strategic Implications of an Integrated European Financial Market for Major Participants

Numerous economic, technological, political, and even global factors of varying importance converge at different speeds to influence the integration of European financial markets. The key strategic implications of such influences for the various participants in an increasingly integrated European financial services industry are discussed in the remainder of this chapter.

European Financial Services. Up until the mid-1970s, European financial intermediaries assumed rather specialized roles that were created by national and international financial deregulation and market competition in each country. Due to market saturation in core banking businesses, however, banks have subsequently turned to diversification of products, services, and customer segments.

The initial effect of this continued diversification drive will be a downward pressure on product margins as competition intensifies. As margins in these new areas are squeezed and the subsidization of losses from the slim-margin traditional business becomes impossible, only the most innovative or highly efficient small banks will survive. Unless such banks focus their managerial effort in certain market niches (such as a strategy of "offer all things to some people," or vice versa), they will find the demands of multibusiness management in banking too complex and too costly in terms of attracting the necessary trained management.

The excessive competitiveness of this environment is being exacerbated not only by the appearance of new nonfinancial entrants (such as retailers and industrial company financial subsidiaries) but also by the EC legislation in the financial area. The shakeout of this process is already leading to national consolidation of participants (either through mergers and acquisitions of entire banks or through the sale of individual nonstrategic business units).

On the European level, balance-sheet type consolidation will probably not take place until nearer to integration and may even continue well beyond that. In the meantime, the larger European banks may opt for strategic alliances (ranging from vaguely defined versions to very specific joint business developments in a particular product or client segment), while the smaller banks may seek to be acquired by larger foreign banks. Interestingly, to date very few banks (regardless of size) have deliberately taken a truly pan-European approach: most have contented themselves with a wait-and-see strategy to deal with the "integration question," while pursuing an active defense strategy for their home market positions.

We argue that three generic bank types will prevail, with differing levels of success: pan-European universal banks, pan-European specialized banks, and large national universal banks. For competitive reasons, it is unlikely that many smaller national specialized banks will survive beyond the middle 1990s.

There is room for only a handful of pan-European universal banks offering full services in most EC countries. Successful players in this group will need to develop numerous skills that center on the management of complex banking institutions. Success will be determined, in part, by those institutions that innovate and perfect a product or client business system within *any* given national market (not necessarily the home market) and quickly tailor and transfer the approach to each of the other national markets (in other words, innovation should be encouraged). This would require decentralization of managerial control downward to each country or region.

The pan-European specialized banks could be those that take either a product-group focus or a client-segment focus. While their managerial task is made somewhat easier by the fact that they are not burdened with a complex matrix of products, clients, and countries, they also have less ability to rely on the profits of one business area to support another during lean years. Nevertheless, their very focus is also their competitive advantage, giving them flexibility in reacting to changes in the demands of their end-clients. Additionally, a European field of operations will enable them to build economies of scale and diversify their business risk. The skills necessary for this group will include all of those cited above for pan-European universal banks, but, in addition, they will need the strategic skill of choosing the right segment and defining its characteristics and parameters. Moreover, they will need to fight the natural tendency of most specialized institutions to start diversifying in response to competition instead of further improving operational efficiencies.

As pan-European universal and specialized banks will be utilizing their respective competitive advantages to enter local markets, large national banks will find life extremely competitive. The potential strengths of large national banks are their typically vast branch networks and loyal clientele. Capitalizing on these advantages will require a separation of the strategies that need to be developed for the retail and wholesale client sectors. On the retail side, essential skills will include managing individual branch profitability through micro-marketing techniques (which the other two banking groups may not be able to afford to undertake) and managing product offering that captures cross-selling opportunities without increasing fixed costs excessively. On the wholesale side (corporate and institutional clients), large national banks may find it advantageous to collaborate with players from the first two groups by focusing on certain aspects of the business system (for example, funding and marketing instead of new product development or off-loading of paper in secondary markets).

The European Retail Consumer. One of the major outcomes of EC legislative reforms should be the proliferation of new products and services across Europe offered not just by local banks and securities brokers but by other European institutions. The ability to offer services throughout the EC with only one license will result in European financial institutions trying nontraditional marketing channels, often based in their home country. Coupled with this, the freedom of capital movements will give retail consumers greater mobility in their borrowing and investing practices.

If European financial integration is achieved on schedule, the following should be an altogether realistic scenario in retail banking in the 1990s. An Italian office worker in Milan uses a local national bank for his current account needs; takes a low-interest-rate Deutschmark mortgage loan from a British building society marketing out of Madrid, which also sells him an exchange-rate coverage; places his savings in ECUs with a German universal bank based in Luxembourg; and purchases lira-denominated variable life insurance from a Dutch company, by mail from its Rome office.

That this will be the scenario for the average individual may be highly improbable. Therefore, although we observed in our discussion on potential price reductions in financial services that consumers stand to gain *on average* in terms of lower borrowing costs and higher investment returns, this remark needs to be qualified. Hence, our hypothesis that European financial integration should disproportionately benefit the financially sophisticated individual who can see the checkerboard pattern of individual product cost differentials across Europe and selectively "shop around" for the best price-value mix.

There are many pitfalls involved in pan-European shopping, requiring the development of new skills. National consumer protection legislation may diminish as home country supervision becomes the guiding rule. When accounting rules become more standardized, foreign intermediaries may publish financial statements in a limited number of languages, hence making risk assessment more difficult for some. The first five postintegration years may turn out to be a somewhat volatile period, as financial intermediaries go in (and out) of new businesses and markets. This will make client commitment to, and reliance on, any one institution difficult to sustain.

Assuming that progress toward unified monetary and fiscal policies may take us well into the next century, European retail equity and bond investors will have to contend with evaluating various currency risks, general economic risks, and industry-specific market risks before embarking on a pan-European investment strategy, which for reasons discussed below should become easier.

The European Corporate Client. European companies are beginning to explore nonbank sources of funding. Domestic bond and equity markets are becoming vibrant, and national and international deregulatory tendencies are jolting both national exchanges (which fear foreign and over-the-counter market competition) and domestic brokers into modernizing their infrastructures and operating practices in order to build more efficient markets. Encouraging this process are the various EC legislative reforms that will allow intermediaries to operate freely across all EC markets. For corporate managers, these developments have opened a whole new choice of financing options that were unavailable in the past for all but a few large corporations.

While the government sector currently dominates most national bond markets, and tapping the Eurobond markets is still the prerogative of large and well-known companies, a number of factors point to a widening of the domestic corporate bond markets. These factors include the future ability of banks to underwrite and trade corporate bonds (as universal banks), the trend toward increased merger-and-acquisition activities in general and leveraged buyout (LBO) activities more specifically, and a potentially greater demand from Europe's growing institutional funds for higher-return corporate bond paper over domestic government paper.

Likewise, various factors are expected to push the use of European equity financing, including privatization programs, off-loading of universal banks' equity holdings in light of possible EC requirements, the future ability of brokers to trade for their own account, and the growing awareness of equity risk and consequent demand for equity paper among retail and institutional investors for diversification purposes.

European equity exchanges, especially in the major financial centers, are rapidly modernizing their infrastructures and self-liberalizing in order to be viewed as operationally efficient by corporations and investors alike. Rules and practices on exchange membership, transaction commissions, and clearing and settlement systems are being streamlined and slowly standardized at a Europe-wide level.

Whereas even the large European companies will gain from these improvements in the functioning of securities markets, it is especially the small- and middle-market companies (traditionally neglected by the banks) that will reap the most benefits. In addition, the small- and middle-market companies have had little hope of being nurtured by the securities houses, which are prohibited until integration from holding and trading securities for their own account in most European countries. Faced with the reluctance of investors to hold small corporate paper, the securities houses had no motivation for putting much effort into this sector.

The situation should change for several reasons. In addition to the improvements in securities market conditions discussed above, we must mention the changing nature of competition for corporate business. With the advent of universal banking, well-capitalized commercial banks will start competing with brokers on the upper end of the corporate market to underwrite and make secondary markets in their shares either on or off the exchanges. Most of this action will take place among a handful of players and is expected to gravitate toward the key financial centers of Europe, with London predominating. The vast majority of European banks and brokers should then begin to focus their attention on understanding the credit and equity risks of middle-size companies, proposing tailored financing packages to them (that should include an open-market securities portion), literally growing the relationship.

Success in serving these nontraditional corporate financial needs will not be easy for most banks or brokers. New skills, sophisticated integrated systems, and a highly flexible, yet integrated organizational framework are needed. For instance, pan-European intermediaries wishing to tap small and middle-size companies will need to build credible research capabilities through acquisition, internal development, or strategic alliances with research houses in multiple European countries. In addition, intermediaries will have to integrate their operating systems and tailor their organizational and business systems approach to the client segments they are targeting. For a universal financial intermediary, an integrated one (from origination to distribution) may be advantageous for the middle market, but will be extremely costly for the upper end of the size category of companies. On the other hand, focused intermediaries, say, brokers, specializing throughout Europe in certain industry categories may find it cost-effective to serve across the business system, across the size spectrum, and across countries, provided that operating scale and synergies are achieved.

European Institutional Investors. The primary impetus to the growing importance of European institutional investors is derived from the continued development of mutual and pension funds. At the time of writing, the European mutual funds market was estimated at over 420 billion ECUs and further growth is expected from both the retail and the institutional sides, seeking higher returns without forgoing too much liquidity. European pension funds are rapidly shifting from a redistribution system to a capitalization system. In the former, contributions made by individuals currently working are immediately redistributed to current pensioners, whereas, in the latter, funds collected from individuals are invested for future distribution according to certain investment criteria. The effect of this trend will be to increase the current size of funded pensions.

As the funds grow in size, the institutions that manage them will increasingly play a greater role in molding the evolution of securities markets. Typically, institutional market participants transact in vast quantities of securities. Hence, they will have larger effects on price movements in any individual securities market, especially those with limited depth (that is, liquidity). This implies in turn that these institutional investors will tend to gravitate their transactions toward those financial centers where they can take an active approach to managing their large portfolios rather than in those where they are forced to take a "buy and hold" attitude. In addition to the importance of liquidity, these institutional investors will naturally favor those financial centers where trading information is readily accessible, intermediaries are cost-effective, and settlement and clearing processes are efficient.

As the funds grow in size, we can also expect their composition to be enriched by national and EC reforms. For example, EC directives enabling free movement of capital and Europe-wide offering of financial sevices will make it extremely difficult (in some ways practically impossible) for governments to dictate the composition of pension funds (as, for instance, insisting that certain percentages be kept in government paper). In addition, the managers of these funds should be increasingly pressured by their end-investors to produce superior results. This may force many institutional fund managers to enhance the risk-return profile by adopting more sophisticated and research-intensive portfolio management strategies, which may be viewed increasingly on a European basis (Hawawini and Jacquillat, 1989).

Several factors will aid this pan-Europeanization trend. The sheer size of the institutional funds will lead them quickly to outgrow their traditional home markets, which can no longer provide the rich portfolio mixes that would be possible on a pan-European basis. As European institutional investors grow and become more sophisticated in their investment strategies, it goes without saying that financial intermediaries will rapidly need to develop strategies that meet the requirements of these investors. As institutional investors trade in large blocks of securities, they will favor intermediaries who can serve as dealers (those with an ability to position securities for their own books) over simple brokers (those who trade only on behalf of customer orders). This, in turn, has significant implications for the capitalization of European brokers. While EC reforms will enable them to position for their own account, they will also set guidelines for capital requirements for various types of instruments. Currently, brokers are thinly capitalized in many countries. Hence, we may witness increased levels of acquisitions of such brokers by major well-capitalized banks wanting to develop their capital markets business.

We stressed the importance that institutional investors will place on excellent research and market information, increasingly so on a Europe-wide basis. In other words, successful intermediaries will be extensively called upon for their informational capability (that is, their knowledge of who the buyers and sellers are), in addition to their execution capability. This implies that purely national brokers and dealers may need either to develop or to acquire these capabilities in other EC countries, or to develop strategic alliances with other players in the form of a clearly defined consortium. Pan-European universal banks may opt to offer services across the institutional investment business system (from in-house research in each country to active secondary market–making in all major EC markets). Others may choose to specialize in one aspect of the business system, but on a European basis (such as research capabilities in each of the twelve countries, tightly integrated by sophisticated telecommunications networks).

The Role of National Governments in Influencing Security Markets. Government ownership of banks is still extensive in many European countries. Primary domestic bond markets are generally dominated by the state and quasi-state sectors. Many governments still impose investment criteria for insurance or pension funds that emphasize the holding of government securities. Governments in certain European states continue to control the criteria by which intermediaries (especially foreign) could enter and participate in domestic capital markets. And, last but not least, until recently many governments tightly imposed controls on private capital movements.

The situation described above is rapidly changing. Privatization programs are increasing in popularity as deficit-ridden governments successfully tap the relatively buoyant equity markets. Although the government role in domestic bond markets will continue to be paramount, we expect an increase in the corporate share of the primary market, especially arising from an increase in bond issuance from corporate restructuring. In addition, EC reforms concerning freedom and capital movements, and freedom to establish and offer products and services, should also diminish the current importance of governments in the financial markets.

As the role of European governments in national financial markets continues to wane over the next decade, governments may have to progressively view themselves as competitors for capital with other borrowers. In addition, European financial integration implies a more holistic view of national monetary management, one that is indeed more European in perspective.

Without the captive investors discussed above and without the ability to impose capital controls, the creditworthiness of governments will increasingly be judged by national investors in a way similar to that by which local corporations are evaluated. Governments are used to this scrutiny and investment evaluation at the international level of fund-raising (for example, in the London syndicated loan market). But most are barely prepared for local investors to start to regard them as one of many investment options. Governments will also need to understand the buying criteria of retail and institutional investors and begin to tailor their instruments to these preferences. For many, this may mean a radical change of mentality from the days when whatever they chose to issue in whatever period of the year was simply absorbed by investors who had limited alternative investment opportunities.

In a financially integrated Europe, monetary management will become exposed more and more to external factors frequently beyond the control of the national government. For certain countries with excessive deficit financing, interest rates may have to rise as the capital markets equilibrate themselves in terms of capital allocation with a European perspective. And in the postintegration era the significant players in national markets may often be nonlocal, with no particular vested interest in buying specific amounts of government paper in order to be on good terms with the respective authorities.

Related to the diminishing profile of European governments in an integrating financial market, national governments will systematically need to consider Europe as the national market when evaluating the impacts of regional macroeconomic policies on their region's financial system. In other words, national debt financing can no longer be viewed from a local perspective. To give an example, movements in Italian money supply should trickle through the various European capital markets more rapidly than in the past and have repercussions on Danish and Belgian government financing patterns. National governments will find that what was once a locally manageable concern becomes far more intertwined with the actions and reactions of other EC states. In turn, this implies the need for greater skills in European-level negotiation and coordination of monetary and fiscal policies.

The Two-Tiered Structure in Financial Services. The structure of European financial markets is evolving into what can be characterized as a two-tiered market. Under this structure, a few key financial cities will serve as "hubs" attracting major corporate and institutional clients from across Europe, while other major cities will serve as "satellites" of differing importance that focus on smaller national companies and retail clients. Nevertheless, an interesting and important distinction needs to be made when speaking about the implications of this market tiering for the banking sector or the securities sector. For numerous reasons, London is consolidating its position as the key center for the Eurobond and Euroequities markets. At the same time, cities such as Frankfurt, Paris, and Amsterdam are vying to build strong positions in their home markets in order to keep the upper end of those markets from drifting to London and to attract some of London's business through promotion of their nascent bond and equity-related derivative markets.

London's developing role as the European link in the global equity market stems from the following factors: its vast market size and concentration of activity; the existence of cross-links to other major capital markets such as bank debt syndication and foreign exchange; the enormous investments the city of London has made in data processing and telecommunications equipment to enhance its operational efficiency; and the combination of the previous three factors, which enable London to provide liquidity for block-trading and derivative markets.

In banking, however, a different form of two-tiering should occur. London may still be predominant, but only for certain banking products and services (activities related to key capital market products such as Eurobonds, major private placements, more sophisticated and esoteric parts of the swaps market, and foreign exchange). Indeed, London-based banks (especially the American ones) will try to penetrate continental markets for mergers and acquisitions, investment management, and the like, but increased alertness and rapid innovation on the part of major continental banks should make the success of this attempt far from automatic.

Instead, we should be seeing each major country consolidating its banking activity in one center, which should serve as the hub for all the other minor commercial centers within the country. Yet, these individual national centers for banking will not be operating in a manner unlinked to the other European national centers, due in part to the increased application of telecommunications technology (this will be a prerequisite for the growth of the pan-European universal banks discussed earlier). In other words, European financial integration should not mean the increased concentration of all banking activity in one or two centers on a European basis, as is likely to be the case in the securities markets (which tend to have a wholesale characteristic).

These structural developments have important implications for financial intermediaries. Building viable positions will require them to start with an assessment of where they stand now and what their short-term capabilities and competitive advantages can allow them to reach within the next decade. For instance, for a regional intermediary, it may turn out to be wiser to pursue a strategy of direct alliance in the form of a cooperative agreement with the hub bank in its own country than to try to jump this step and embark on an acquisition strategy abroad.

Likewise, it may be more prudent for major national banks to develop better ties with smaller companies than to try desperately to attract the debt- and equity-new-issuance business of their major corporate clients, whose needs in this particular area may be better met by London-based intermediaries. Similarly, brokers and dealers in London with excellent secondary market capabilities may be better off allying themselves with continental research firms for local advice and continental brokers for local trades rather than trying to create mini–home offices to duplicate their secondary market skills in less liquid continental markets. How well European financial intermediaries undertake the assessment of their capabilities in light of this evolving market structure will determine the winners and losers in the integrated European financial markets.

Conclusion

A fundamental evolution is taking place in Europe's financial services industry: twelve formerly independent markets laden with twelve different historical experiences and developments are blending together to create one integrated financial sphere. In comparative terms, the final goal of this process goes far beyond what the United States or Japan has achieved to date in the financial arena. The expected financially integrated Europe will not only explicitly enable interstate banking, securities, and insurance under home state supervision; in tacit recognition of the blurring of traditional functional roles and the globalization of financial services, it will also permit financial intermediaries to freely adopt the universal banking structure of financial activities throughout the twelve EC nations.

Considering the numerous differences in regulations, standards, informal attitudes, and practices in the twelve disparate financial markets, we have seen that January 1, 1993, is only a symbolic point in a long and arduous process of integration that has already been characterized by fits and starts. In other words, participants in Europe's financial markets, ranging from financial intermediaries, securities exchanges, governments, corporations, and investment funds to retail clients, may not see the true benefits of financial integration until well after formal integration. Our examination of what these benefits may be indicates that they are well worth waiting for.

As financial intermediaries consolidate in type and number at a European level, operationally inefficient and un-innovative banks and securities houses that are financially viable only under protected circumstances will find themselves restructured in some form or another. The cross-shareholdings and strategic alliances under which these players are now taking refuge may end up in outright mergers and acquisitions, as financially healthier intermediaries with new value-propositions to the end-clients become bolder in the pan-European arena. And the buyers of their financial products will certainly gain from being served by more innovative and efficient intermediaries who will now be faced with competitive pressures at a European, rather than national, level, namely:

- Corporations should find themselves presented with a larger range of funding options, either via financial intermediaries from across EC countries or, gradually, by tapping directly into more dynamic national and European securities markets.
- Individuals, in addition to gaining from efficient consumer loan markets, should also be able to choose from a panoply of investment opportunities on a pan-European level.
- Investment fund managers, in recognition of the fact that cross-border investments can reduce risks without reducing returns, will progressively attempt to diversify their portfolios on European and international levels.
- European securities exchanges, most of which have remained stagnant backwaters of global financial markets, are already rising to the challenge of the new financial environment, vying with each other to provide differentiated and operationally efficient trading arenas linked technologically to other European and international financial centers.
- European governments, long used to playing a heavy-handed role in controlling (and, in some cases, stifling) national financial markets, are awakening to the short-term cash benefits of privatization and the longer-term tax-income benefits from profitable financial entities.

However, as we have indicated, the enormous benefits of an integrated financial market may be neither equally distributed nor available without a price tag—that is, the repercussions of structural readjustment to the respective participants. These are the anticipated side effects of the European Commission's voluntary "dynamic disequilibria."

In order to survive in this period and—better yet—prosper, new skills will have to be acquired. In the ensuing competitive turmoil, weak financial institutions may suffer and be absorbed by stronger, frequently nonlocal players. Uninnovative corporations and individuals used to viewing the bank as the only recourse for their financial needs will find that other buyers of such services have either reduced their funding costs or improved their risk-return profiles. And as capital flows freely to its most efficient destination within the EC countries, individual governments will find national monetary control and government deficit financing a trickier task.

One should not view these transitory side effects as reasons for not going forward with the mandate for integration laid by the European Commission. As aggressive and innovative participants already understand, the needed skills can be acquired, the pitfalls avoided, and the challenges tackled, as the opportunities and stakes are well worth pursuing and defending.

References

Commission of the European Communities. "The Economics of 1992." *European Economy*, 1988, *35*, 91.

Hasse, R. "Costs and Benefits of Financial Integration of Europe." In D. E. Fair and C. de Boissieu (eds.), *International Monetary and Financial Integration: The European Dimension.* Dordrecht: Kluwer Academic Publishers, 1988.

Hawawini, G., and Jacquillat, B. "European Equity Markets: Toward 1992 and Beyond." In J. Dermine (ed.), *European Banking Strategies for the 1990s.* Oxford, England: Basil Blackwell, 1989.

PART FIVE

1992 and Beyond:
Perceptions and Realities

CHAPTER 14

The Impact of the
Single Market
on European Business

A Case Study

Bernard Majani, Danielle Majani

It has become increasingly apparent that the construction of a unified European market might be hampered by delays in fiscal harmonization, the opening up of all government procurements, and the agreement on national sovereignty versus centralized power in Brussels. Nevertheless, in most cases, the delays created by politicians are more than compensated by the investment decisions of businessmen anticipating the creation of a single market of 325 million people. Such an integrated market, where goods and capital flow freely, will generate not only new opportunities for them, but also dangers, as their competitors will also have equal access to this market.

For capital-intensive industries like the pulp and paper sector, the full liberalization of the capital market is of major strategic importance. It is not always fully recognized that the Treaty of Rome, or at least its hitherto partial implementation until the Single European Act (SEA) was signed in 1987, created a major distortion in business strategy. It led to the development of a preferred policy of investing at home in order to export

329

abroad to other EC countries and evaluating the success of private companies by their ability to export. Moreover, governments were providing considerable incentives to those national firms that were exporting without regard for the profitability of such exports. Somehow it was thought that exporting on its own could increase national wealth, since it improved the trade balance and increased employment.

The liberalization of financial services and the free flow of capital within the community, however, are encouraging both EC and non-EC companies to invest anywhere in Europe. Thus, investment decisions are no longer influenced by national considerations (that is, "let us invest at home no matter the consequences to the economy or our profits"), but by rational criteria aimed at improving the firm's competitiveness and productivity, and reducing its production and distribution costs. The implications of a pan-European investment strategy will open the floodgates of EC-wide investment, thus bringing benefits to pulp and paper firms (as the Treaty of Rome opened up the floodgates to the free flow of the paper and pulp trade within Europe).

The costs of not being unified, as estimated by the EC Commission, are therefore not only the cost of the physical, technical, and fiscal barriers, but also the cost of not being able to optimize business investments on a communitywide basis. In our view, this is as high a cost as that of all other barriers combined. Furthermore, as far as the business strategy of paper and pulp companies is concerned, its implications are of critical importance.

During the past few decades, the EC countries with the greatest forest resources and thus pulp and paper potential (France, Portugal, and Spain) have suffered dismal economic performance. In the early 1980s, France applied outmoded, socialist economic policies; Portugal went through a disruptive economic and social revolution; and Spain stagnated through a long political transition. These three countries, together with a more combative Great Britain, are now experiencing a major investment boom in the pulp and paper industry. Foreign and domestic companies are investing billions of dollars to purchase competitors and create state-of-the-art production facilities. So great are the current investments, and so huge the potential for additional ones, that the implications of this new investment strategy are bound to have a real impact on paper and pulp companies not only within the community and the European Free Trade Association (EFTA), but also in North America and other non-European countries. These implications are not yet universally recognized by all paper and pulp executives in European countries, or indeed around the world.

The Treaty of Rome: An Export Boom

The White Paper on the Completion of the Internal Market could just as well have been called the White Paper on the Completion of the Treaty of Rome. Indeed, the major success of the Treaty of Rome in the 1960s and 1970s was limited almost entirely to the full removal of customs duties among the member states and between the countries of the community and their partners in EFTA. This free-trade policy played a very important role in promoting productivity and economic growth, at least in the 1960s and the early 1970s, and made it possible for companies to invest more by achieving economies of scale that could not otherwise be attained in the single home market of each firm.

The economic growth of the EC member states was very strong throughout the 1960s. The GNP of the three main EC countries (Germany, France, and Italy—the United Kingdom did not join the community until 1972) grew on average at a rate of 4.7 percent per year. The community paper sector also achieved record growth during this period, while growth in its major segment (the printing- and writing-paper grade) was exemplary.

During the first fifteen years of the Common Market (1957–1972), the six founding member states increased printing- and writing-paper production by 8.9 percent per year, from 1.7 million tons to slightly more than 6 million tons. The only mediocre performer was France, with an annual production increase of only 6.9 percent. Over the following fifteen years (1972–1987), paper production growth was considerably slower and yearly growth rates dropped from 8.9 percent to 3.3 percent. (See Table 14-1.)

The United Kingdom, Denmark, and Ireland joined the Common Market in 1972. In the same year, various treaties with the EFTA countries were signed or were being prepared. After a transitional period of ten years (instead of five, as for other goods), Austria, Switzerland, and the forest-rich Nordic countries were given free access to the large EC markets for pulp and paper. The treaties undoubtedly led to a reduction in paper production in the EC member states, although the slower growth in production was just as much the result of the countries' poor economic performance from 1974 onward. West Germany, however, kept increasing its production of printing and writing paper at the average rate of 4.5 percent a year throughout this period, a rate double that of its partners. Such an excellent performance in a country not endowed with large forest resources is due to the high quality of management and the capital resources provided by the employees' pension funds, which allowed companies a huge pool of funds for investment. This means that the paper industry of even countries not possessing large forest resources could have performed better than it had done from 1974 onward.

Between 1957 and 1972, printing- and writing-paper production in the EC grew slightly faster (8.9 percent per year) than

Table 14-1. EC Production of Printing and Writing Papers.

	Tons			Annual Growth Rate	
Country	1957	1972	1987	1957–1972	1972–1987
West Germany	587,100	2,228,800	4,294,000	9.3%	4.5%
France	595,300	1,620,000	2,309,000	6.9	2.4
Italy	268,200	1,283,600	2,025,000	11.0	3.1
Netherlands	143,100	515,400	603,200	8.9	1.1
BLEU[a]	96,100	401,600	603,100	10.0	2.7
Total	1,689,800	6,049,400	9,834,300	8.9	3.3

Source: Authors' compilation from various paper industry sources.

[a] Belgium-Luxembourg Economic Union.

consumption (8.7 percent per year). Over the next fifteen years, the opposite was true. Consumption increased by 3.6 percent per year while production increased by only 3.3 percent per year. The single and major exception was Germany. Between 1972 and 1987, paper production in that country grew 4.5 percent per year while consumption increased by 4.0 percent per year. The German paper trade deficit was thus reduced from 305,000 tons in 1972 to 245,000 tons in 1987. If this trend continues, it will not be long before West Germany becomes a net exporter of printing and writing paper. (See Table 14-2.)

The original six Common Market countries need few imports to satisfy their consumption needs. (Net imports of pulp or paper represent only 7.8 percent of their consumption, whereas the equivalent figure for the United States, with its immense forest resources, is 11.4 percent.) In 1987, however, the United Kingdom imported 1,553,000 tons of printing and writing paper (representing 16 percent of total EC production). In this sense, the United Kingdom is set apart from the other major EC paper producers, and therefore it presents great opportunities for both local production and exports from other EC countries.

If the paper potential of Spain and Portugal is taken into account, it is quite reasonable to expect that the EC will achieve self-sufficiency in printing and writing paper within the next decade or so. Self-sufficiency, however, does not mean that there

Table 14-2. Balance of Trade in Printing and Writing Papers (Thousands of Tons).

Country	1972	1987
West Germany	− 305	− 245
France	− 103	− 349
Italy	+ 131	+ 25
Netherlands	+ 5	− 176
BLEU	+ 55	− 82
Total	− 217	− 827

Source: Authors' compilation from various NORTHSCAN data sources.

will be no trade between the EC and other countries. Nor does the low level of imports of printing and writing paper in relation to consumption recorded by the six founding EC member states between 1972 and 1987 (7.8 percent) indicate a low level in the trade of paper among European countries. On the contrary, intracommunity trade (as well as extracommunity trade) has reached extremely high levels. At present, intracommunity trade represents more than a fourth of the total production, while in 1972 it was less than 20 percent and in 1957 it was a mere 3 percent. Similarly, exports within other EC countries amount to almost 40 percent of the total production of the twelve EC members—an enormous percentage for countries that are net importers of paper—and show the extent of the interdependence of the twelve community members as well as the importance of trade within Europe.

   In 1987, the consumption of printing and writing paper in the EC (excluding Greece and Ireland) totaled 14,808,700 tons (see Table 14-3).

   At 6,939,000 tons, in 1987 total imports for the ten countries amounted to 46.9 percent of consumption. About half the tonnage (3.3 million tons) was imported from EC member states and the other half from EFTA countries. Only 300,000 tons was imported from countries outside the EC or EFTA (see Table 14-4).

Table 14-3. EC Consumption of Printing and Writing Papers, 1987 (Thousands of Tons).

Country	Production	Imports	Exports	Consumption
West Germany	4,294	1,821	1,577	4,539
France	2,309	1,087	738	2,658
Italy	2,025	491	516	2,000
Netherlands	603	746	570	779
BLEU	603	548	465	686
United Kingdom	1,243	1,774	221	2,796
Denmark	126	182	59	248
Spain	826	261	138	949
Portugal	167	29	43	153
Total	12,196	6,939	4,327	14,808

Source: Authors' compilation from various NORTHSCAN and other data sources.

Table 14-4. EC Import Sources for Printing and Writing Papers, 1987.

Country	Tons	Percentage
EC	3,367,400	48.5
EFTA[a]	3,258,700	47.0
Other	312,500	6.5
Total	6,938,600	100.0

Source: Authors' compilation from various NORTHSCAN data sources.

[a] Sweden, Finland, Norway, and Austria only. (Imports from Switzerland and Iceland are not included, as they are not of significant magnitude.)

The "export-or-die" mentality so prevalent before 1985 was developed because of the widespread belief in giving priority to as high national production as possible. Exporting bulk goods like paper, however, is a relatively costly operation, especially given the inefficient and highly regulated transportation system that existed in Europe and the delays involved in border crossings. The lower profitability of exports was overlooked and potential foreign investment opportunities neglected because of the many barriers to the free flow of capital across European countries. With the Single European Act, new strategies have become possible as intracommunity investments flourish and non-EC firms fight to obtain a share of the new EC-wide cake. As a result, paper production in the EC countries will increase at a rate higher than consumption between now and the year 2000. In some countries, this growth rate in production will be as much as double that of consumption.

In addition to customs and noncustoms barriers and investment strategies based on narrow national objectives, paper and pulp consumption and production were hindered by the poor economic performance of the EC countries during most of the 1970s and 1980s.

A Dismal Economic Performance

Over the past ten to fifteen years and up until quite recently, European governments tended increasingly to intervene in the economy (see Chapter Ten). The results are all too evident: the European Community has done poorly, not only when compared with its own economic performance in the 1950s and 1960s, but also in comparison with the results obtained by its major trading partners, which can be seen in Table 14-5.

Thus, during the 1980s, the gross domestic product (GDP) of Japan, Canada, the United States, and the EFTA countries progressed more than that of the EC, where economic growth slumped to a meager 1.9 percent per year. Every EC country suffered the same sharp downturn. Even Germany did quite poorly, with a GDP growth rate of only 1.6 percent in the 1980s, compared with 2.8 percent in the 1970s. The EFTA countries did not fare much better than the countries of the EC (2.1 percent yearly growth versus 1.9 percent for EC countries). The overall economic slackening resulted, not surprisingly, in a slowdown in the consumption of all sectors of pulp and paper, where growth rates dropped to almost a third of those of the pre-1972 period (see Table 14-1).

The 1970s and 1980s were characterized by the tremendous growth of spending in the public sector, which started increasing after the first oil shock in 1973. The average government spending of the twelve EC countries increased from about 38 percent of GDP in 1974 to 49.1 percent of GDP in 1986 (the last year for which homogeneous data for all EC members is available). This spending is by far greater than the 36.9 percent of the United States and the meager 33.1 percent of Japan.

Table 14-5. Gross Domestic Product Yearly Growth Rate.

Country	1969–1979	1979–1988
Canada	4.9%	3.1%
Japan	4.7	3.9
United States	2.8	2.9
EFTA	2.5	2.1
EC	3.1	1.9

Source: Eurostat Statistical Office of the European Communities, Luxembourg, 1990.

The low GDP growth of the European Community resulted in near stagnation of its industrial production, which grew by only 1.5 percent between 1979 and 1988. The EFTA countries did a little better, while the United States grew by 3.0 percent, Canada by 3.5 percent, and Japan—the leader among OECD nations—by a staggering 3.8 percent.

The more taxes a government collects and the greater the public spending, the less money is available to be invested by firms, as governments rarely use the huge sums of money they collect to promote investment. Instead, this money is used to help the poor and improve social welfare. If gross capital formation is taken as a measure of total investment made by a nation, it becomes clear that such a formation did not increase at all in constant value, between 1974 and 1987, among the twelve countries of the EC (in some cases it even decreased). This means that all GDP gains were used to increase consumption rather than improve investments and modernize the community's industry. On the other hand, Japan's and Canada's rates of capital formation were in excess of 3.0 percent throughout the 1980s; moreover, Finland and the United States, both major players in paper and pulp, also increased their rates of capital formation to above 2.4 percent a year. This put the EC pulp and paper industry at a disadvantage, as the Canadian, U.S., and Finnish firms that increased their investments were able to modernize at much faster rates than their European counterparts.

A Change for the Better

Recently, all European governments, with the probable exception of Greece, have accepted that they cannot continue to favor increasing consumption without investment. Moreover, labor unions and political parties (even socialist ones) are much less inclined to fight for pay increases that lead to inflationary pressures, which in the final analysis erase the benefits of such increases. This means that company profits are increasing throughout Europe at a much faster pace than in the past and that investment has started to grow faster than GDP—an excellent remedy for the economic ills of the past fifteen years.

If the European Community countries have in the past applied economic and social policies leading to stagnation, it follows that a policy promoting investment will bring faster growth. The coming liberalization of financial services will encourage both EC and non-EC companies to invest anywhere in Europe in the same way that they have invested at home. The free flow of capital will push firms to seek and go beyond their own national boundaries for the best investment opportunities. This optimization of capital investment may well turn out to be the most important benefit from the Single European Act. The increasing rate of EC investment and optimal allocation decisions are having an unexpected and highly positive impact on the effectiveness and return of investments.

Countries where investments have been low in the past fifteen years, and capital-intensive industries that have suffered the most from the lack of investment funds since 1974, stand to benefit most from the Single European Act. The pulp and paper industry is not an exception, and in particular that of Southern Europe, where investments in plant modernization have been meager or nonexistent.

Major Investment Boom in the Pulp and Paper Industry

The pulp and paper industry covers a number of segments with very different growth outlooks and market potentials. Packaging, for example, depends on manufacturing for its growth. Printing and writing paper is influenced by advertising and office work. It is therefore linked to services rather than production, and is consequently the fastest-growing sector of the industry. Thus, the pulp and paper industry can grow without undue influence from any single sector.

It is worth noting that from 1979 to 1989, demand for printing and writing paper rose by 4.3 percent in the Common Market countries — a higher rate than the 3.2 percent of the previous decade (see Figure 14-1). This rate was achieved despite the slump in economic growth (a mere 1.9 percent over the same period). Since we believe that the advertising and office sectors will increase faster than the remaining ones in the economic

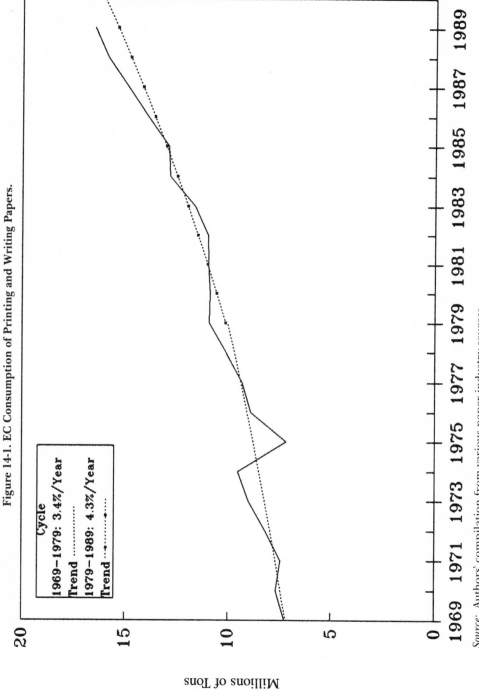

Figure 14-1. EC Consumption of Printing and Writing Papers.

Cycle
1969–1979: 3.4%/Year
Trend ....
1979–1989: 4.3%/Year
Trend ..-■--......

Millions of Tons

1969 1971 1973 1975 1977 1979 1981 1983 1985 1987 1989

0   5   10   15   20

Source: Authors' compilation from various paper industry sources.

sector, we predict high growth rates for the consumption trend that can be expected between now and the end of the century. Allowance must be made both for the exceptionally high growth rate achieved over the last ten years and for the positive impact of the single European market.

It is apparent in some advanced countries such as Germany that some printing paper markets have started to stagnate. Direct mail, which has been the fastest-growing advertising segment in recent years, is no longer progressing in leaps and bounds. Concern is also being expressed about the growth in the consumption of office papers. Despite some people's overhasty predictions about the advent of the "paperless office," offices are still cluttered with enormous volumes of paper, in particular since photocopying is becoming much faster and considerably cheaper. At the same time, electronic data transmission systems, for both internal and intercorporate communications, have already resulted in lower demand for continuous form computer printout paper. Additional factors must also be considered, such as the development of desktop publishing and faxes, which further increase the demand for paper. Taking all these market changes into account, we estimate that the growth in EC consumption of printing and writing papers should drop by about one percentage point between now and the year 2000 to an annual growth rate of around 3 percent per year. This loss will be more than compensated by the positive impact of the single European market, which is bound to increase consumption.

For instance, the liberalization of financial services will increase the consumption of printing and writing paper as more direct mail and higher newspaper and magazine advertising appear. Moreover, higher economic growth of the EC countries will also increase paper consumption, and might bring annual growth rates in excess of 4 percent, thus compensating for the 1 percent loss cited above.

In addition to increased consumption, the major impact of the single European market will be felt in the production of paper. Apart from Germany, the production growth rate of printing and writing paper was less in the 1980s than the corresponding rate of consumption. While significant progress in paper production was made (a 3.6 percent increase between 1972 and 1987), most of the increases were obtained by improving and modifying existing facilities to produce printing and writing grades on machines previously used for other types of paper production (for example, newsprint). Until recently, very few new, faster, and more modern paper machines were installed. In France, for example, the last of such major investments aiming to modernize production were made as far back as 1974.

The prospects of a unified market and the untapped investment potential for manufacturing various paper grades in France are considered so important that many new paper machines are now being planned. More specifically, two newsprint paper machines are currently being built and two more are planned for before 1995. Once they come into operation, France will be producing 1.2 to 1.5 million tons of newsprint, against its current 350,000 tons. In Great Britain, the situation is quite similar to that of France, as new investments are under way; increases in investment spending are also expected in Spain and Italy. Thus, by 1995, the Common Market will, in all likelihood, have the most modern newsprint industry in the world. Producing 80 percent of its newsprint needs, it will clearly be on its way to self-sufficiency. This is a big change, as the Common Market imported 55 percent of its newsprint consumption requirements in the past.

Large production increases in printing and writing grades are also currently being built or planned in the European Community. In France alone, four large machines with a total capacity of one million tons are under construction. Two more can be expected before 1995. These new state-of-the-art machines will represent about 50 percent of the existing production capacity. Thus, in France as well as in other EC countries (Spain, the United Kingdom, Belgium, and Portugal), production growth may well be double the rate of consumption. These investments will reduce production costs, increase supply, intensify competition, and certainly bring prices down, thus further increasing consumption.

The prospects of the free flow of goods, people, and capital, and the creation of an integrated market of more than 325 million people are the main factors behind the decision to invest billions of dollars in the EC paper industry. The investment climate has definitely changed. Today, American, Canadian, New Zealand, Norwegian, Swedish, Finnish, and even Japanese companies, in addition to European ones, are investing heavily in the community's paper and pulp industry. For instance, German companies are heavily investing in France and Spain, as the administrative and other barriers that hindered investment in the past have now been eliminated. Similarly, a multinational company of British origin is investing in Portugal. This flow of new investment in the paper industry will continue to increase as more announcements are made that force the undecided companies to invest — if not for any reason other than the fear of being left behind.

In the pulp and paper industry, the unified European market is attracting considerable attention from non-EC competitors. Such competitors are now becoming a major force with which to contend, although they had rarely invested in this market before. Thus, it appears that EC paper manufacturers, and EFTA producers as well, must accept and rise to the challenge of the industry's losing its domestic and even European orientation and becoming a truly global player, if they are to prosper, or even survive, as the twenty-first century approaches. The trend toward globalization requires a reappraisal of strategies that European companies will have to follow. As many companies are accustomed to the Europe of the 1980s, they seem to have difficulty in figuring out the true consequences of the single European market. A recent survey, for instance, concluded that many of Europe's paper industry leaders viewed the impact of the Single European Act mostly as a means to facilitate the free movement of goods, people, and capital from one country to another. In our view, this misses the true implications of the Single European Act — that is, the huge possibilities for pan-European investments. Investing at home with a view to exporting is now too narrow and outmoded a criterion on which to base a company's strategy. The time has now come to change attitudes and to optimize Europe-wide operations. Most often, this means investing away from home in places that combine abundant resources (in this case, forests) with proximity to major consumption centers so as to minimize transportation costs.

Finally, European executives must realize that investments and investment opportunities are inevitable in other sectors as well. Higher capital spending will accelerate economic growth and, consequently, consumption. Higher economic growth and more consumption will necessitate further investments and will require a mentality different from that of the past, where new investment in order to modernize facilities and improve quality and customer services will probably become the key to strategic ingredients for success in the future.

CHAPTER 15

Future Challenges for Single Market Europe

Feedback from Business and Government Leaders

Spyros G. Makridakis

The completion of the internal market is not the end of the road. After the single market will come the single economy. What lies beyond that is a matter of which history rather than what the present generation of politicians will determine.

> Lord Cockfield,
> EC Commissioner,
> author of the 1985 White Paper

A French businessman staying in Tokyo saw a beautiful French tie in the window of a shop in his hotel lobby. Although the tie was French it cost around 180 Fr (around $30), half what the same tie would have cost in Paris. The next morning the businessman went into the store and asked for the tie. Since this was his last day in Tokyo and he still had yen left, he decided to pay in cash. He therefore gave the equivalent of around 200 Fr in yen to the salesperson. To his surprise he was told that the money was not enough. The tie wasn't 4,500 yen but 45,000 yen. At this point he realized that he had made a mistake when translating the yen into francs—he had omitted a zero! Needless to say, he did not buy the tie. He loves to repeat the story, however, which illustrates so well the exorbitant prices at which foreign imports are sold in Japan. The consequence is that high prices kill demand or lower it to the point where selling foreign products in Japan becomes in itself a rare event. Small boutiques selling ties, for example, have low fixed costs and need no huge investments, yet their prices differ so greatly from those charged in Paris, London, or New York that the question is raised as to why this should be so. Somehow, it would seem, the Japanese distribution system is controlled to such an extent that no retailer can get around it by buying directly from abroad and therefore providing goods and services at prices compatible to those in other capitals. There are even those who claim that retailers could sell Japanese products in Japan at considerably lower prices if they bought the products in another country before reselling them inside Japan itself.

This chapter, as its title indicates, summarizes the opinions of European government officials (including the EC officials) and business leaders in Europe (who are not necessarily European). The material used has been collected from person-to-person interviews, personal letters, long discussions held with executives attending INSEAD's executive programs, and published interviews in the press. The purpose of the chapter is to present as broad a range of opinions as possible.

The Japanese: A Challenge or a Threat?

One of the few topics on which the overwhelming majority of European business and government leaders unanimously agree is the Japanese challenge and/or threat (see Exhibit 15-1).

Throughout our interviews with EC commissioners and business leaders, the most common response when asked about their greatest anxiety concerning the future of the European Community had to do with Japan. Similarly, in public statements and published interviews, the Japanese question figures prominently.

Moderate critics agree that market access and general treatment of European firms trying to sell inside Japan are not akin to what is accorded Japanese firms selling in Europe. Middle-of-the-road leaders like EC President Jacques Delors have even stated publicly that Japan wants to apply its own rules

Exhibit 15-1. Opinions About Japan.

They are no better than we [Europeans] are—their virtue lies in their ability to pick up good ideas and commercialize them successfully.

We can catch up with them; we have the resources and the human potential. We need to take the [Japanese] challenge seriously and not underestimate their determination to succeed.

Japan's fears of Fortress Europe ring hollow in view of its own reality—one of the most tightly sealed economies in the free world.

Japan and the United States cannot make additional bilateral deals to benefit each other to the detriment of Europe.

For almost two decades, the Japanese have advised Westerners to be patient with them. But long-promised changes have not arrived, and the Japanese are still asking for more patience.

European firms are excluded from any competitive bidding in Japan (in particular in the public sector).

Even if you live in Japan for years and become fluent in their language, you are always treated like a foreigner. You never feel that people (even your close collaborators) really tell you what they think. You cannot get to know them.

Four or five years ago, there was no way of penetrating the Japanese market. Now there is hope, but European businessmen must try hard in order to succeed.

European companies can beat Japanese ones if management puts its mind to it and works hard. The problem is that many European firms don't want to make the effort or allocate the resources to compete with the Japanese. They prefer easy profits with little or no risk.

The quality of Japanese products is excellent. The Japanese worker is much better trained, more motivated, and harder working than the European one. That is what makes Japanese firms successful. The Japanese set ambitious long-term objectives and invest heavily to achieve them, even if it means losses in the short term. We are not willing to invest as heavily or take risks.

They are doing a terrific job. They can sense market changes much quicker than we can and they get their act together and bring out new products before we even realize that a change is taking place. This is their secret to success, not protectionism or unfair competition.

Japan has the world's most highly integrated economy, superbly geared to produce what people want. Their investments cost much less than those in Europe because interest rates in Japan are much lower than ours.

We should not stop the Japanese from investing in Europe. Last year (1987) their investment here was close to 8 billion ECUs—double the amount of the previous year.

Our view of Japan is at least ten years old.

---

to the international trade game. These are rules that generally result in strictly limiting market entry and competition from abroad at home, while making extensive use of the European policy of open entry and unrestricted trade within the countries of the community. The accepted rules of free trade as understood in the West "simply don't work in Japan," Delors says. Moreover, he believes that Japan is not evolving toward a more open economy. At the extreme end, there are businessmen who believe that Japan is striving for economic dominance of the world. They hold that the Japanese will use any tactics, including dumping products at prices well below cost, to achieve their goal of destroying any foreign competition.

Both groups (the moderates and the extremists) demand tough measures to deal with Japanese "economic imperialism." They envisage import restrictions on Japanese goods coupled with guaranteed market shares in Japan for products and services coming from EC countries. For them, reciprocity must extend to highly protected Japanese sectors such as banking, construction, insurance, and even agriculture. They believe that, until Japan opens up its complex, tightly controlled distribution system and radically reforms its archaic land-use laws, it will be practically impossible for foreign firms to have opportunities equal to those of domestic ones. The only way to get equal access is by pushing the Japanese hard at the negotiating table and achieving perfect reciprocity, to the point where an equilibrium in the trade balance between EC nations and Japan is accomplished. These businessmen do not think anything else will work. Access to the Japanese market is not getting any easier, despite the repeated promises made by Japanese officials, who, critics maintain, are somehow neither capable of keeping such promises, nor willing to keep them.

European government and business leaders are afraid of a repetition in Europe of what happened in the United States, where the Japanese virtually wiped out whole segments of American industry. With a few exceptions, they advocate tough action to defend European industry. At the same time, business leaders are taking steps to improve their competitive positions (alliances, mergers, joint R&D projects, and so on) so that they can achieve a position where they are capable of dealing with the Japanese threat. They believe that by taking such action they are not fortifying Europe but rather responding to Japanese "economic imperialism." At the same time, some business leaders are afraid of the consequences of any form of protectionism or, rather, of its potential for disguising governmental interference. "Job saving" and "helping infantile [European] industry" are alibis invariably invoked when governments intervene in trade. These leaders also point out that American protectionism aimed at Japanese products has hurt the U.S. economy further because it has resulted in higher prices for American products, which, in turn, have made the Americans less competitive globally and thus have in fact benefited Japanese firms (see also the last section of this chapter).

Fortress Europe

Few if any businessmen or government leaders within Europe advocate protectionism (see Exhibit 15-2). EC officials are quick to point out that article 110 of the Treaty of Rome states: "Member States aim to contribute, in the common interest, to the harmonious development of world trade, the progressive abolition of restrictions on international trade and the lowering of customs barriers." They call attention to the fact that the objectives of article 110 were reaffirmed by the European Council of Heads of State and Government, which declared in June 1988 in Hanover that the goal of the single market was not to create a "Fortress Europe" by raising external trade barriers, but rather to create a European partnership that will stimulate world trade. Moreover, as officials in Brussels are eager to point out, the EC has expended considerable effort and a great deal of political will on the General Agreement on Tariffs and Trade (GATT) and will abide by its agreements and principles. Export is too important for EC countries to become protectionist in their own lands. No country, however, can expect to discriminate against EC products or services and enjoy free access for its own products in the various EC countries.

Exhibit 15-2. Opinions About Fortress Europe.

I would like to express my astonishment at the emotional reaction to the word *protectionism*. The fears that Europe would erect a barrier around itself are groundless.

Impossible: Europeans are strongly committed to free-market institutions and free trade and have an impressive track record.

There is a huge amount of basic research to be done in the natural sciences, and the funding of basic research is a proper role for public authorities. This has nothing to do with Fortress Europe.

Quality of life is important to us. Our legislation aims at maintaining quality rather than excluding foreign firms. If they want to operate in the community, they must follow our laws and regulations.

What is shown on TV does not fall into the same category as soap and detergents. We cannot treat culture like any other merchandise.

Today the strongest companies doing business across Europe are American. Integration will change that—it will allow European firms to meet the challenge. That is not protectionism; it is self-defense.

That is not an issue for us, as we are already established in Europe. Our affiliates are European.

It is natural for Europeans to want to protect what they have.

Countries must have something to offer when asking for favors. We shouldn't give anything for nothing.

As long as there are prosperity and growth there will be no problem, but when hard times come—you will then see Fortress Europe.

The European demand for reciprocity might create serious problems for non-EC firms.

The whole idea of reciprocity can be so easily used and abused as the pretext for protectionism.

No firm can compete against the four governments subsidizing Airbus.

Look at the quotas on Japanese cars and chips imposed by the U.S. government. They did not help American industry. On the contrary, they increased Japanese profits, as well as increasing the prices of American products, and thus they benefited the Japanese rather than the Americans. How can anyone expect that quotas will benefit Europe?

High-ranking officials in Brussels complain that their policies are not well understood outside of the community, often because there is little will to understand on the part of outsiders. They point out that the single market program is expected to add significantly to the rate of economic growth of member states. Because of today's interdependence among all countries, this will increase global demand to the benefit of everyone and not just the community countries themselves. Moreover, officials state that even in the area of agriculture, where the complaints about Fortress Europe are loudest, the community is the largest single importer in the world and the second largest exporter (thus running up an agricultural deficit). The fact that European consumers do not want to eat meat coming from animals treated with hormones, for instance, should not be seen as a form of protectionism but rather as a genuine public concern for health and welfare. Finally, community leaders argue that EC agricultural subsidies are smaller per full-time farmer than in the United States or Japan. As Europeans are unwilling to see their farmers fall below the poverty level simply to avoid being labeled protectionist, agricultural subsidies must be viewed in a social context—as part of an integral social policy in place throughout Europe.

Another concern about Fortress Europe relates to technical, safety, and health standards. Non-EC countries claim that such standards discriminate against products made in countries other than the EC. EC officials and government leaders are quick to respond that similar standards exist in all countries (including the United States and Japan) and are justified for reasons of health, safety, and environmental protection. Thus, the Europeans wonder why the application of similar standards across all community countries should pose a problem for the Americans, whose uniform standards across the fifty states (as far apart as Alaska and Hawaii, which are much farther apart than Ireland and Greece, for example) are of long standing. If some firms using these standards on a large scale are able to gain competitive advantages (because of economies of scale) over others that produce less, this cannot be viewed any differently to European firms producing in Europe according to U.S. standards, because they, too, are at a competitive disadvantage vis-à-vis U.S. firms that produce on a much larger scale.

Both EC officials and business leaders feel that the issues run much deeper. What is at stake is European competitiveness, which has been improving and will continue to do so because of the movement toward integration. Moreover, EC bargaining power has increased considerably since the countries chose to speak with one voice rather than with twelve. Improved competitiveness and increased bargaining power, however, are shifting global patterns of industrial leadership and creating anxieties that lead to accusations about Fortress Europe. Outsiders object to the fact that Airbus Industries is challenging Boeing's monopoly and that Philips' and Thomson's proposed standards for high-density television, if accepted, will threaten Japanese dominance in television manufacturing. In the view of Europeans, however, these examples are not part of the foundations of a Fortress Europe, but the legitimate strategic responses to the existing competitive structure of the global business environment. Europeans, like their Japanese and American counterparts, intend to compete on a level playing field while respecting international agreements, such as those included in GATT, and the established rules of international competition.

The overwhelming majority of European industrialists who participate in the European roundtable are adamantly opposed to any form of protectionism. They know that government interference and protectionist measures will backfire, bring almost certain retaliatory action from the victims of any protectionism. At the same time, a large number of them have worked in and know well both the United States and Japan. They are, therefore, aware of "Blockhouse Japan" and the "Great American Stronghold" and judge the U.S. and Japanese reactions as self-projections — what *they* would do (already have done to a certain extent) if *they* were Europeans.

European business leaders welcome foreign investment. They feel comfortable with companies like IBM, Ford, and Coca-Cola operating in Europe. These companies have made a genuine effort to implant themselves in Europe, create local employment, and become "European." Great concern exists, however, among European leaders about "screwdriver plants" where, in one case, even the small "Made in Scotland" label is in fact manufactured in Japan. To them, a free EC market should not be abused. Limiting the extent to which the kind of operations where products are merely assembled from parts imported from Japan can succeed is less a case of building a fortress than one of shutting the back door on unwelcome guests whose sole interest is to abuse Europe's hospitality. (By claiming that the product is made in one of the EC countries, extra-EC products have unrestricted access to the other eleven EC countries.)

Finally, EC officials point to their track record and their wholehearted commitment to increasing, rather than decreasing, competition within Europe. They remind critics that they have repeatedly obliged EC governments to stop outright subsidies or aid to local producers. They are behind the liberalization of the financial service sector and the opening up of public procurements. They strongly favor deregulating the road and air transportation industry and have blocked mergers and acquisitions whose aims were to decrease EC-wide competition. The protection of the consumer is as much a goal of the single market as is improving the competitiveness of European firms. Thus, since protectionist measures will ultimately lead to higher prices for consumers, leaders are opposed to such measures unless there are sound reasons related to unfair practices.

Beyond Integration

Although almost everyone agrees on the need for and usefulness of a single market, there is considerable disagreement as to how far and how fast things should advance (see Exhibit 15-3). There are arguments and counterarguments as to why European integration is moving too slowly or too quickly, or why Brussels has too little or too much power, and so on. Pragmatists point out that such concerns don't really matter. Whether European integration will take five, ten, or fifteen years is, according to them, irrelevant. What matters is that the process has started and that it is irreversible. It is not even conceivable to go back to having twelve separate countries, each dealing

Exhibit 15-3. Opinions About 1992 and Beyond.

By a large majority, both politicians and the general public support the construction of a single European market.

Business executives must accept that their market is the whole of Europe. Then they must understand the community and the way it works. Otherwise, they cannot take advantage of the integrated market.

What Europe is doing is gigantic.

The psychological benefits are tremendous. The investment boom is real and its benefits will be higher than the most optimistic estimates.

We were planning to invest more in Europe but the Single Act has increased the pace and intensity of our investments.

1992 is not affecting us, as we are already operating across Europe.

Europeans must agree on a common stance concerning Japanese car imports to the community.

Many business executives are still ignorant about the benefits and changes that Europe 1992 is already bringing.

Both our strategy and operations are bound to change as a result of 1992. My view is that our company is not moving fast enough in its Europeanization.

The big losers will be small and medium-sized firms. Excessive concentration might hurt rather than help competition in Europe.

Everyone seems happy but not everyone knows how the single market is going to affect him.

If 1992 does not hurt anybody, it will not achieve anything, either.

---

with its own problems. With this everyone agrees. Thus, the pragmatists say, "Why worry?" It is only a question of time. Integration is bound to come.

Others talk about missed opportunities and the necessity for bold prescriptions for Europe. For instance, Helmut Schmidt, former chancellor of Germany, advocates accelerated integration going beyond that envisioned in the White Paper. Schmidt proposes a joint European defense force, a single European currency, and a single central bank (modeled on the U.S. Federal Reserve Bank) that can resist inflationary government pressures aimed at financing budget deficits. He thinks that Europe must become unilaterally independent and that this can only be achieved by creating a single defense force and adopting a single currency. The rest, he feels, is squabbling about unimportant details such as abolition of border controls or imposing common standards, which amount to little as long as a country maintains its own defense, monetary, and fiscal policies.

At the other extreme are those who are fearful of Brussels Eurocrats creating a monstrous "Eurocracy." Their free market instincts oppose regulations and protectionism even in retaliation against foreign countries that do not treat European firms fairly. They argue that if some countries want to sell their products below cost in Europe they should be allowed to do it— European consumers can thus benefit from low prices. Furthermore, European firms can play the same game. If companies located in non-EC countries can sell below cost and still survive long enough to establish market leadership and make handsome profits, then why can't European firms do the same? Why do they demand government protection in order to make huge profits, which are, in fact, subsidies coming from the European consumer?

Brussels commissioners fervently argue that the middle-of-the-road approach they are currently following is the only realistic alternative. They point to the case of the United States and its huge trade deficits as an illustration of the results of remaining passive in the face of external threats. They also mention the uniqueness of Europe with its built-in social welfare policies. The commissioners say that it is impossible to talk about free market forces while at the same time maintaining the minimum welfare levels that everyone expects in the EC nations. How, they say, can you deal with a recession when life employment is considered a right? Similarly, can you allow large numbers of big firms to go bankrupt when there is widespread concern about short-term unemployment? Europeans are not willing to accept the misery caused by higher rates of unemployment, and their elected politicians are not willing to take that risk, either. These are constraints that cannot be ignored. Thus, there is a thin line between protecting the European consumer and helping European firms to become and remain competitive on a worldwide scale. The same dangers exist on the narrow road between maintaining as high a level of employment (and social stability) as possible and interfering as little as possible with the mechanisms of free trade.

Euro-officials in Brussels argue that they walk this tightrope better than the individual countries can. They are thus asking for more power and greater flexibility. Delors fears that the community is becoming "an intergovernmental institution paralyzed by waffle." He therefore suggests far-reaching changes. His proposals include weekly meetings of the deputy prime ministers in Brussels in order to coordinate policies, recommend action, and make public statements with a single voice. Alternatively, he suggests turning the commission into a stronger, more executive-type body with a transfer of national sovereignty on matters such as trade and pan-European coordination. In addition, there are ambitious commission projects for two consecutive conferences—one on speeding up the European Monetary Union, the other on reforming the EC constitution. These proposed changes are wholeheartedly endorsed by several European countries and many business leaders who want a more decisive commission. Nevertheless, there are still some members who oppose them and suggest more caution. Margaret Thatcher has probably best expressed the dilemma of "more Europe, less transfer of power." Her three, by now classic, statements affirm this clearly:

> And let us be quite clear, Britain does not dream of some cozy, isolated existence on the fringes of the European Community. Our destiny is Europe, as part of the Community.
>
> September 1988

> We haven't worked all these years to free Britain from the paralysis of socialism only to see it creep in through the back door of central control and bureaucracy from Brussels.
>
> October 1988

True democratic accountability is through national
parliaments.

November 1989

Many businesspeople and political commentators believe
that the effects of integration have already started to arrive and
will continue regardless of national governments' public statements. They point to the most impressive outcome of the Single
European Act: the investment boom currently under way in
Europe (since 1986, the rate of investment has tripled in comparison with that of the previous decade). Economic growth
rates have consequently increased and are expected to stabilize
at around 3.5 percent in the medium term. Unemployment is
sliding down for the first time since the early 1980s. In the view
of many businesspeople, this optimism is the most concrete
benefit of integration. It has turned around the pre-1986 climate
of pessimism and, by reducing the perceived risks of investment
(huge opportunities are now seen to be the result of the single
market), has spurred capital spending. No one talks about "Eurosclerosis" anymore. Moreover, firms that were undecided
about investment have imitated those that were investing readily,
as the former were afraid of being left behind. Imitation effects
have thus encouraged even greater investment. Finally, business
leaders point to increased non-EC investment in Europe (for
instance, U.S.-originated investments jumped from $12.5 bil-
lion in 1986 to almost double that amount one year later).

The EC economies are already so interdependent that
there is limited freedom of action on the part of national governments. Firms, institutions, labor markets, and currencies are so
closely linked that it is difficult to envision any degree of national independence. According to knowledgeable observers,
the only question is to what extent governments will accept this
reality and move forward with EC-wide institutions in order to
facilitate the functioning of a pan-European economy and improve the ability of that economy to adjust to shock.

This is where many, including some of Thatcher's own
advisers, did not understand England's attitude toward speeding up European integration. They pointed out that England

has little choice but to follow the economic policies of other EC nations. They argued that English inflation has recently been the highest among the EC countries, while the pound has been devalued even though it is not part of the European Monetary System. Moreover, British interest rates, already among the highest in Europe, had to be further increased in October 1989 when the Germans decided to raise their own. Even in areas like social policies, Britain cannot afford not to follow EC legislation, as British workers can theoretically find employment in any of the other EC countries.

Still, EC officials in Brussels and some government and business leaders talk about the need for a "quantum leap" to achieve the single market, so that the momentum will not be lost and possible regression toward nationalism will be avoided.

Knowledgeable EC observers argue that true unification will depend on the ability of European government leaders to work out acceptable compromises, as well as on the intensity of pressures for increased and faster integration coming from business leaders. These observers point out that recent events point to both progress and deadlock on these two fronts. On the positive side, the heads of the twelve countries have agreed to subject mergers and acquisitions to EC antitrust rules rather than self-serving national regulations. In addition, they have opened up the telecommunications, banking, and insurance markets to communitywide competition. The consequences of these agreements — much sought by business — are far-reaching. On the negative, side, there has been no agreement on harmonizing VAT rates or handling of Japanese car imports. This is why EC observers conclude that progress will depend greatly on not only the compromise position of the EC countries but also external events such as the unification of Germany and the ability of Gorbachev to hold on to his power and further liberalize the Soviet Union.

Visionaries want more than just economic integration. They talk about a federal Europe that, in addition to the twelve EC members, will include the EFTA countries (or at least those who choose to join) and even the Eastern European nations. They see the strength of such a federal Europe as the only way to achieve true European independence from the United States. In addition, federal Europe could play a balancing role between the United States and the Soviet Union simply by acquiring the status of a superpower positioned both geographically and ideologically between the two.

Perhaps progress toward European integration and eventual union can best be envisaged in a long-term context. The younger generation of Europeans see their fellows in other EC countries as compatriots rather than foreigners. Although they might not speak the same language, they share the same values, ideals, and anxieties. These young people, born and growing up in relatively prosperous, peaceful times, see no need for national identities or rivalries. They increasingly perceive themseslves as Europeans. They can travel, study, or work in any of the EC countries. Their friends are in many parts of Europe, and they are all used to watching television programs and listening to records without even thinking about the language they hear. In the view of many, the younger generation of Europeans are certain to create a united Europe if their parents fail to do so. They are Europe's best chance.

A good example of this new generation is the ten-year-old Spanish girl who proposed a newspaper entitled "Our Europe — For Children." The editorial of her newspaper, entitled "The European Community," reads as follows: "Spain, Ireland, France, Italy, Greece, Luxembourg, Belgium, Portugal, Denmark, West Germany, the United Kingdom and the Netherlands will form one European Community and one country in 1992. From this date we will no longer use pesetas, francs, pounds, and so on, but ECUs. When we go from one country to another, we won't need to show our passports or identity cards. To go to a European University, we will need to know two languages of the Community. This Community will be very important for us" (quoted in Jaurequi, 1989).

Thus, to paraphrase Lord Cockfield, it is the new generation that will create the Europe of tomorrow. The signs are that young people perceive Europe as a single entity and will do their utmost to see a unified Europe encompassing the entire continent. In the view of the optimists it is only a question of *when* the United States of Europe will be created.

Reference

Jaurequi, J. A. "1992 Now." *IBM Europe*, Oct. 1989, p. 6.

Index